FARM BOY TO FLYBOY

DARREL F. SMITH

FOR
DAN AND KATHY

BEST WISHES

Darrel F. Smith

27 FEB 2020

Copyright

Quotes

Writing is its own reward.
- *Henry Miller*

I can't write five words but that I change seven.
- *Dorothy Parker*

I realize that I know nothing about writing; therefore, my goal has been to tell true stories that hopefully are reasonably interesting.
- *Darrel Smith*

Proofread carefully to see if you any words out.
- *Unknown*

Every writer I know has trouble writing.
- *Joseph Heller*

Be obscure clearly.
- *E. B. White*

Writing goes more easily if you have something to say.
- *Sholem Asch*

A person who publishes a book willfully appears before the populace with his pants down.
- *Edna St. Vincent Millay*

ACKNOWLEDGEMENTS

Larry R. Gibson: Major USMC Retired, College Professor

Larry, an old Marine Corps buddy, wrote a book, *Recollections of a Marine Attack Pilot*, and insisted that I also put the stories of my life into print. Without his encouragement, editing, and expert advice this book would never have existed. I will forever be grateful.

Glenda M. Smith: my wife

Glenda has been a steadfast partner during the many facets of my life. She has supported and accompanied me on many of the adventures that are presented in this book. There is no way of knowing the number of times I asked, "Glenda, how do you spell ------?" She always paused from whatever she was doing and patiently spelled the word. She always got it right. My computer's spell checker did not work.

Gary Ferguson: editor of Contrails magazine

Gary chose to publish several of my stories in that great publication. He surely recognized that I was a fledgling writer but still chose to include my efforts. Thanks, Gary, your support has been a valuable motivational influence.

Kelly L. Smith: our daughter

Kelly had heard and read a number of my stories. She had on occasion indicated that she enjoyed them. At a family gathering she simply stated, "Dad, I can publish a book of your stories if you would like." She has made good on her promise.

Others:

This book was "in the process" for about six years. During that time many people read, made suggestions, and edited my stories. These people contributed valuable input. Thank you.

Bob Jarboe; a fellow Marine
Bob Gould; a fellow Northwest pilot
Cherie Ruppe; a fellow Northwest employee
Anne Dougherty: a longtime friend
Jerry and Carol Stiles: friends
Jo Harrison; a book club friend
Gyla Sturgeon; a bridge friend
Randy and Marie Powell; hiking buddies

PREFACE

Over the years, I have often wondered what my parents and grandparents were doing and thinking as they made their way through life. It would have been interesting to know what their lives were like and maybe even some of their fears, hopes, and dreams, but none of them left a written record. With this in mind I have attempted to document some of the events of my life which are presented as "stand alone" stories. This type of writing sometimes requires a bit of repetition but allows the stories to be read in any order.

These stories are true but may contain minor errors since they came from my memory alone. Hopefully, a reader will get some idea as to the life that Glenda and I have lived and the adventures we have experienced. Even though the stories are arranged in the approximate order in which they occurred, this book is not intended to be an autobiography, and even though I have written of my experience in Vietnam, it should not be considered a war story. My stories could possibly be described as a collection of memories.

During the process of writing I have come to recognize and appreciate the many opportunities that have come my way. I will forever be thankful for the individuals who contributed in so many ways toward whatever successes I have enjoyed.

The writing of this book has greatly enriched my life, in that it has brought to mind memories from as far back as my early childhood. Your interest is greatly appreciated.

Glenda and I are thankful for the adventures that this life has offered. With luck, there are still unknown exciting places and events that we can experience. We had a small framed "saying" that was displayed on the driver's console of our motorhome that stated, "Not all those who wander are lost." J.R.R. Tolkien should be given credit for this phrase, but to be honest, we were lost quite often.

We hope you enjoy reading these stories. I truly believe that age should not be a factor in our dreams. If you can think it, it can happen.

This book will allow a peek into the lives of Darrel and Glenda Smith. I was born on a farm but made a career of flying--hence the title, Farm Boy to Flyboy.

ALONG CAME LARRY

2013

On rare occasions during my life, I have felt a mild urge to write. I didn't even know what the word meant. My weak command of the English language and my poor spelling skills were enough to keep me from any serious attempt. The vague desire was there but the motivation was missing. The idea of writing stories that would hopefully be somewhat interesting was very intimidating.

Twenty-five or more years ago, I made a weak effort by attempting to write two or three stories about events in my life. I shared these stories with a few people and even received some favorable comments. However, the motivation to pursue the documentation of my life just never became strong enough to incite any real action. Deep down I felt that my life's stories would be of little interest. Therefore, why should they be put into print?

As an adventure, Glenda and I chose to live and travel for several years in a 40-foot diesel-powered motorhome. One fall, Wayne Anderson, a friend from Northwest Airlines, suggested that we try the "Valley of the Sun" as a place to park our home-on-wheels for the winter. That winter was the first of many that we have spent in Arizona. We truly enjoy the Phoenix area with its warm weather and beautiful desert scenery.

In early January of 2013, we settled into our rented winter quarters, as the motorhome was long gone. Our plan for the next three months was to play a little golf, do some reading, and do some hiking. There was a real possibility that boredom would raise its ugly head, but we were willing to accept this as the price to pay for enjoying the warmer weather.

Then, along came Larry.

Out of the blue, Larry R. Gibson, nicknamed Long Range, a buddy from my Marine Corps days, made contact after many, many years. In 1964 Larry and I, fresh out of flight school, had reported to VMA-332 as our first operational Marine Corps squadron. This unit was located at Marine Corps Air Station Cherry Point in Havelock, North Carolina. We young pilots were eager and excited to pursue our military aviation careers.

The squadron was forming up with mostly young pilots who had recently completed flight training. We would be flying brand new A-4E Skyhawk attack aircraft. Our group was full of pride and confidence, but much was yet to be learned. We didn't give it much thought but most of us were destined for combat duty in Vietnam. We trained hard. A year or so later we were considered combat-ready attack pilots.

Larry and I became friends, partly because we were both from the South--Kentucky for him and Tennessee for me. There seemed to be a common bond since we both had our own type of country or mountain accent.

Along with most of the squadron pilots, Larry and I eventually received orders to a Marine Corps air base that had recently become operational. We would soon be given the opportunity to test our skills and aircraft in actual combat. We soon learned the "joy" of living and flying at the Marine air base at Chu Lai, Vietnam.

During that year in Vietnam, Larry and I were never in the same squadron, but our paths crossed regularly. On several occasions he gave me and others haircuts, since he had brought clippers from home and taught himself to be a barber. He initially cut his own hair and did a darn good job. Thankfully, he could not see the back of his own head!

During that entire year we flew only one flight together, and that flight was out of Japan. My squadron had been sent out of country for training and to take on new pilots. Larry was one of only two Marines I knew who were fully qualified to deliver a nuclear weapon. In order to maintain that qualification, he had to undergo specific training at regular intervals. We flew one of his training flights together.

We both completed our twelve-month tour of duty honorably by doing our best on any and all assignments. Upon returning to the States I chose to leave the Marine Corps when my current enlistment expired. Larry decided to pursue a military career.

After serving for more than twenty years of active duty, Larry retired from the Marine Corps in 1983. Almost immediately, his second career as a college instructor was launched. He had completed his BS and MS in engineering prior to joining the Marine Corps and easily slipped into teaching math and physics. His advanced education served him well and he taught for more than thirty years.

The commercial airlines were expanding and therefore hiring pilots. I was fortunate to secure employment as a pilot for Northwest Airlines and served in that capacity for 30 years. During those years, Larry and I met and talked on only a few occasions. Separated by many miles and absorbed in the pursuit of different careers, we gradually drifted apart.

I was surprised and excited when he initiated contact after all those years. Through emails and eventually telephone calls we were able to rekindle our friendship. It was good to hear his voice and to reflect upon our many common experiences.

Larry informed me that he had written and published a book that was composed of stories about events in his life, many concerning his military career. He had begun by writing stand-alone stories about these events and initially had no plans to write a book. When the number of completed stories exceeded fifty, he made the decision to publish. His straightforward approach and non-technical descriptions make his book very readable.

He encouraged me to write stories documenting some of the experiences of my life. His thinking was that unless these stories were put into print, they would be lost forever. Initially, the thought of writing a book or even a few stories was too much for me to consider. I tended to agree with his thinking in that none of my relatives had left any written record of the events of their lives. The stories that they could have told are now lost.

Larry sent a copy of his book, *Recollections of a Marine Attack Pilot,* and continued to stress the importance of documenting my life. Because of his prodding, I finally decided to give it a try. His short story format seemed to be something that I could possibly attempt.

My first attempts were a struggle, but I began to reflect upon events and experiences that had long been forgotten. I had put all that "stuff" into the back of my mind and without Larry that is where it would have stayed. His insistence that I write brought back a flood of memories.

That winter of 2013 was filled with my feeble attempts at trying to write a few readable stories. The possibility of drifting into boredom disappeared completely. It was a slow and painful process, but Larry took my hand and attempted to lead me toward improving my stories and writing skills. He was kind enough to edit my stories and willingly served as my mentor. This book would not exist if not for his encouragement and help.

This literary contact with my old friend happened in 2013. My life has been infinitely richer due to this rekindled association. I have spent an untold number of hours trying to find the very best words that would make every sentence as good as it could be.

Larry invested time, effort, and money into publishing a book concerning the events of his life. His stories are very interesting, especially since I lived many of the same experiences. I am in awe of his dedication and determination. As a Marine he was "One of the few," and now in his mentoring he is again "One of the few."

Larry, my old friend, thanks for stirring a chord deep within my being. I promise that I will strive to write more and better. I *do* understand that I will *never* come close to matching your story-telling skills. Thanks for your continued encouragement.

Darrel and Larry in MCAS Iwakuni, Japan
Neither had considered writing. They both wrote a book.

"Two Out"

1950
Ten years old

My maternal grandmother, Ethel Williamson Rhodes (Mama Rhodes to us grandchildren) had lived a hard life trying to raise a family on a small farm in Tipton County, Tennessee. She had given birth to seven children and shouldered the responsibility of bringing them up with very little money or support. Oscar, my grandfather, seemed to be uninterested in manual labor but loved to travel. He was a self-proclaimed doctor and believed he had devised a treatment that would cure cancer. He spent much of the time away from home visiting people who requested his services.

Mama struggled through. Upon the death of Papa Rhodes, she dreamed of a better life and insisted on moving to the big city of Memphis. She was able to buy a home on Linden Avenue, which at that time was in a relatively nice neighborhood. In future years, this area would decline and was eventually bought, demolished, and rebuilt as a huge medical facility.

My mother had married young and was also living a hard life. For a bit of relief, she would occasionally persuade my dad to make the 25-mile drive to Memphis for a visit with her mother.

On some of these visits, my dad would mysteriously disappear for a few hours in the afternoon. We finally challenged him as to what he was doing. The Memphis Chicks, a minor-league baseball team, played their home games at Russwood Park stadium which was within walking distance of Mama Rhodes' house. He loved baseball and truly enjoyed going to these games. Once exposed, he occasionally agreed to let some of us kids tag along.

Man was that ever an experience for a farm kid! The perfectly groomed field and the opportunity to see a few of the great players of that time, either on their way up to stardom or drifting downward, was a delight. A few of these famous player's names will always be remembered. Roy Campanella, Pee Wee Reese, Louis Aparicio, Luke Appling, and others pop into my mind when I reflect upon those games.

We always sat on the third-base side of the stadium as did a local character who usually downed more than his share of the beer. As the beverage took effect, he would begin yelling over and over again, "Let him hit, Luke." Luke was the manager of the hometown team. The players, the stadium, and the atmosphere made for a very exciting day.

One warm Sunday afternoon I completely lost interest in the game. A group of men and women were sitting in the row of seats just ahead of us. They had consumed a few cold ones and were in a very festive mood. A man in the group thought it would be great fun if one of the ladies would remove her bra, right there, during the game. She was reluctant. Every conceivable argument was made to persuade this woman to attempt this feat.

At my tender young age, this exchange was of extreme interest. The beer flowed, and the pleading continued. She finally agreed. To this day, I do not understand the maneuvers that are required to remove a bra while the blouse remains in place. She struggled this way and that and finally pulled the bra from the arm hole of her blouse. One of her male friends stood and raised his arm with two fingers displayed and loudly proclaimed, "Two out!"

I do not remember the teams that competed that day, but I will never forget the thought of this woman braless only one row in front of me. I was young but realized that something important was going on. The world was keeping secrets from me. As I grew older, some of these secrets became known but I will probably never fully understand.

In the years to come, I spent many days playing on various baseball teams. As an infielder, it was my duty to remind the outfielders as to the progress of the game. After the second out in an inning, I would turn toward them, hold up two fingers, and shout "Two out!" These words often triggered the memory of that long ago warm southern Sunday afternoon. I could never resist a smile.

First Hunt

Tennessee
1950

There was no alarm clock, and none was needed. He had been wide-awake for at least an hour and for the third time slipped from beneath the covers to peek out the window. As the family had grown, the attic had been converted into a bedroom for the boys. This upstairs vantage point allowed him to look through the window, past the roof of the kitchen and the old barn, to the woods only about a quarter of a mile away.

He was convinced that the woods which contained oak, beech, and black walnut trees could be seen in slightly more detail. Could the sun be making its way toward the horizon? Yes, now was the time.

His blue jeans, work shoes, and shirt had been carefully laid out so that he could dress in the dark. Before going to bed he had put five shotgun shells in his left jeans pocket, and six in the right. After loading his single-shot shotgun from his right pocket, he would have five shells in each pocket. Shells were expensive, and he had learned to account for each one.

This was his first solo squirrel hunt and he shivered with excitement. With nervous hands, he buttoned his shirt and pulled on his jeans. Hoping to creep out of the house without waking anyone, he descended the stairs as quietly as possible, but the squeaky steps gave him away.

His mother, who in his mind never seemed to sleep, said, "Son, be careful," and he answered, "Yes, ma'am, I will." He was only ten years old and always said "ma'am" when speaking to his mother, as was the custom here in the South.

After opening the screened door and negotiating the three concrete back steps, he finally felt free to take a deep breath. He stood for a moment, feeling and smelling his surroundings in the darkness. As always, there was the earthy smell of the farm. The odor of cow manure, the aroma of their molasses-laced feed, the wet green grass, and the freshly cut hay, filled his senses. This was his home.

Walking toward the old barn, he crossed the lane that led to the milk house and climbed over the wooden gate into the cow lot. The milk cows looked at him with only idle curiosity, since they were accustomed to seeing him every day. These gentle giants watched him pass within only a few feet, with very little or no reaction. The back gate was scaled, and finally he was clear of the farm buildings.

This little farm was located on a ridge line that, if followed, led to the woods. He easily found the dusty cow path that ended at a small spring-fed creek near the location of his intended hunt. During the years of his youth, no matter how hot and dry the summer, this little stream never stopped flowing.

In the hollows on either side of the ridge, he could see a thin layer of fog caused by the ever-present moisture in the southern air and the slight drop in temperature during the hours of darkness.

He followed the cow path along the ridge, and then down into the hollow to the left. He paused near a very large beech tree that for years had housed an active wild honeybee hive. These bees had never been a threat, only a point of interest. At this spot, he took a shell from his right jeans pocket and loaded his gun.

So far so good, but the dark woods seemed very intimidating. What was that noise? Did he just see something move?

He was very familiar with these woods and knew without a doubt that they held nothing that would harm him. And yet, the darkness created a totally new dimension. His imagination was working overtime. Could there be a lion, tiger, wolf, or even Satan himself waiting in the darkness?

Mustering what was left of his waning courage, he steeled himself and walked into the face of his fear. The faint light of the sun that was still below the horizon only vaguely lighted his way. He saw things that he had never seen during the daytime. That black lump and those white spots seemed very menacing.

Crossing the little creek, he stepped into the two-inch deep water. The gravel bed made a crunching sound that made him cringe. He feared that this horrific noise would cause any squirrel within a mile to stay safely in its den for days. In his mind, the hunt was over before it had even begun.

Although discouraged, he found his intended hunting spot, sat down, and waited. Nothing happened. As the sun slowly flooded his neck of the woods, the only sounds were the drops of dew falling from the leaves, and the occasional chirp of a bird awakening from a night on its roost.

The black lump turned into an old rotting tree stump. The white spots were exposed wood from where tree limbs had been broken by the ice storms of the previous winter.

Time dragged. He could easily hear the sounds of the equipment being readied for the morning milking. He was accustomed to being part of this daily procedure and felt a twinge of guilt. He should be there doing his part.

The inactivity and the familiar sounds made him drowsy. No matter how hard he tried to fight it, his eyelids seemed very heavy and wanted to close. He realized that he was not playing the part of a great hunter.

Suddenly, from behind and above he heard a leafy branch shake. He was immediately wide awake. A squirrel traveling through the trees makes a sound that is unmistakable. The ears of an experienced hunter will perk up since there is no doubt as to the source of this sound. It is magical, addictive, and causes the heart to beat a little faster.

Slowly turning his head, he looked for what he thought surely must be a squirrel. He caught a slight glimpse of movement in a large beech tree. Holy Cow! This was the real thing. His heart pounded. Then, nothing.

He saw no further movement and his neck began to ache. Had he really seen a squirrel or was his mind playing tricks on him? He faced forward and his shoulders slumped. Failure.

There was activity above and to his front. He looked up and there, in full view, was the furry little animal that he was hunting. There was no time to think--he pulled the hammer back on his shotgun, aimed and fired. To his surprise, the squirrel tumbled from the tree and crashed to the leaf-covered ground. It lay there completely motionless.

Now what? He sat for a few minutes, stunned into inactivity. He heard the dairy-barn sliding door open allowing the "boss cow" into the three-stall parlor-type milk barn. Morning and evening at milking time, the cows lined up in the same order. The milking machine compressor started--the morning milking began.

Gathering himself, he stood and walked to the downed squirrel. This muscular little animal still didn't move. He picked it up by the tail and returned to the spot where he had been seated.

He looked the squirrel over very carefully but saw no blood or wound. Could this little guy be playing possum? He had heard of other animals using this tactic to fool predators. They would remain motionless until the opportunity arose and then they would quickly make their escape.

What was he to do? Looking around he saw a broken limb of about three inches in diameter. It might hold his squirrel in place if it was in fact playing possum. He pulled the limb over and carefully placed it on the squirrel.

He watched it for what seemed a long time and it still did not move. His excitement got the best of him. He was eager to tell the family of his success. He also knew, deep down, that the tree limb would never hold the squirrel in place. He took his trophy and made his way back to the farm.

This first hunt was the beginning of a lifetime of going into the fields and woods in search of game. As he grew older his focus turned to the white-tailed deer that were becoming more plentiful in this area.

He always enjoyed the process of the woods coming alive as the sunlight slowly illuminated the surroundings. Even at seventy years of age the sound of a squirrel traveling through the trees still makes his heart beat a little faster. On that quiet morning in those damp Tennessee woods, hunting became a part of him that would indeed last a lifetime.

FIRED

My Lucky Day
1958-1963

"You *will* get a college education because we want you to have a better life than we have had. You will *not* play football because it is dangerous, and you could get hurt." These are the words that my mother preached to me for as long as I can remember. I assume my dad agreed but I don't remember him saying so.

During the first eight years of my schooling, I played baseball but not football. I was confident in my ability to perform athletic activities as well or better than my classmates but was honoring my mother's wishes. The coaches and school principal would approach me from time to time and chat about the possibility of my joining the football program. I avoided the issue by feigning lack of interest.

I showed up for the first football game of my freshman year and took a seat in the bleachers, intent on cheering my team to victory. As the game progressed, I became distressed and could hardly sit still. The home team lost the game and it was obvious that they needed help. My football career began as I showed up for the very next practice. My mother outwardly expressed disappointment, because of her concern for my safety, but she soon began to show considerable pride in my football achievements.

There were several good athletes that attended our small-town school. We worked on our fundamentals and grew bigger and stronger as the season progressed. We started to win a few games, along with having a lot of fun. It is much more fun to be on a winning team.

Tipton County, Tennessee was a very rural area in those days. There were only two towns of any significant size. Munford, the location of my school, had a population of about eight hundred folks and Covington, the county seat, was overflowing with maybe thirty-five hundred residents.

Our team had never won a game when playing this larger school. In my senior year the game drew a big crowd. We had won most of our games and Covington always fielded a good team. It was a hard-fought battle, but our team was victorious. A short time later I was in Covington wearing my letter jacket. A Covington resident approached me and said, "Now I suppose you will want to move the courthouse to Munford."

It was twenty years or more before Munford again defeated the Covington team. This second win featured my nephew, Clifford Dewayne Smith, catching the winning touchdown pass late in the fourth quarter.

I achieved a fair amount of success during my high school career. The team had winning records every year and received considerable favorable press. Near the end of the football season of my senior year, much to my surprise, college scouts started attending the games. They showed interest in me and one other player, Harris Pritchett. Until that time, it had never crossed my mind that I might have enough talent to play college ball.

Coach Hatley, the Memphis State University head coach, offered scholarships to both of us. Our college education would be totally free if we could make the team. Two country boys were off to the big city and were in for a big surprise.

Growing up on a small farm milking cows, driving tractors, and working in the fields was a part of my early life. Dad needed help, and as the oldest son I was pressed into service. I feel that because of this early activity, my parents trusted me--maybe too much. For example, they allowed me to go hunting with a shotgun at only ten years of age. Remember, my mother didn't want me to play football but allowed me to carry a gun!

Looking back now, I subconsciously knew that leaving for college football camp was an end to my life on the farm. It was important for me to take one more trek into the woods that had been so much a part of my growing up. The day of my departure, I rolled out of bed very early, took my old shotgun and quietly walked to my favorite hunting spot. I never again went squirrel hunting on that old farm.

Harris Pritchett's dad, who was also the high school principal, drove us to Memphis for our first taste of college football. Wow! We were amazed at the large number of big, strong, and fast players that had gathered. Some had strange accents since they came from distant parts of the country—all were there to try to make this football team.

The big surprise, which turned out to be bad news, was that the coach who had recruited us had been replaced. The new coach and his staff had never heard of the two boys from the small town of Munford. It was obvious that this coach had brought with him many players that he already knew. Maintaining our scholarships was going to be an uphill battle.

Practice in those days seemed to be an exercise in seeing how much punishment the players could take. Hot and humid conditions, two-a-day sessions, and being driven to exhaustion were enough to make many players sneak away during the night. I guess I was too dumb to quit. The thought that kept going through my mind was, "They can fire me, but I ain't quittin'."

Well, they *did* fire me. In my opinion, the coaches did not allow me to demonstrate that I was worthy of that scholarship. I was called into an office and told that my services were no longer needed. The assistant coach didn't seem to be interested in my comments about not being given a fair trial. It was the most painful disappointment of my life.

The Memphis State football program floundered. I don't think any of those football players were ever very successful. Years later, while serving as a Marine A-4 attack pilot in Vietnam, an enlisted Marine identified himself as one of those players. He told me of the pain, confusion, and frustration that the team experienced during the period following my being "fired."

That first academic quarter at Memphis State was a time of licking my wounds and trying to adjust to college life. I was surprised to be contacted by Bob Carroll, the head coach of the University of Tennessee, Martin Branch football program, offering me an opportunity to try out for his team. Shortly after this tryout session, he offered me a full-ride scholarship. I had found my football home for the next four years.

Harris also left the Memphis State football program and joined the team at Martin. He was a strong and fearsome player. He dominated for a while but decided to devote his time and energy toward his farming operation. He had purchased a farm near Dresden, Tennessee and made it a lifelong occupation.

After playing my freshman year as the backup for Bobby Fowler, an all-American and future NFL player, I assumed the starting fullback position. During my remaining college career, the team always had winning records with considerable success and honor coming my way. Each year a new group of big, strong, and fast fullbacks, many with accents, would show up to compete for my position. They were never able to take my job.

There are times when it seems you are having the worst day of your life. In my case this bad day turned out to be a very lucky one. It set me on the road to success in many aspects of my adult life. I am fortunate to have been fired on that day so many years ago.

Notes:

Coach Carroll and I were inducted into the UTM athletic hall of fame.

Coach Carroll devoted his entire professional life toward the betterment of the university. His achievements are known by many. He will go down in history as the winningest football coach in the history of UTM.

The University of Tennessee – Martin Hall of Fame

Darrel F. Smith

Smith was named Williamson All-American as a fullback in 1962, concluding an outstanding four-year career. He was the team's most valuable back for three seasons.

He led the Volunteer State Conference two seasons in rushing. He was an all-conference selection three times and was third among the state's colleges and universities with total points scored in 1960. He also lettered in baseball one year.

After graduation, he was commissioned as an officer in the U.S. Marine Corps. He served a tour of duty in Vietnam flying single-engine attack jets.

Darrel – UT Martin Branch

Roast Pork

Seventeen Years Old
1957
Baseball, Civil War and Prison Food

Our entire group gathered before a four-foot wide heavy steel door. On command, this massive door slid slowly to one side and we were told to step forward. Another security door stopped our progress as the first slowly closed behind us.

We were trapped between these doors. Only a few seconds later, the second door opened allowing us to walk into a room occupied by a large group of prisoners lounging about in their prison attire. With a loud metallic clang, the door locked behind us indicating that we were in prison.

We had just entered the Fort Pillow State Prison in West Tennessee, located on a bluff above the Mississippi River. Each year this prison fielded a baseball team but due to the backgrounds of their players, all the games were home games. There was no traveling squad. We were a small-town independent baseball team and on this Sunday afternoon we were to test our skills against the prison team.

The noise of that second door slamming shut heightened my apprehension. Suddenly, a large black prisoner threw his arm around my neck and aggressively tried to pull me toward the floor. My fears were confirmed. I was only seventeen, but it was abundantly clear that my life was over.

This prison was located near the original Fort Pillow, a Civil War fortification of dirt and logs, named in honor of Confederate General Gideon Johnson Pillow who oversaw its construction in 1862. Only a few months after its completion the Southern troops abandoned it due to the Union Army successes in the near vicinity. There was a real possibility that they could have been cut off from the main Confederate Army.

Union forces took over the vacated facility and used it to protect shipping along the Mississippi River. About two years later the celebrated southern general, Nathan Bedford Forrest, who had been raiding in the West Tennessee and Southern Kentucky area, made the decision to attack and eliminate this Union stronghold.

General Forrest's army attacked on April 12, 1864. The battle raged for several hours but it soon became apparent that the defenders, about half of whom were recently freed slaves, could not hold off the superior Southern force.

It was reported that many Union soldiers tried to surrender but were shot down even though they had already put down their weapons. This battle has gone down in history as the worst massacre of the Civil War. There were a total of about 600 men at the fort when the battle began and only 150 survived.

That summer I played on three independent baseball teams. This was possible since their games were scheduled on different days of the week. The home field of this particular team was Kerrville, Tennessee, a very small town consisting of one store, one cotton gin, and only a very few houses. The majority of the team's players were farmers from the surrounding area who worked hard in their fields day after day but dropped everything in order to take part in the weekly game. They loved the competition.

About halfway through that summer we were shocked and excited to be issued the first real uniforms of our lives. We were never to know who financed these uniforms.

My dad loved baseball. I think as a young man he had dreamed of growing up and becoming a professional baseball player. In his mind, this would rescue him from the drudgery of living in poverty on small farms as his family had always done. His love of the game was a gift to me. Regardless of the work that had to be neglected, he always allowed and encouraged me to play on these teams. On every possible occasion, he would attend my games as a spectator.

As I grew into my teens, it was evident that I possessed some of the skills required to play the game. I could throw hard, run relatively fast, and consistently hit the ball. I think my Dad thought these skills might enable me to play at a much higher level. He was wrong.

"Robert! Robert? Is that you?" This young, strong, and seemingly aggressive black prisoner was an old friend. We had worked and laughed together many times as we went about our duties on my parents' little farm. He seemed to be very excited to see me, and his pretending to rough me up was his way of showing it.

He had been arrested and found guilty of theft to such a degree that he was now in the "Pen." He was a good-natured young black man who had slipped off the straight and narrow and ended up in trouble. I never saw him again and have often wondered what sort of life he lived.

Our team was escorted through the prison's main building out to the baseball field. Home plate was located in a corner of the fenced prison yard. Bleachers had been set up outside the fence to accommodate family, friends, and other spectators.

The main prison building, with a large coal storage facility attached, was in deep left field. As the game progressed, we learned that this coal bin would receive many homerun balls, none from our team but a bunch from the prison team. Some of these guys were really good.

We could only watch in amazement as the inmates demonstrated their considerable skills. One big young man seemed to possess the ability to play professional baseball. On one occasion he came to bat while I was playing third base. His extremely hot grounder zipped by me so fast that I had absolutely no time to react. In the end, I was just happy to get through the game without serious injury.

Some of us commented to the coach of the prison team that this player appeared to have real possibilities. The coach sort of chuckled and replied that he did possess tremendous ability but upon his release from prison at the age of 64 he might be a bit old for the big leagues.

Well, our little country team never had a chance, the prison team scored at will. We were relieved when the game and our humiliation came to an end. The game ended with our Kerrville amateurs on the receiving end of a good-natured thrashing.

We had not been briefed as to what would happen next. Licking our wounds, the team was gathered and escorted through the main prison mess hall. The inmates were seated at long tables eating from metal trays. The meal of the day was a serving of some sort of gray soup and a large square of cornbread. It looked rather unappetizing.

We filed through this depressing room into the guard's area where we were seated in a comfortable and well-lighted dining room. Prisoners, dressed in white uniforms, immediately supplied our tables with platters of some of the best food I had ever tasted.

Back home on the farm the standard for cooking was frying—if it was destined for the dinner table it was most likely fried first. I loved that food and never dreamed that there was anything different available.

The platters of steaming roast pork and succulent vegetables were beyond my wildest dreams. It may sound strange, but this was an astonishing gourmet delight. Man, was it ever delicious.

For this farm boy this unimportant episode was a small step into the wonders of the world. I loved it.

My wife Glenda, also from a small farm, and I have been fortunate to have traveled the world. During these travels, we have sampled the foods of many cultures in many countries. That roast pork dinner boosted my courage to seek and sample the many varied offerings of this world in which we live. I will always remember that day, since the food opened my mind to things that were beyond anything that I could ever imagine.

PAPA RHODES

Memories

My grandfather, Oscar Franklin Rhodes, and I share the same middle name. I remember him as being a tall, strong, and overbearing man. I was afraid of him. His loud and forceful voice seemed to indicate that he was a mean man and should be feared. I did not like him.

He ruled his family, including my mother, with an iron hand. He would often allow the family to fend for themselves as he disappeared for extended periods of time. My grandmother Mama Rhodes, a gentle soul, was left to run the farm and raise the seven children. Survival at that time was difficult but even harder when the patriarch was missing for a good portion of the time. He seldom took part in the physical labor that was required to keep a small farm operational.

His father had died of cancer which motivated him to search for a cure for this horrible disease. He came to believe that he had concocted an effective treatment. Folks who were afflicted became aware of his claims and in desperation often requested his help. His reputation was such that people started calling him "Doc" Rhodes. The general populace was poor and oftentimes could reward him with only meager gifts such as chickens and vegetables.

Many stories exist of this man and his interaction with his family. On one occasion, his sons had been given a lovable little puppy in Munford, Tennessee, the town where their school was located. Unable to ride the bus with the dog, they walked the five miles home with their prize. Papa took the situation into consideration, picked up the puppy by its back legs, and smashed it against a tree. The dead body was discarded in the locust tree thicket behind the house.

On another occasion, he brought home some sort of leg coverings and demanded that my mother wear them to school. This type of garment was not something that kids wore at that time. She was embarrassed but had no choice. Dressed in this undesirable uniform, she and her siblings left home for the quarter-mile walk to the school bus stop. When they were out of sight of the house, the offending clothing was removed and replaced by something more acceptable. He was a hard man, but his children learned to work around him.

There is no way to know for sure, but it was told that he had another family. In those days transportation and communication were very slow or non-existent. According to rumor, he had another complete family and life only a few miles away from the farm. It was reported that at his funeral an unknown group of people attended. Again, rumor has it that a son from that other family was a war hero who was killed during WWII. We will never know.

The stories of Papa can never be confirmed or disproved. It is ancient history now. I do know for a fact that he was a great storyteller. I remember him having supper with our family, after which he announced that he would tell a story. He demanded that we kids sit in a particular chair and remain quiet. He insisted that there be no moving about, which was easy since his story and delivery kept us mesmerized.

His Story:

Times were hard. Families were having a difficult time putting food on the table. As a teenager, Papa would go into the woods and attempt to bag wild game to help feed the family. He went quite often, and each time passed a neighbor's home on the way to the woods. That family included two boys who were maybe ten or twelve years old. Each day as he passed, these boys would beg to accompany him on the hunt. He finally allowed them to tag along.

His gun was loaded for small game such as squirrels, rabbits, or birds--a light load. They had walked the woods all day without making a kill. The boys made too much noise and repeatedly asked him to fire the gun, but he had refused.

The sun was making its way toward the western horizon as they headed back toward home. Papa heard an unusual sound. In the distance he heard a mountain lion which seemed to be following them. It came closer. He fired his gun in order to load it with a heaver load. The boys were happy, but they too, soon heard the lion.

Papa carefully developed this story and was talented at creating realistic and detailed word pictures. We were fascinated and hung onto his every word.

They walked, and the lion followed. They were nearing the edge of the woods when the lion was spotted only a short distance away. They stopped walking and watched. The lion hesitated near a tree that had a large branch that reached far out and nearly touched the ground. It seemed to consider the situation as it stood in full view.

It looked this way and that, finally climbed onto that limb, walked to the end, and leaped into the brush. It disappeared, and Papa and the boys continued their walk toward home.

One of the boys had peed his pants and the liquid made a sloshing sound as it had been collected in his over-sized, second-hand shoes. The boys never asked to go hunting again.

We were never to know how much truth there was in this story. It certainly kept us quiet for a while. As I said, he was a great storyteller.

I have occasionally stated that none of my family had left any sort of written record, but this statement is not completely true. Papa Rhodes once wrote an account of a dream from his past. He had been visiting a family in the hills of middle Tennessee and walked outside before going to bed. The clear dark night had impressed him; he felt that he could reach out and touch the stars.

That night he dreamed that he had made a visit to Hell. After feeling his way along a dark stone wall, he was admitted without obligation. He saw and conversed with people that he had known and then was allowed to leave unharmed. This dream seemed to have left an everlasting impression upon his life. I cannot know, nor can I judge what this effect might have been. It is reported that during his last few minutes of life he said, "Don't let them bury me any deeper than the law allows."

This man was stern and demanding but a simple story may give some insight as to his moral makeup. At that time, life was very difficult. A neighbor came walking up the dirt road one day toward Papa's modest house. He and Papa Rhodes stood looking at each other, eye to eye. The neighbor said, "Mr. Rhodes, my babies are hungry, I'm going to take some corn from your barn to feed them." Papa stood aside and allowed this event to happen.

Stories of the people of that era indicate that they were patriotic, caring, brutal, honest, dishonest, unfaithful, loving, and lovable. Papa Rhodes probably possessed a little of all these traits. We are left to form our own opinions after considering the stories and rumors.

I feel an unusual connection to this hard and complicated man.

Burr

"Don't Step on Me"

It was well into the third quarter of a hotly contested small college football game. Our team, The University of Tennessee, Martin Branch, was on the offensive and making some progress in that the ball was being steadily moved downfield. In the huddle our quarterback, Vernon Prather, called a play that had been somewhat productive. In those days there was no direct communication between the players on the field and the coaches. Vernon knew the plays and called the one that he thought would work.

This play was designed for me as fullback to take a handoff from Vernon, run to the right and then make a hard left turn downfield over our right tackle. Wilbur, my friend and backfield running mate, was to lead the play and block anyone in the area to the outside, allowing me to make that turn into the hole.

As the team broke the huddle, Wilbur turned his dirt-stained and sweat-soaked face toward me, looked me in the eye, and said, "Don't step on me."

The play developed as planned. Vernon took the ball from the center and smoothly slipped it to me as I charged toward the right side. Wilbur, running just ahead, had no choice but to engage a defensive lineman that probably outweighed him by a hundred pounds. This confrontation was a standoff at best. Wilbur fought this huge defensive player to a draw. My intended path was momentarily visible, and I planted my right foot as hard as possible and slammed into the collapsing opening.

Wilbur Garner Edmiston was a year ahead of me in high school in the small town of Munford, Tennessee. He and I, like most of the students, were born and raised on small farms. We were both required to get up early each school day and catch the school bus for the long trip into the town of about 800 residents.

Mother nature decreed that Wilbur would be a late bloomer in the weight department. Soaking wet, he weighed a meager 115 pounds on his high school graduation day. This lack of size was offset by a surplus of natural athletic ability.

As we progressed through our high school football careers, we both had our share of triumphs and defeats. Our small-town team had winning seasons every year. Upon graduation, I had received enough recognition to be offered a football scholarship at Memphis State University in Memphis, Tennessee, although I still had to make the team. Wilbur took a different route, trying several different jobs in his search for a career. Unfortunately, I failed to make the team at Memphis State and was dismissed.

During the year after high school Wilbur gained about 40 pounds and his athletic abilities also grew by leaps and bounds. Our paths crossed again when I was invited to try out for the University of Tennessee Martin Branch football team. This tryout took place in the spring and Wilbur happened to be a walk-on tryout at the same time.

Robert Carroll, the head football coach at this University had become aware that I had been "fired" from the Memphis State team. It was my lucky day when he gave me a chance to tryout. Shortly after spending an afternoon attempting to demonstrate what I could offer his team; I was offered a full scholarship.

Wilbur, a much better natural athlete, was offered no financial aid whatsoever. This would be a "burr under his saddle" for his entire college career and even until today. I can only say that his blossoming physical attributes were only just becoming evident—nobody knew how good he had become. He was convinced that he was better than me and therefore was incensed that I received a full scholarship while he received nothing.

He later shared with me that he had been devastated, since he desperately needed some help paying his college tuition. Having no other choice, he showed up for the beginning of fall football practice along with the rest of the hopefuls.

Throughout his early life he was small of physical stature but large in the personality department. During that one year after high school he had become an exceptional athlete, the best natural athlete that I had ever personally known. For instance, he could stand flat-footed and jump over the average living room couch.

Wilbur was and is a comedian, always seeing the comical side of any situation. The first memory I have of him was at some forgotten place where we were changing clothes to practice basketball. He was on a raised portion of the dressing room and was entertaining everyone. He had been issued an old uniform shirt that sported long tails. These tails were designed to be buttoned between the legs. I had never seen a shirt like that before and have never seen one since. Wilbur enjoyed himself and entertained the rest of the team by demonstrating his interpretation as to the proper way to wear this garment.

The Edmiston family's natural athletic genes were also shared with his siblings. I remember his older brother, Clinton, telling the story of his first football game in college. The coach had little knowledge of his abilities, just like Wilbur's experience at Martin, but finally put him into the game. He took the ball and ran for a touchdown. The coach quickly devised a new play called "Give the ball to Clint."

Wilbur was not perfect—he had acquired the habit of smoking. The first two weeks of fall football practice were called "two a day." This was a period of conditioning. We were required to be on the field in the early morning while the inevitable southern dew was still on the grass, then again in mid-afternoon in the hot sun. It was a punishing and exhausting ordeal.

We were pushed to near total exhaustion and then forced to run around the track. I could barely put one foot in front of the other and yet we were required to walk, jog, and then sprint, over and over again. Coach Carroll would start each new phase with a short blast on his whistle. This drill seemed to go on forever.

Every part of my body was in pain, desperately needing water and rest. Wilbur, even though he smoked, would always be out in front, prancing along. Sometimes he even taunted the rest of us by running backwards. I hated him. I was sure the coaches thought the rest of us were "dogging it" since Wilbur was so fresh. If I could have caught him I would have tried to choke him.

I don't remember the details, but the coaches soon realized that Wilbur was a diamond in the rough. He was therefore awarded his coveted full scholarship. As I write this story we are in our mid-seventies. Even today, I could easily start a lively but friendly argument by bringing up the fact that I was given a full scholarship well before him.

That before-mentioned college football game from so long ago has no meaning today, but on that particular day, it was very important to our team. Even today Wilbur and I share a little chuckle should one of us mention it. Wilbur had momentarily slowed the huge defensive lineman but was soon overwhelmed and pushed backward. In his effort to protect me he placed his left hand on the ground. The opening was just large enough for me to attempt to slip through.

You guessed it. When I planted my right foot to make that hard turn it came down directly on Wilbur's hand. He stumbled back into the huddle holding his cleat-scarred and bloody hand in front of my face. He yelled in pain, frustration, and anger, "I told you not to step on me." The two of us had played many years and games together. He had never before and never again asked me not to step on him. I had never before and never again actually stepped on him.

We have remained friends over the years. In the spring of 2014, we shared several enjoyable days in Gold Canyon, Arizona. It is still fun to reflect upon our college days of so many years ago. I am often tempted to ask him to show me his left hand so that I can "check out" my cleat marks. He was always such a wimp.

Notes:

Wilbur G. Edmiston, Coach Robert Carroll, and I were eventually inducted into the UT Martin's Athletic Hall of Fame.

My experience at Martin set me on track to experience a very eventful and successful life.

A scholarship sponsored by Wilbur is now in force at The University of Tennessee Martin. This fund is used to support young athletes who travel a path similar to the one he trod.

Coach Carroll dedicated his entire professional life toward the betterment of the university. His achievements are well known by many and he will go down in history as the winningest football coach at UT Martin.

PETE AND OLD BLUE

Clad in full flight gear, he walks across the flight deck to the FA-18 that sits quietly waiting, bristling with weapons. In a short time, this war plane and pilot will be hurled from the deck of the carrier into the sky to engage in possibly mortal combat.

The tiny Piper Cub floats just above the grass, then touches one wheel in the slight crosswind. The pilot in the back seat is careful to guard against the ever-lurking "ground loop."

She strides through the airport terminal, back straight, uniform perfect, cap low over her eyes as she approaches the departure gate and her aircraft. People notice, and eyes follow.

The weathered hand of a seasoned old veteran confidently pushes the four thrust levers forward on a huge Boeing 747. The 200,000 pounds of thrust cause this 800,000 pound "whale" to slowly begin a journey that will end many hours later, most likely in some foreign country.

Pilots, yes. Superhumans? Not. Some might be surprised to know that pilots cannot see through clouds or leap large buildings in a single bound. Just a few hours earlier each of the above-mentioned pilots woke up, put their feet on the floor with bed hair evident, in desperate need of a toothbrush. Pilots are real people.

These people at some point in their lives simply made the decision, and stuck with it, to pursue some phase of aviation as a hobby or profession. All had different backgrounds and overcame different obstacles on the road to the cockpit. With effort and determination, step by step, they achieved their goal. There was no magic—just real people with a dream and a will to work.

Most pilots have interesting stories that could be told, but they seldom attempt to put them into print. Too often, we get glimpses of these stories while reading obituaries. Larry R. "Long Range" Gibson, an old Marine buddy, encouraged me to document some of the happenings of my life.

In keeping with his suggestion, here's how "Pete and Old Blue" helped transform my hard-working hands into those of a "seasoned old veteran" pilot.

The farm of my early years was a place of hard work. Every day was a study of selective neglect, in that there was always more work than could be done with the available manpower. Every member of the family pitched in to do their part toward keeping the operation going.

Until the time of my youth, mules had been used as the primary source of power to till the fields in West Tennessee. A man and a team of mules could cover only so much ground. Sharecropping was a practice that evolved to help alleviate this problem. The landowner would furnish the land while someone unrelated to the farm would perform the labor. That's how I met Pete.

Peter Macklin and his family lived about two miles from our farm. I knew nothing about their background and at six years of age the thought of asking never crossed my mind. They were just there. They owned a car and, on most weekdays, arrived early and stayed late tending to their crops. There were children about my age, therefore it was natural that we played together like family. Oh, did I mention that they were black?

Pete was a farmer during the week but became the Reverend Macklin on the weekends. He served as the pastor of a church located near Millington, Tennessee, about five miles from his home. All accounts portrayed him as hard-working and honest. He was well respected. I would agree with this description, but in my mind, he was also a very wise man. Although he was much older, I always considered him a friend.

My dad owned a pair of mules, Top and Tobe, that could be described as outlaws. They were all things bad--nervous, difficult to harness, prone to running away, and could jump any fence. No one wanted to deal with this team, but eventually Pete asked to be allowed to work with them.

He must have been an early-day horse (mule) whisperer. Within a short period of time these misfits were like puppies. I have no idea what he did or said to them, but they were completely changed. Going to and from the fields, they would follow him with no lead rope attached. A stop could be commanded by quietly saying, "Whoa," and to have them start again, in the same low voice, he would say "Come on." If left alone, they would stand quietly until he returned. The transformation was like magic--they seemed to love him.

Economic conditions were changing for the better and the general population was enjoying a gradually improving quality of life. Most families owned automobiles and more and more farmers were buying tractors. Mules were slowly disappearing from the farms by either being sold or dying.

I lived through this transition from mules to tractors, but I was too young to have worked with the mules on a regular basis. The Old Gray Mare and Old Blue, the last team on our farm, had been partners their entire working life. The few times I worked with draft animals they were assigned to me because of their gentle nature. The Gray Mare left the farm, I don't remember the circumstances, leaving Old Blue the last mule, alone but retired. She ate and hung out with the dairy cattle. We suspected that during her later years she thought of herself as a cow.

Life moved on. I went off to the University of Tennessee at Martin, UT Martin Branch at the time, playing football to pay my way. During my sophomore year the Marine Corps convinced me to join their ranks as a prospective officer. The Marine PLC (Platoon Leaders Class) program required that I spend six weeks at Quantico, Virginia during two separate summer breaks. Upon successfully completing this training and earning a college diploma, I was designated as a Marine Second Lieutenant. My wife Glenda pinned on those gold bars.

In the spring of 1963, there was a lot of activity as Glenda and I prepared to leave for Pensacola, Florida, my first active duty station as a Marine. Pete was around but remained very quiet and subdued. As departure time approached, he took my arm and led me aside. He looked me in the eye and said, "You are going out into a big world. There will be times when things will get really tough and you may even feel like quitting. If you feel that you don't have the strength to carry on, don't worry, just come on back to the farm. Old Blue will be hitched to the plow waiting for you."

I never saw or talked to Pete again and Old Blue died about a year later. Pete's words stayed with me. Many times, things did get tough and it would have been much easier to just quit. When those occasions arose, I thought of my wise friend Pete, his comment about quitting, and of Old Blue. I always pressed on. I will always appreciate the words of wisdom and advice from my wise friend the Reverend Macklin, Pete.

PENSACOLA, FLORIDA

A "Takeoff" into Our Future
Preflight
1963

Glenda and I arrived in the Pensacola, Florida area with no concept of how or where to look for a place to live. As per my official orders, I was reporting for Preflight, the very first step in becoming a Naval Aviator. We bought a local newspaper and searched the "houses for rent" section. One of the first ads we read offered a duplex on Perdido Bay about five or six miles to the west of town on the Lillian Highway.

Our landlord to be, Mrs. Island, informed us that the place was still available and that the rent was $85 a month. We did not have that much money. This small duplex was on the bay, only about fifty yards from the water, and we wanted it. I was afraid to ask but finally got up enough courage to offer her thirty dollars up front with the remaining balance promised about a week later, after my first pay day. Thank goodness, she agreed. This was our first home as a married couple.

We considered this little house on the bay a perfect home. Living near the water was so very different from our growing up on small farms in West Tennessee. We didn't have much money, but we realized that we were taking our first steps into a world of adventure.

These were very exciting times. We were newlyweds and I was beginning the long process of attempting to become a Marine pilot. Our knowledge of the world, outside of Tipton County, Tennessee, was almost nil but we eagerly embraced our uncertain future.

The walls of our new home were very thin, and sound traveled freely between units. The floor plans were such that the master bedrooms were located with only a wall separating them. Our neighbors in this little duplex, originally from Wisconsin, were similar to us in that he was also a beginning pilot trainee and they too had been recently married.

It so happened that his wife was very vocal during their sexual activities. She would give specific and demanding instructions during the entire process. We don't recall ever hearing him say a word but could imagine the sweat on his brow in his effort to fulfill her requests. He soon washed out of the flight-training program and they moved away. I have often wondered if his failure was due to his inability to grasp the fundamentals of flight or the extreme stress, he encountered at bedtime each night.

The association with these folks was short-lived but one event stands out in our memory. In our farm background, the common way to cook most everything was to fry it. One evening they fired up a small charcoal grill and cooked steaks. The smoke that drifted through our windows was one of the most wonderful aromas that we had ever experienced. It was our first knowledge of grilled food. What a pleasant awakening.

Going to Pensacola Beach and playing in the surf is one of Glenda's most vivid recollections. She could not swim but we had a great time playing in the big waves in the Gulf of Mexico. On one occasion Elbon and Mildred, her parents, brought her younger sister Cindy for a visit and we all enjoyed a great day of sun, sand, and waves at the beach.

The bay near our house was normally calm and at times as smooth as glass. Even though Glenda was afraid of the water, we could wade as much as 100 yards from shore with the water coming only to our waists. She decided that she wanted to learn to float. The water was a bit salty and she eventually learned to lie on her back and completely relax. She could float.

Glenda found a job at the Metropolitan Life Insurance Company, which was the same company she had worked for in Memphis, Tennessee. Her duties were the same; therefore, she fit right in. I believe she enjoyed this brief employment. I remember that her boss lived nearby and gave her a daily ride to work.

Even with this additional income we were still always short of cash, but I don't remember that we worried about it very much. Our income was what it was, and we just learned to live within our budget.

Reflecting on that time in our lives, we do not remember even having a television. I do remember that we bought a single deck of cards and by studying the enclosed instructions, we learned the game of solitaire. The card deck was passed back and forth allowing each of us to play the one-person game that we knew. I also remember that we once drove toward Pensacola until we were within range of a radio station. A boxing match between two famous fighters had been highly hyped. We do not remember their names or who won.

Living on the water was a special treat. We learned that there was an abundance of crab in this brackish water. The locals told us that chicken necks were the best bait for these little creatures. Strings were tied around the chicken necks and they were tossed into the water. The string was either held or tied to some solid object. It would hang loosely until a crab went into the attack mode. As our quarry tried to drag the necks away, the string would gradually grow taut. The crabs were determined little guys and would not give up their prize. The "crabber" would simply pull in the string and lift the bait and crab out of the water.

We had several in a bucket when our landlord stopped by to see what we were doing. She informed us that these crabs were delicious. We were shocked. Neither of us had ever seen a crab and certainly had never considered eating one. We do not remember if we actually tried to eat them.

During the first few weeks of our preflight training my class attended ground school at the Pensacola Naval Air Station. We were new officers trying to learn how we were expected to act as junior aviation candidates. Now that we were officers, we were amazed that the instructors were not constantly in our faces yelling, as had been our experience in OCS, Officer Candidate School. The enlisted men even called us "Sir" and saluted as we passed. Wow!

These weeks of ground school included classes in aerodynamics, engines (we studied the reciprocating type) aircraft systems, and physical conditioning. One of our frequent drills was to run several miles to the obstacle course, do several timed runs over this monster and then run back to our starting point. I had played football in college, but the heat, humidity, and exercise made for a demanding day.

The only aircraft we saw were in the hangars as we ran up and down the sea wall near the maintenance area. Climbing into a cockpit and going flying seemed a distant and almost impossible dream.

I learned that our next duty station, where we would take our first flight, would be Saufley Field, which was only a few miles from the Pensacola Naval Air Station. On a day off, Glenda and I drove to that field to see what we could learn. There were T-34 aircraft everywhere. As many as twenty or more with engines running were making their way to or returning from the active runway. I could not even imagine being a part of this beehive of activity. My anxiety only increased as I observed this organized confusion.

Everyone in my class successfully completed ground school and we moved on to the next phase. At Saufley we settled into what would be the norm for the remainder of our flight training. One half of the day was dedicated to ground school and the other to flying.

I have always been amazed how the instructors led us, one step at a time, from knowing nothing to confidently performing the maneuvers that were required. Luckily, I was able to function in this training regimen and consistently moved forward.

As was the tradition after a student's first solo, my instructor lopped off my uniform tie with a scissors. As was also the tradition, I produced a bottle of booze as a gift of appreciation. I gave him a bottle of Cutty Sark, a blended Scotch whiskey, that set us back about eight bucks. That was a lot of money and it put a dent in our budget, but it was tradition and I would have it no other way. At this point in my life I had never tasted any sort of alcoholic beverage.

At the end of this first stage of training the students were sent along one of two "pipelines." The ones with the better grades were sent to jets at the Meridian Naval Air Station near Meridian, Mississippi. The others were sent to props, where they would be trained to fly transports or helicopters, at Whiting Field, near Milton, Florida. I was fortunate that my grades were considered good enough.

Shortly after learning that I had qualified for the jet pipeline, I was told to report to the squadron duty office. I was introduced to the head football coach of the Navy Goshawks. This team, based at NAS Pensacola, had a reputation of always fielding a quality team. I was asked to join that team. Howard Caughran, a teammate in high school and college, was playing for the Goshawks. He had probably mentioned my name to the coach along with a positive recommendation.

I told the coach that I had been selected for jets and sincerely wanted to follow that course. He informed me that he could guarantee me jets after playing on the football team. I had my dreamed-of assignment in hand. I had taken a physical beating during four years of college football but had been lucky enough not to have any major injuries. I decided not to play football and to follow my hope of flying those aircraft with no propellers. I have often wondered how my life would have been different if football had been chosen.

Glenda and I packed our meager belongings and proceeded to

Meridian, Mississippi, pulling a small U-Haul trailer behind our 1962 Ford Fairlane. This training facility is located in the rolling wooded hills of east central Mississippi.

I was proud to have completed that first phase of flight training. Glenda and I were having the best time of our lives. We still had so much to learn.

JETS

Wow!

During my initial flight training I became aware that the pilot trainees with the better grades at Saufley Field in Florida would be considered for assignment to jets. I had very little experience, but the idea of becoming a jet pilot became very important. After only about thirty hours of flight time the decision was made as to whether the trainees go to jets or props.

Reflecting upon that system, I feel there were many beginning pilots who were directed in the wrong direction. What if a student pilot and his first instructor did not get along personality wise? What if that student was a slightly slow starter? It did not matter; the die was cast. Some pilots were mistakenly sent to jets which caused them to struggle and sometimes fail. The opposite was also true, some who were sent through the prop pipeline could have become excellent jet pilots.

Having absolutely no previous flying experience, it was difficult for me to judge how my training was progressing. After each flight my instructor would debrief me without a lot of criticism but also did not give me much praise. I finally asked him if my progress was normal. He told me to stick with him and we would get through "this thing." Evidently, my grades were good enough. I was sent to fly jets.

Glenda did not look for a job but became the perfect wife and support person. All the help I could get was greatly appreciated as the flight training had become very demanding. At times I felt I was struggling up a very steep mountain. There was more work and stress than had ever been experienced in any other phase of my life. The fact that I was flying military jet aircraft daily was almost beyond my comprehension but a great motivator.

As in our first phase of training our workday consisted of half a day in the classroom and the rest on the flight line. My progress must have been acceptable since none of my flights resulted in a *down*, an unsatisfactory performance that required extra training. A phrase from my earlier life often came to mind: "They can fire me but I ain't quittin'."

We befriended a young woman from the neighborhood who had a baby girl that was just beginning to walk. They visited our trailer often, maybe too often, but we adored the little girl. Even at this early stage of our marriage we decided to attempt a child of our own. Conception happened almost immediately. Our future was totally uncertain, but we were expecting and very happy about it. What were we thinking? We had only been married and living together for a few months.

On 22 November 1963, dressed in my flight suit, I paused at the doorway of the scheduling office. My intention was to check the date and briefing time for my next training flight. At that moment someone announced that President John F. Kennedy had been shot and killed. It is said that nearly everyone remembers where they were and what they were doing when they heard this news.

I had recently joined a local gun club which had organized a deer hunt for the next morning. None of us knew how we should act so soon after our President had been assassinated. During telephone conversations we came to the conclusion that no matter what we did this tragic event could not be changed. We went hunting.

We gathered well before daylight and were transported in pickup trucks to our assigned stands along the property line of our leased hunting area. We hunters waited as the sun, still below the horizon, began to push the darkness from the pine woods. In the distance, sounds of the dogs (Beagles) being released could be heard. Using dogs to move deer around in the thick woods was an accepted and legal method of hunting in the state of Mississippi.

The woods became very quiet and frankly it was hard not to allow my mind to wander. Suddenly, I heard the sound of large animals running through the woods. Two whitetail bucks with large antlers ran from right to left within fifty yards of my posted position.

With my heart pounding, I aimed and fired at the larger animal. The woods again became very quiet but soon, I heard noises that indicated that my trophy was down. I found it a bit sad that I had killed this magnificent animal.

As part of our training syllabus we were introduced to formation flying. What a tremendous psychological boost. There, only a few feet away, was another actual military aircraft. It looked so sleek and even though my flying was very rough, I could now say that I had flown in formation. This action made me feel that becoming a Marine pilot was possible.

I think that my first attempts must have made my instructor laugh but I soon learned to maintain the proper formation position without even thinking.

Glenda's Ford had a few mechanical problems, but I don't remember that they were serious. However, we made the decision to trade that car for a VW bug. I remember that we paid about $1600 for that little blue 1964 ride. It served us well during the first years of our marriage.

The few months that we were based in Mississippi passed quickly. I was very excited that my introduction to flying jets had been successful. The Naval Aviation flight program had proved to be very demanding but also very rewarding. I still had so much hard work remaining.

The U-Haul was towed behind our little VW as we made our way back to Pensacola for yet another phase of flight training. This training segment was scheduled to be fairly short, only about two months. We found another mobile home which proved to be comfortable housing during this limited training cycle.

So far so good— "They can fire me but I ain't quittin'."

JET SOLO

"Look Ma, No Propeller"
Fall 1963

During the circling approach the runway was visible through the left side of the canopy. The green vegetation, the blue sky, and the runway markings will forever be etched into my mind. My instructor standing on the airfield tarmac probably said a small prayer and watched but could do nothing. This was my first solo approach and landing in a military jet aircraft.

I knew very little, but jets seemed to be the most desirable next step. During my initial training there was no way of knowing how my grades were stacking up against my fellow students. I just worked hard and hoped for the best. Oh, man. The more I thought about it, the more I wanted to fly those cool machines.

The T-2 Buckeye was a near perfect aircraft for our transition into the world of jets. Its straight wings and honest handling characteristics made our first steps achievable. The rotating propeller on my first trainer had caused some vibration but the jet was exceptionally smooth. On my first flight, the instructor pulled the nose up slightly and performed an effortless aileron roll. He allowed me to perform the same maneuver which took my breath away.

The first few flights were structured to allow us students to become familiar with the aircraft and improve our flying skills My progress seemed to be acceptable, and as per the training syllabus, the day finally arrived for me to solo. After making several practice landings at an outlying field my instructor told me to taxi clear of the runway and come to a stop. With the canopy open and the engine running, he secured the backseat harness and made his way to the ground.

On command, the canopy moved slowly to the closed and locked position. I was alone. The aircraft was taxied to the runway and with my gloved hand the thrust lever was pushed forward to the stop. The rush of conditioned air was louder than the sound of the engine.

After spinning busily, the engine instruments stabilized at near maximum power. Everything seemed to be working properly.

Canopy:	Closed
Instruments:	Checked
Heart:	Racing
Brakes:	Released

The aircraft, slowly at first, started accelerating down the runway. At the proper speed I eased the nose up to the takeoff attitude. Just as had happened with an instructor in the back seat, the wheels lost contact with the runway. Airborne.

As instructed, the landing gear and the flaps were left in the landing position. Only slight control input was required to start a climbing left turn. I was soon established in level flight heading in the opposite direction. After passing the landing end of the runway a shallow descending turn was started. Upon completing ninety degrees of turn, the entire runway could be seen through the left side of the canopy. The aircraft was soon aligned with the runway centerline and was flown to a landing. My first solo attempt to get this jet back on the ground safely had been a success.

This entire maneuver had seemed quite normal. The repetitive training had given me the confidence and skill that were required. Another small step forward had been taken.

It was impossible to keep from smiling as I realized that with this maneuver, I had done something that was more than I could have ever dreamed. I was on my way to proving that I was good enough to be called a Naval Aviator.

CARRIER QUALIFICATION

Pensacola
1964

The very soul of Naval Aviation is the fact that Navy and Marine pilots operate aircraft from the decks of aircraft carriers. Upon demonstrating that he or she has the determination and skill to be considered ready, the student pilot is sent to the carrier in an attempt to qualify. I feel that the events of that day will forever be etched in the memories of these pilots. It is a special achievement and would probably be somewhat envied by most pilots.

Although often feeling overwhelmed, I had successfully completed each phase of training on my march toward becoming a Naval Aviator. In only a few months, the instructors had turned a farm boy who knew nothing about flying into a pilot who was ready to hit the boat.

After successfully completing initial jet training at the Naval Air Station at Meridian, Mississippi, the students were sent to Pensacola, Florida for carrier qualification and initial gunnery training. We young hopefuls flew many approaches to runways that had been set-up to look like an aircraft carrier's flight deck. The markings and the approach light system were exactly like what we would see as we approached the ship.

On a normal training day, after making a number of approaches, we students made full-stop landings and parked our aircraft. A very small and basic building, furnished with worn-out couches and plastic chairs, was located near this parking area. We seated ourselves in this humble structure and waited for our debriefing.

The LSO, Landing Signal Officer, had carefully observed each of our practice approaches and taken detailed notes. He evaluated each student pilot's performance, response to his instructions, and the probable end result of each pass. This was great stuff. We were making progress.

This phase of training also included our introduction to air-to-air gunnery. We would launch with loaded guns and make repeated live runs on towed banners. Each aircraft's 50-caliber machine guns were loaded with ammunition that was painted a different color so that it could be determined whether that pilot had scored hits. I must confess that even with my best effort those banners proved to be very elusive. The ground crews searched carefully but found that my color bullets had not in any way violated the banner. Hits were not required to successfully complete gunnery. Thank goodness.

A thought had started to form in the back of my mind. During our early training the emphasis had been on pre-flighting, starting, taxiing, taking off, performing a few maneuvers, returning to the airport, and making a survivable landing. Subtly, a change had begun to take place. The operation of the aircraft was beginning to be taken for granted and the mission was being pushed to the forefront. We were now expected to be able to fly the aircraft.

The Navy made every effort to keep the entire family involved and enthusiastic about our ongoing flight training. The wives of the student pilots were invited to board the USS Lexington, the aircraft carrier used for training, for a day at sea watching student pilots attempting to qualify. There was a rule that a wife could not go to sea on the day that her husband was flying.

I have never gone to sea on an official naval vessel—Glenda has. I recently asked her to tell me about her experience that day. She remembers that she, in fact, did spend a day on the carrier, but the details have been forgotten. Only 50 some years have passed so I question the fact that she does not remember the details.

We think that she was escorted aboard, shown about, and positioned so that she could observe the day's carrier operations. She does not remember what they were served for lunch or any other detail. We both are confident that she observed T-28s, a propeller-driven training aircraft, as the student pilots put forth their best effort to achieve carrier qualification.

When in port, the Lexington, a massive aircraft carrier, was tied up at the Pensacola Naval Air Station. As we progressed through our early training its presence loomed over our budding group of student pilots. To maintain our physical fitness, we were required to run along the sea wall on a regular basis. I had never flown an aircraft, but the image of this ship was subconsciously imprinted in the back of my mind. Before I had performed even one takeoff and landing, I knew that if my training was successful, I would eventually approach this huge machine in an aircraft with hopes of making arrested landings.

The highly anticipated day finally arrived. Years later, I discovered that Larry R. Gibson, "Long Range", a longtime friend and my writing mentor, and I "hit the boat" on that very same day. We could possibly have been in the very same four-plane flight.

We young pilots manned our aircraft, became airborne, joined in formation, and headed out to sea. The early morning view of the Pensacola area was breathtaking. We soon had our destination in sight. The Lexington was a huge ship, but it looked so small. We were expected to approach this ship and make arrested landings without killing ourselves. I am happy to report that every pilot in that four-plane formation was able to accomplish this feat.

Needless to say, there was a certain amount of anxiety. However, our intense and repetitive training had served us well. The radio calls, the voice of the LSO, and the approach lighting system were as we had seen and heard so many times during our training.

Our four-plane flight approached the carrier in the direction that it was traveling. After passing overhead each pilot made a steep turn to the left in order to create nose-to-tail separation. It was now a one-aircraft operation as far as each pilot was concerned.

After slowing, we dropped the landing gear, extended the flaps, and made the proper radio calls. We were now in the proper configuration to approach the ship. We had been instructed to make our first passes without dropping the tailhook. During these first passes, we were expected to make touch-and-gos. As our aircraft made contact with the carrier deck, we were trained to immediately apply full power and fly into the air for another pass.

The LSO watched each approach, offering guidance as needed to ensure that we students made safe and acceptable passes. He evaluated the way we flew the pattern, spoke on the radio, responded to his instructions, and our presence of mind. All things considered; he eventually deemed each student good enough. We were individually instructed to drop the hook.

These LSOs seemed to be almost superhuman. On one of my approaches he calmly said, "You will need a little power." I was perfectly aligned, on glide slope, and on airspeed. In my mind I said "Bullshit, I'm good" but almost immediately the aircraft started to settle, and additional power was required. As I snagged a wire and came to a stop he said, "Told you so." These guys were phenomenal.

A landing in a tailhook aircraft is in fact a controlled crash. As my aircraft hit the deck, I added full power and prepared to go around. Suddenly, I was looking at a deck hand, with my engine at full power, who was aggressively giving me instructions via hand signals to reduce my power to idle and raise the tailhook.

I recently read the account of another pilot describing his first arrested landing. In the excitement of the moment he was slow to reduce the power to idle. According to him the air boss said, "It's okay, son, we have you now. You can reduce your power. You can't make the ship go any faster."

It happened so fast. I reduced the power and raised the hook. I was told to follow the directions of a taxi director. At some point, a steering bar was inserted into my nose wheel and the only control I had was power on, power off, and brakes.

Within only a short time I was positioned behind a blast fence that had been raised behind an aircraft that was about to launch. The fence disappeared, and the skilled hands of the taxi director put me into the proper position. I was on the cat. There was all sorts of activity on the deck around my aircraft. Suddenly, I could feel that something very powerful had seized my plane. The wheel struts seemed to be completely compressed.

Someone to my left, I later learned that this crew member was called "the shooter," gave me the signal to run up my engine to full power. The shooter shouldered the responsibility of the overall safe operation of a cat shot. He checked that all crew members were in their proper places, the pilot was responding properly, the catapult was properly set, and the area was clear. I did as directed and attempted to check my engine gauges. Everything was a blur.

The shooter was looking directly at me, waiting. The only thing I could remember was to salute. I did this and placed my head against the headrest. There was noise, tremendous acceleration, and suddenly I was over water and flying. Holy Cow! I had just successfully completed my first arrested landing and cat shot.

Within only a very few minutes I was again on deck with the same deck hand telling me to reduce my power, raise the hook, and to follow instructions. I would guess this guy to have been less than twenty years of age and yet he expected prompt and proper compliance with his commands. Training.

I made the required arrested landings and cat shots to be considered carrier qualified on only two occasions during my Marine Corps experience. On both days the weather was great—calm and sunny. Hats off to you Navy and Marine pilots who flew on a regular basis from a carrier deck. You must take great pride in that experience. It scares me to even think of pitching decks and night landings. I will always wonder if I would have had the right stuff. I stand in awe. You did it and survived but never bragged.

Glenda and I found it interesting that while we were in Pensacola this second time, we experienced an unusual happening. During a cold front passage, our little rented mobile home shuddered in the wind and suddenly there was a noise that we had never heard. Something was going on outside. We rushed to the door and peeked out to find our lawn covered in ice pellets. Weather of this type is very rare in Florida.

All in all, flying state-of-the-art jet aircraft was a big deal for this "hillbilly" from a farm in West Tennessee. I survived. To this day at 78 years of age I cannot resist looking skyward when the sound of an aircraft reaches my ears. I surely must love it and always will.

I may be kidding myself, but with a bit of training, I feel that even today I could complete a safe approach and landing in a Boeing 747. However, this event would have to be scheduled at a time other than my normal nap time.

Kingsville, Texas

Advanced Jet Training
1964

In my quest to become a Naval Aviator, I had successfully completed each required phase of training. There was only one giant step remaining. My initial training had been at NAS Pensacola Florida where my class had completed preflight ground school and flown our first training flights. I had known nothing about flying and on my first flight I proved it by making full use of the airsickness bag.

The program was designed to take someone like me, who had no flying experience, step by step toward receiving those Wings of Gold. On numerous occasions, I would find myself performing maneuvers with an aircraft, that a short time before, would have been beyond my wildest dreams. Two of my most vivid memories are of my first formation flight, and the day that I made arrested landings on, and catapult launches from, an actual aircraft carrier. The flying had become more exciting and demanding with every step along the way. Was I good enough to become a Naval Aviator? "They can fire me but I ain't quittin'."

Advanced Jet Training was the final and possibly the most demanding phase of our training. The student pilots arrived in Kingsville, Texas knowing that they would be flying swept-wing and afterburner-equipped aircraft which required totally new skills and techniques.

Glenda and I were assigned to base housing, a two-story townhouse, located only a mile or so from the main gate of the base. At night we could easily hear the maintenance crews running up recently overhauled engines in a static test cell. I loved this sound. It indicated that I was becoming a part of a very powerful and dynamic organization.

One afternoon I was sitting in the sun on the front step of our townhouse. Suddenly, a young girl started to scream and cry as she pointed into the shrubbery. I immediately rushed to her aid. Looking into the bushes, I saw a huge Tarantula crawling along the wall of our house. Now, both of us were screaming, crying, and pointing. This big spider was not a threat to us, but we had never seen anything like it. All our lives we had been taught to hate and fear spiders. This was a small but interesting event in our introduction to the world beyond West Tennessee.

Glenda had become pregnant months before in Meridian, Mississippi and was showing a bit. In fact, she was showing a lot. We both were anxious for our first child to arrive. It was a stressful and exciting time.

The program in advanced jet training required the students to fly in two different squadrons. Initially we flew the F-9 Cougar, which was our first experience with swept-wing aircraft. In our final training squadron, we flew the sleek, afterburner-equipped F-11 Tiger. During these final months we concentrated on weapons delivery, air-to-air tactics, and instrument flying.

During the entire training program, I worried that my performance on a flight would be below the normal standards causing the instructor to give me a "down." The dreaded "down" required the student to receive extra training and to refly that particular flight. This never happened – I was lucky. The closest I came to receiving an unsatisfactory grade was on a solo night flight when I started my initial taxi without having the aircraft position lights turned on. An instructor pilot noticed and berated me over the radio. Upon completing the flight, he told me that I should probably be given a "down" and be required to refly the mission. He chose not to write me up and allowed the incident to pass. I have often wondered how I would have reflown that flight. I assume I would have gone through all the procedures up to the point of turning on the position lights. Problem corrected; flight successfully completed.

Flying swept-winged aircraft was a demanding departure from everything that we had been taught. This design enabled the aircraft to fly faster and be more maneuverable but demanded more attention in the landing pattern. Even though we had gone through extensive training, a few pilots were unsuccessful in making the transition. This was a dangerous business in which a mistake could easily be fatal. This fact was pushed to the back of our minds. The dangers were overshadowed by the fact that we were flying swept-winged, high performance, military aircraft.

I had worked harder and experienced more stress than ever before in my life. Upon successfully completing all required phases of the flight training program, nine young pilots, including myself, were summoned to an office where we were awarded those coveted "Wings of Gold." We still had so much to learn. Two of the pilots that received their wings that day were killed in action during the war in Vietnam. I fear that others in the group met the same fate.

Glenda had flown from Texas to Tennessee with the expectation of giving birth at the Memphis Naval Hospital in Millington, Tennessee. After receiving my wings, I drove the Volkswagen to join her. I had been granted a long period of leave, and therefore expected to be present for the delivery. Our daughter Kelly did not cooperate. My leave expired, and I had no choice but to report to my new duty station.

Many times, Glenda, as the wife of a Marine Corps and commercial pilot, was left on her own to deal with tough situations. This was the first.

MCAS CHERRY POINT

Naval Aviator?
Yes.
Training all done?
No way.

I checked into VMA-332, my first active duty Marine unit, at Marine Corps Air Station Cherry Point in Havelock, North Carolina. At that time, I was stressed because of my concern for Glenda, who would soon give birth to our firstborn. She had been left in Tennessee to endure the birthing process while I was hundreds of miles away.

This attack squadron was forming up with mostly young pilots who had recently earned their wings as Naval Aviators. We would be flying new A-4E Skyhawks and man, did they ever look cool all lined up on the ramp.

Upon checking in at this base, a few pilots knew enough to request a certain type aircraft, or even a specific unit. I didn't know about such stuff, so I accepted the will of the Corps. I was very fortunate to have been assigned to an attack squadron. I soon learned to love the aircraft and the mission.

I was assigned to base housing and arrangements were made for Glenda and our daughter, Kelly, to join me in North Carolina. Our little duplex, older but adequate, was located only about a mile from the main gate. There was no garage or parking area—we parked on the street but there was a sidewalk that led to the front door.

This was an exciting time. We were still newlyweds but also had a new baby. I was engaged in flying advanced warplanes and we had a house of our own. Kelly was a joy—she was happy, playful, and seemed to get a kick out of my arriving home from work. We played hide and seek and wrestled on the floor. Glenda was the perfect young wife and mother. We were a great little family.

The flying was demanding and stressful, but we met new friends and tried to enjoy our day-to-day life. We explored that part of the world and enjoyed showing our families around when they came for visits.

Shortly after we were established in our new home, I noticed a shiny red Vespa motor scooter that sported a "For Sale" sign. We had no money, but I wanted it. We bought it. My squadron hangar was only about two miles from our house. This little scooter was dependable and easy to operate--it was the perfect commute vehicle. Glenda now had full use of our 1964 VW Bug for household chores.

Janice, Glenda's sister, and her husband Challice came to visit. I decided to give him a demo ride on the scooter. We rode along the highway for a while, then turned onto a sandy road that ran through a pine forest. The scooter was probably overloaded but it clipped along easily. Suddenly, a large rattlesnake was spotted in the middle of the road.

We both saw the snake at about the same time. I slammed on the brakes and Challice, who was holding my left arm and right shoulder, clamped down with both hands. I claimed that it took weeks for the fingernail scratches on my arm and shoulder to heal. To say that he was not fond of snakes would be an understatement.

The entire squadron was sent to Puerto Rico to continue our training. As flights of four, we departed Cherry Point for NAS Cecil Field in Jacksonville, Florida, where we were refueled without shutting down our engines. The flight over the Caribbean, with its clear blue water and numerous islands with white sandy beaches, was breathtakingly beautiful.

This deployment was my first time to leave the United States mainland. It was exciting. The weather was warm and sunny. We started flying within a day or so and flew nearly every day. The bombing target that we used was located within thirty miles of our base, therefore a flight could be completed in less than an hour.

The food was good, our accommodations were adequate, the beach was nearby, and the jets were fun to fly. Life was good. The one disadvantage was that I was separated from Glenda and Kelly.

Some evenings, after the aircraft had been parked for the day, a group of the pilots would gather at the Officers Club for a social hour. This club was not fancy, but I was impressed with the hilltop location, the relaxed atmosphere, the available outdoor seating and the featured steel drum band. I did not drink but was aware that the rum drinks were very cheap--less than 50 cents each.

On one of the first nights, I walked away from the group and stood in the darkness while looking at the lights across the countryside. I had to smile. The Caribbean, music, tropical aroma, moist air on my face, and being a part of a group of eager young pilots, made me realize that I was again experiencing more than I could have ever dreamed.

The United States had steadily increased its involvement in the war in Vietnam and Marine Corps attack pilots were in demand. Most of the pilots from that squadron would be sent into that conflict. I was no exception.

Our happy days in North Carolina came to an end as we moved Glenda and Kelly to a small duplex only about a mile from my Mom and Dad's farm in Tennessee. Glenda's parents lived only about eight miles away. I was confident that Glenda, who was pregnant, would have a great support team during my absence. We will forever be grateful for their help. I soon stepped onto an airplane in Memphis with plans to be gone for a full year--a very long year.

A DOSE OF REALITY

Cuba
1964

I was awarded my Wings of Gold as a Naval Aviator in July of 1964 after about 15 months of very intensive training. The low-key presentation ceremony was in no way representative of the effort and stress required to earn those wings.

There is an old rhyme that has circulated through Navy and Marine Corps aviation history. Many times, military flying is stressful and dangerous and when things got really tough this saying would surface. It went: "Wings of Gold, Bars of Brass, you can shove them up your a--." It was a sarcastic utterance and spoken as a showing of dark humor.

This type of dark humor played into our effort to deal with the stress of flying combat attack missions. A fellow pilot had been assigned a tough mission in Vietnam. A friend asked, "If you don't make it back, may I have your air mattress?"

On graduation day there were nine of us, four Marines and five Navy, who were very unceremoniously presented our hard-earned wings. There was no parade, no crowd, no band playing patriotic music, and no family or friends to shower us with congratulations. A Marine officer simply pinned the wings to my shirt and shook my hand.

I had been issued orders to the Marine Corps Air Station Cherry Point in Havelock, North Carolina. I honestly had no idea what to expect. Flight school had demanded that I spend my time focusing on what was scheduled for the next day. I gave very little thought as to what would come next should this training be successful.

Some Marine officer in some unknown location carefully studied the list of new pilots and assigned them to squadrons where, hopefully, their budding skills could best be used. I was assigned to an attack squadron.

I had been willing to accept any assignment that the Marines Corps felt would best serve me and the Corps. Being sent to VMA-332, an attack squadron, was a very lucky day in my life.

Still thinking of myself as a pilot in training, I was surprised to be called, along with other squadron mates, into a special briefing. We were informed that we had been assigned targets in Cuba, an island located about 90 miles south of Key West, Florida. Cuba had been in the news a few years earlier when the Soviet Union had attempted to install missiles on this island that could have been launched against targets in the United States.

The designated pilots assembled at our Group Headquarters building, and after a briefing, were escorted into a secret planning room. This room was filled with tables which displayed detailed maps of Cuba and the southern part of the States. Each pilot was assigned a specific target on this tropical island that he would attempt to attack if it became necessary.

Should an armed conflict occur, my air group was to fly unarmed aircraft from North Carolina to Key West, Florida. At this southern naval base, the aircraft were to be loaded with the proper weapons. As required by my assigned mission, my aircraft was to be armed with Shrike anti-radar missiles which I would do my best to deliver.

My specific target was a radar site on the Isle of Pines. The plan was for all attacking aircraft to become airborne and cross an imaginary line at about the same time. Hopefully, the Cubans would not be aware of the impending attack until only a few minutes before we released our armament.

The delivery of my specific weapon required that I fly at high speed and low altitude until reaching a specific initial point. At this point, under full power, I would pull my aircraft into a steep climb. At about 10,000 feet I was to roll inverted and pull the nose of my A-4 down to the approximate direction of the target, roll the aircraft to the upright position, and fire the missile. If all worked as planned, the weapon would detect the radar beam and track it to the facility. At the programmed altitude it would detonate and hopefully disable the site.

Even though all my training had been dedicated to learning how to use this great aircraft as a weapon, it was still somewhat of a shock that a real mission was being planned.

The details have now been forgotten. The people in power were able to work out a solution that did not require us to fly those attack missions against the Island of Cuba. However, we would soon be tested by fire in a totally different situation and part of the world.

This non-event was my first realization that my chosen profession would be a very serious business. I had been trained and was expected to fly my aircraft into the face of danger should the United States Marine Corps feel that it was necessary.

I risked my life many times. I am fortunate to have lived to tell my stories. Some of my mates were not as lucky.

Outdoors at Cherry Point

North Carolina
1964

Marine Corps Air Station Cherry Point, my first assignment as a Marine pilot, served as my duty station for almost two years. Reflecting upon that time, I now realize that I participated in more outdoor activities than I could have imagined. The following is an attempt to put some of my memories into print.

Bow Hunting

Larry R Gibson, a fellow Marine pilot, and I became interested in learning to shoot a bow. We both bought some inexpensive equipment and on occasion would practice together. Gradually, we honed our skills to a point where most of our arrows hit on or near the target. My intent was to become skilled enough to hunt the whitetail deer that roamed this sprawling base.

My knowledge of how deer lived and moved about their range was very limited, maybe even nonexistent. I obtained the proper license and took the time to search for a likely hunting spot. On this base there were woods, small creeks, and large swampy areas, excellent habitat for deer.

Before daylight, I quietly made my way to a promising spot and took a position that was very near a well-used deer trail. This vantage point proved to be much too close to the action. In the predawn darkness a deer passed within only a few feet of me. I could have touched it with an outstretched hand. That deer never seemed to know that I was there. I realized that at this close range the deer would have never given me the opportunity to raise my bow to take a shot.

My next selected spot allowed the deer to see me well before I had a chance to put my bow into action. On that second attempt I had chosen a clump of small trees right in the middle of the trail. On several occasions deer showed up but I was directly within their line of sight. They stood only a few feet away looking suspiciously at this strange "thing" trying to hide in this little bunch of trees. They knew that something was not normal and quickly dashed away.

I then chose a spot about ten yards to the side of their trail. Two deer passed before sunrise but in the darkness, it was impossible to make a reasonable shot.

I made one last attempt to bag a deer on the base. I arrived early and stayed late but not even one deer showed up. I think they were now aware of my tactics. They must have giggled as they discussed the inept human hunter. I gave up.

Bow in hand, I headed to the car but took a moment to sit on a log that was lying across the trail. My slumped shoulders gave evidence that I had failed as a bowhunter. The woods were completely quiet, but I felt a "presence." I very slowly turned and looked over my shoulder. A deer was standing only about three feet behind me. It stood absolutely still and was looking directly at me. This beautiful animal and I made and held eye contact for a few seconds. It suddenly seemed to realize that this was again the inept bow hunter and bounded away.

Of course, I never bagged a deer at Cherry Point.

Flat Fish
Neuse River

In casual conversation an enlisted Marine told me of harvesting flounder at night from the sandy shallows of the Neuse River, only a few miles from our base. I expressed some interest and he encouraged me to tag along on his next trip.

The flounder and several of its cousins are fish that, upon hatching, look like all other fish. However, within a short period of time this fish turns onto its side and the lower eye migrates to the top side. These fish feed by burying themselves in the sand and waiting for some unsuspecting creature to venture nearby. The prey has little chance of survival as the flounder explodes from its sandy hiding place.

My Marine friend, using an inflated car tire inner tube, had devised a float upon which he had mounted an automobile battery that illuminated a powerful light. This light allowed us to easily spot the shape of a sand covered fish. This contraption was towed behind us with a thin rope. Upon seeing a fish, we were able to slowly approach and pin it to the bottom with a barbless spear that was mounted on a broom stick.

These small fish with their white meat and mild taste made for a gourmet delight.

Bass in the Creek

A slow-moving creek was located near the east end of the east-west runway system at the Marine base. The water was clear but had a reddish color that reminded me of tea. Maybe twenty feet wide and two miles long, this fishing site was somewhat protected from the wind and held a good population of largemouth bass.

Boats were available from the base special services outlet. After launching, we would paddle our small watercraft up the creek (we did have a paddle) while casting lures toward bushes and logs near the creek banks. Our technique was to allow the artificial lure to lie motionless for a few seconds and then give it a slight twitch. Quite often the water would explode, and the fight would be on. It was common to catch five or six of these healthy two or three pounders in only an hour or so.

When aircraft were landing to the west they would fly very low over our heads during the final portion of their approach. They were very noisy, and their wake turbulence would disturb the water and give the trees a good shaking. All said, this activity was a great way to put aside the pressures of our never-ending training. This creek was no more than one mile from our house.

Bugs a Plenty
A Deer Hunt

In our younger years my brother Jerry and I had hunted rabbits and squirrels on the family farm in Tennessee. We heard and read of hunting big game, but this type of hunting was impossible since no big game inhabited our area and we could not afford to travel to hunt.

Soon after arriving at MCAS Cherry Point in North Carolina, I discovered that whitetail deer were common in the area. I secured the license and permit that made me legal to go deer hunting with a rifle. I knew very little as to how to go about this type of hunting.

The deer had the advantage. I selected several different spots, never saw a deer, and became the hunted. Hordes of mosquitoes found me right away. The area around my head became a dark cloud of these pesky beasts.

This may have been the shortest deer hunt in history. Very soon, no more could be endured. I fled for home.

Wild Goose Chase
Lake Mattamuskeet

Several pilots in the squadron made plans to go goose hunting at Lake Mattamuskeet, which was about a two-and-a-half-hour drive north of Cherry Point. I became a part of this hunting expedition.

We departed in the middle of the night and arrived at our planned hunting area well before daylight. The leader of the group had made arrangements to hunt in a farmer's cornfield, in which pit blinds had been dug. Upon arriving at the farmers home, we were driven to our assigned blind in an old pickup truck. We were to stay in that spot for the entire day.

As the sun made its way to the horizon we were treated to an amazing spectacle. A horde of geese began flying from the lake to their feeding grounds. The sky was filled, and the noise was shocking. Thousands upon thousands of hungry geese were looking for food, but not even one chose our cornfield.

We sat there all day without firing a single shot. Late in the afternoon, very near and probably past official sunset, three or four geese finally flew low over our position. Some of my friends fired, probably out of frustration, but I never fired a shot.

One goose was downed. Legally? Who knows? I certainly did not bag a goose, but the experience will always be remembered.

The Major and I
Doves

There was a major, a large man, who had a somewhat gruff demeanor. He liked to hunt and smoke cigars. It became known that he was going dove hunting. I did not know him very well but agreed to meet him at his hunting spot. Only the two of us showed up.

It was hot. The doves were not flying, happy to be resting in the trees around a large soybean field. The major and I trudged about trying to get the birds to fly. His cigar took a beating and soon started to unravel, which left long strips of tobacco leaf hanging in shreds. I still have this mental picture of him thrashing through the brush, clothing sweat-soaked, cigar in disarray with his shotgun in hand.

The birds finally did start to move about, and we had a great day of shooting. In those days I was pretty good at knocking them out of the air and took pride in finding nearly every bird that I had downed.

After leaving the squadron, I never saw or heard of this major again.

Glenda

Wife, Mother

As I write about these outdoor activities the thought of, "What was Glenda doing?" crossed my mind. She never got a day off in that she was taking care of Kelly, keeping house, and cooking.

She never complained, and I feel she encouraged me to get out and do things that would take my mind off our never-ending training. She surely felt that these outdoor adventures were good for me.

Reflecting upon Glenda, over the many years of our marriage, I am sad to say that I have probably been guilty of taking her for granted. She has been a great companion and support person. I fear that I have never given her enough credit.

There are few women who would have endured the hardships that she has shouldered. She should have some sort of special award.

NOT IF BUT WHEN

Plowshares into Swords

Approaching the Marine Corps Recruiter in the Student Union Building at the University of Tennessee, Martin Branch, I noticed posters of young Marines with painted faces armed with rifles. Pictures on the nearby walls were of tanks, aircraft, and ships all engaged in some phase of warfare. The Marine on duty had an array of ribbons displayed on his chest, earned for participating in conflicts in several foreign countries. Even with all these hints, it didn't register in my mind.

As I was signing the enlistment papers the recruiter asked if I had any interest in aviation. I was only vaguely aware that the Marines Corps operated aircraft. I stammered but answered in the affirmative—not realizing that I had just chosen my weapon of choice. Another hint but I just didn't get it.

My enlistment into the PLC (Platoon Leaders Class) program required that I complete two separate six-week training sessions at Quantico, Virginia. Upon successfully completing this training and graduating from college, I would be designated a Marine Second Lieutenant. During those summer training sessions, we Marine officer hopefuls received instruction in physical conditioning, weapons, hand-to-hand combat, and tactics. I still didn't understand.

During one of these training sessions at Quantico, our platoon was having a less than stellar day on the drill field. In frustration our DI, Drill Instructor, called us to a halt and, in his "gentle" voice, informed us that our performance was well below that of even the worst Marine. He further informed us that unless we got our act together, we would not be returning to our college studies. According to him, we would be issued weapons and sent directly into combat. At the time I was not aware of any war that was in progress but chose to keep this information to myself. I chose not to comprehend.

Upon graduation from college I was ordered directly to flight school at Pensacola, Florida. The next 15 months were the most demanding of my life, both mentally and physically. We were taught how to use our aircraft to its limit. Our training included dropping bombs, firing machine guns, air-to-air combat, and carrier landings. My future was cast in stone, but I ignored it.

My first year in a Marine Attack Squadron was a continuation of this training. We young pilots sharpened our skills in every aspect of flying and weapons delivery. These were exciting days for me and my fellow Marine aviators. I still chose to disregard the evidence that was so obvious.

United States combat troops had been in Vietnam for nearly a year. Pilots in my squadron were now considered combat-ready attack pilots. There was no doubt, soon every trained pilot would be sent into combat. I had no choice. I had to face reality. I finally understood.

All my Marine training had been designed to prepare me to go to war. All my learned skills had one and only one purpose, which was to engage and try to kill men who were trained to kill me. An enlistment in the United States Marine Corps is, in effect, signing a blank check for up to and including your life. These are not my words, I don't know who originally spoke or wrote them, but they accurately described my agreed upon obligation.

I surely knew that all this training was to prepare me for war. I had allowed this fact to lie dormant in the back of my mind. Upon reflection, from the very beginning, it was, "NOT IF, BUT WHEN" I would be tested in actual combat.

I had orders in-hand and there was no doubt as to my destination. I could not help wondering how I would react when an actual combat situation occurred. Would I cower and shake in my boots or would I do my job as trained? I was confident that I would choose the latter, but one never knows until that moment arrives.

I hereby report that every combat mission was accepted and flown to the best of my ability. There were times when things got very tense and on occasion mistakes were made. Thankfully, my aircraft was never hit by enemy fire, the engine never failed during flight, and my mistakes were not fatal. I am proud to have served as a United States Marine Attack Pilot.

I was not unique in that there were hundreds of pilots that served with honor and some lost their lives. These pilots flew combat missions almost daily and never, in my observation, complained or showed any fear. Oh, there was almost continuous bitching, moaning, swearing, and grumbling, but never about the flying or the mission. Damn, I loved those guys.

I served proudly as a Marine Skyhawk pilot and was lucky enough to live to write of the experience. I loved the "Scooter," as the A-4 was fondly nicknamed. It proved to be a dependable and effective weapon.

TOP

A Story of George
1964

They called him "Top." This handle may have been created due to his bright red head of hair.

Looking back on those days, some fifty years ago, it seems that we were a group of young boys attempting to be Marine/Navy Pilots. Pictures seem to confirm this image in that we looked like a bunch of high school seniors.

Upon receiving my wings, I hoped that the pressure that we had endured during flight school would be relieved. My hopes were dashed. The intense training in pursuit of mastering our aircraft never let up. We were slow to realize it but there was no doubt that we were being prepared for actual combat in Vietnam.

The weather at Marine Corps Air Station Cherry Point was generally quite mild. However, a cold front had passed through during the night. There had been blustery winds, rain, and the temperature had dropped to slightly below the freezing point.

The morning had dawned cool and clear. On that brisk day George and I, both second lieutenants, were assigned to fly as a two-plane flight. He had been designated as the flight leader and I was to fly his wing.

We accomplished the normal briefing, signed for our aircraft, and felt the chill on our cheeks as we walked the ramp to our jets. The start and taxi had gone as expected. We proceeded to and lined up on the active runway for our briefed "section" takeoff. This type of takeoff is a maneuver where two aircraft simultaneously accelerate and become airborne together.

All seemed normal as I did my best to maintain the proper position during the takeoff roll. I observed his nose wheel leaving the pavement and matched this maneuver as both aircraft became airborne.

George suddenly put his aircraft back on the runway and called, "Aborting, aborting." With a slight right turn I cleared his aircraft and then made a left turn over his line of travel in order to see what was happening. I fully expected to see him come to a safe arrested stop near the end of the runway.

All Marine and Navy runways are equipped with some sort of arresting gear. This runway was equipped with the most basic type. A heavy cable had been installed across the runway at about 1000 feet from the end. This cable was attached to large chains that were laid out along both sides of the runway. These chains were like anchor chain with each link being quite heavy. Should the tailhook of an aircraft engage this cable, these links would be pulled out, one at a time, with ever increasing resistance. This primitive but effective arresting gear would in most cases bring the aircraft to a safe stop, possibly saving both the pilot and the plane.

The big problem on this fateful day was the fact that we had made a "section" takeoff. George, to allow room on the runway for my aircraft, had lined up slightly left of centerline. Upon engaging the cable off-center, more links of chain were pulled from one side than the other. This unbalanced force caused his aircraft to swerve and as it crossed the end of the runway, the turn increased. Due to the rain of the night before, the North Carolina soil was wet and soft. His wheels dug in and his aircraft flipped onto its back and came to rest with the canopy pressed into the ground.

My immediate frantic radio transmission was something like, "An aircraft is upside-down. The pilot needs help, right now." The mental picture after all these years is of a beautiful new aircraft upside down, with its landing gear pointing skyward, its tailpipe smoking, and a fellow Marine pilot in extreme danger.

Thank goodness, the aircraft did not burn. We were told that George was partially out of the cockpit when the rescue crew arrived. The refueling probe had been broken from the aircraft by the crash. A rescue worker attempted to use this probe to break the plexiglass canopy to create an escape route. This probe held jet fuel which spilled on George.

The squadron pilots never received a formal briefing or a written account of this accident. I feel that some instrument, possibly the airspeed indicator, was not indicating properly. George, on the spur of the moment, and who can fault him, had made the decision to abort. In hindsight, the accident could have been avoided if he had simply continued the takeoff and immediately passed the lead. He could have then flown my wing as we returned to the airfield for a landing.

We were engaged in a dangerous profession. Attention to detail was mandatory. A simple wrong decision could easily result in the pilot's death. I flirted with disaster many times and feel fortunate to have lived to tell these stories.

George and most of the pilots in our squadron soon received orders to participate in the war in Vietnam. I learned later that he spent time in the field with the ground Marines but also continued to fly combat missions. He was later involved in an incident very similar to the above but flew the aircraft to a safe landing.

I often wonder what he experienced during his time in Vietnam. Every person has many stories that could be told. George, if it is ever possible, I would love to hear the stories of your life.

George survived that year in Vietnam and remained in the Marine Corps for more than twenty years. After retirement he served as a stockbroker and now lives a peaceful life in Florida with his wife and their beloved animals.

Note: After reading this story, my daughter Kelly contacted George. We have exchanged our versions of this story. This incident happened many years ago, but our stories are very similar. He is in the process of writing a book which will contain stories of his life.

Colonel Grayson

Eglin Air Force Base
Florida
1965

As a newly designated Naval Aviator, I had been assigned to VMA-332, a Marine Attack Squadron that was forming up with mostly "nugget" (first tour aviator) pilots like myself. Our new A-4E Skyhawk aircraft were sleek, powerful, and capable. We didn't put much thought into the fact that we were being trained for combat duty in Vietnam.

Step by step, I had gone from getting airsick on my first training flight to flying modern jet aircraft. I can remember walking from the line shack, a place where we checked the logbooks and signed for our aircraft, toward my assigned aircraft. I sometimes shook my head in amazement, how could this farm kid, dressed in full flight gear, be trusted to take this beautiful and expensive warplane out on a mission? I felt confident and worthy.

We flew nearly every day, practicing the maneuvers and weapons delivery techniques that would be used in actual combat. Our skills and our aircraft were being pushed to the limit. It was a heady time.

With no prior notice, the flight operations department informed me that I had been selected to fly one of the squadron's aircraft to Eglin Air Force Base in Florida to be temporarily assigned to the Air Force. My assignment was to help test the operation of a spray tank and determine the dispersion pattern of a released liquid. I was to fly near a tower which had collectors installed from top to bottom. A harmless but traceable substance was to be released for a specific time while flying at a specific airspeed. After my spraying pass, the collectors would be gathered and

71

processed in a nearby laboratory.

Flat Hat: The act of flying an aircraft too low over or near buildings or people with the pilot feeling that someone, somewhere, must be saying, "Wow!" An old saying: Give a pilot an aircraft and a crowd and he will kill himself in order to present a good show.

This assignment allowed me to legally Flat Hat. After the first few flights, people from the laboratory started to show up on the roof of their building to watch my flyby. I noted this and rewarded them with a second pass which might have included a few rolls as the nose was pointed skyward. I was young and probably foolish.

I had departed Cherry Point alone but with plans for Glenda and Kelly, our new baby daughter, to join me in Florida. There was a layer of low clouds that covered the entire area as I arrived over the Eglin airbase. I requested and received a radar vector into the airport area. Approach Control gave me headings and altitudes that would hopefully enable me to safely fly through the clouds. Breaking out of the bottom of this layer, I was surprised to see a large Air Force transport aircraft that was much too close. I was easily able to maneuver clear but puzzled as to how the radar operator had allowed the two aircraft to fly that close together.

My Marine aircraft and I were an unusual sight at this Air Force base. My assigned parking and servicing area required me to taxi across a rather busy public road. My plane evidently had the right of way since all traffic would stop and wait for me to clear. Early on, I waved to the people in the waiting cars, and they waved back with enthusiasm. Very soon I noticed that the three or four cars that initially stopped to allow me to pass had turned into a small crowd. I felt like a rock star. Kids seemed excited and waved as if I was someone of importance. This daily greeting continued for the entire time of my deployment to Eglin.

Until that assignment, I had had very little contact with senior military officers. The officer in charge of this project was Air Force Lieutenant Colonel Grayson. The shocking development was that we were directed to share the same BOQ (Bachelor Officer Quarters) room. I was terrified. How could a lieutenant sleep in the same room with a colonel?

I soon learned that he was a mild-mannered man and a comfortable roommate. He put his trousers on, one leg at a time, just like me. In the morning his hair was in disarray and a few times he allowed a fart to escape. He was a fellow human being and I learned to respect and like him.

These were the days before cell phones and GPS. I don't remember how we communicated but Glenda, with Kelly in tow, manned the VW Bug and joined me in Florida. Earlier, I had fashioned a piece of plywood to fit the back-seat area of the car. This flat area was covered with a folded quilt and Kelly used it as a playpen and bed. This was the mid-60's and we never considered that she or Glenda should use seat belts. Somehow, Kelly survived her childhood.

I think that Colonel Grayson must have become very lonely. Glenda and I rented a room on the beach near or in Valparaiso, Florida and I moved out of the BOQ. At the time we didn't think that this little event would be considered an adventure. I knew that we could not comfortably afford this trip, but I didn't want to be separated from Glenda and Kelly. Unfortunately, there would be an extreme separation in the not too distant future.

The daily flights were short, 30 minutes or so, with the heart of the mission being a low pass near the collector tower spraying a harmless yet traceable substance. This assignment, with the full support of Colonel Grayson and the Air Force, required me to make twenty or more of these flights.

Glenda and I, along with Kelly, were invited to visit the lab that processed the results of my airborne sprayings. We were treated like royalty. We carried Kelly in our arms and were shown about the lab and told of its mission. I was surprised that one of the technicians was a fellow graduate from the University of Tennessee at Martin.

The employees of this facility became more and more interested in my low-level passes near their building. I continued to fly my official mission but always made an extra Flat Hat or "show off" pass.

After completing this assignment, I flew the plane back to Cherry Point as Glenda returned by VW. Kelly had just experienced the first adventure of her life but today has no memory of the happenings. The success or failure of this deployment was never shared with me. The officials of my squadron, to my recollection, made no comment concerning this assignment. It seemed to be a non-event.

Glenda made a safe and timely trip back to North Carolina and I continued to train for my upcoming deployment to Vietnam.

We were so young, yet so full of life.

This rather mundane story is an effort to pass on tales of our lives. Glenda and I have shared many years and happenings. We remain friends and dedicated partners. She is a good woman and I am lucky to have had her as my copilot throughout my life.

GROUND CONTROLLED APPROACH

On every successful takeoff the pilot must have a plan as to how to return safely to earth. During good weather it is relatively easy to find an airfield and make a landing. This procedure becomes increasingly more difficult as the visibility decreases. Over the years tremendous progress has been made in aircraft instrumentation. Pilots of today's aircraft have unlimited information available and the planes can be programmed to land themselves. During my early flying career, we considered it a luxury to have a single needle that pointed to a station.

A ground-based radar had been developed and used extensively in the years before I began flying Marine Corps aircraft. The controller viewed two radar displays which enabled him to observe the aircraft's course and altitude. Using voice commands alone he could give the pilot enough information to maintain the proper course and glide slope.

The controllers and the pilots became very proficient with this system. The GCA (ground-controlled approach) was used in Vietnam where there could be long periods of low clouds and rainy weather. Very soon after liftoff the pilot and aircraft entered the clouds. The entire mission was flown with no visual contact with the ground. By following only verbal commands the pilot could safely fly the aircraft to a position from which a normal landing could be made.

Today's aircraft are equipped with very sophisticated equipment. The autopilots and instrumentation are capable of landing the aircraft with zero forward visibility. During all phases of flight, the pilot has a visual display of all aspects of the aircraft's surroundings.

My flying career of thirty-five years allowed me to witness and use this tremendous advance in technology. Early on, during an approach in an airliner, after completing all the proper calls and procedures the captain would say, "Landing." This word was an indication to the other crew members that the runway or runway environment was in sight, and the captain intended to make a landing.

During the later years of my airline career my copilot and I (now only a two-person crew) were scheduled to fly into Seattle, Washington which had experienced several days of dense fog. The Boeing 757 was equipped with the latest instrumentation. All the prescribed procedures were accomplished, and we were cleared for an approach and landing.

The approach went as briefed and at the proper time I, as the captain, said, "Landing." On this modern aircraft this word meant that I had carefully observed the approach, all instruments appeared to be normal, and I was comfortable allowing the computers to land the aircraft. We felt the main gear touch and as the nose wheel was lowered to the runway, I began to dimly see the centerline runway lights.

The brakes were automatically applied. As the aircraft slowed to taxi speed, a runway exit became visible and we were cleared to leave the runway. Using the nose wheel steering handle, I attempted to steer toward this exit. The autoflight systems would not allow the aircraft to deviate from the runway centerline. These modern systems had to be disengaged before I could take control of the aircraft.

At some point during our training we, as student pilots, were introduced to flying under instrument conditions (IFR). We gradually learned to fly our aircraft without any external visual reference. The training aircraft were equipped with a canvas device (hood) that could be pulled over the rear cockpit. I clearly remember flying with this shield in place on a flight from Kingsville, Texas to New Iberia, Louisiana.

Even during our takeoff roll I had no outside visual reference. Flying completely on instruments, I was able to climb to the assigned altitude, cruise, descend, and make an approach to our destination airport. The instructor finally said, "I have the aircraft—pop the hood." This was an amazing moment! There directly ahead was a beautiful runway and the aircraft was at the proper position to make a normal landing.

During certain times of the year the weather in Vietnam was cloudy and rainy nearly all the time. The Ground Controlled Approach (GCA) was used on a regular basis and I became comfortable flying my aircraft down to two hundred feet above the ground using only the verbal transmissions of the controller.

Night flights, during poor weather conditions, were stressful to say the least. I can only speak for myself, but all my learned skills were required. The attack portion of the mission was over, the weather was not good, and there was a need to get this aircraft back on the ground safely.

Approach Control gave me directions that put me in the airport area where I was directed to contact the GCA final controller. The aircraft was configured for landing by lowering the landing gear (wheels) and flaps. The controller in a confident and steady voice said, "No need to acknowledge any further transmissions." The weather conditions had not improved but somehow when I heard this phrase, I felt that a weight had been lifted from my shoulders. I trusted these guys!

The controllers were very good at what they did. Their calm voices and continuous stream of information instilled a special level of confidence. By looking at two radar displays these guys were able to keep me on course and on glide path. In every case, as I approached the lowest altitude allowed on this type of approach, the runway lights came into view.

I never knew where these guys were located on the airfield and I never met any of them in person. Should any of them read this story, they should know that by using their learned skills they "talked" me home safely many times. Gentlemen, my life was in your hands! Thank you!

Major Alwan

Vietnam
1967

In March of 2014 Glenda and I were in Gold Canyon, Arizona when we first heard the news of the disappearance of Malaysian Airlines Flight MH370. That commercial flight had suddenly inexplicably been lost to all radio and radar contact. Every effort was made to track and locate the aircraft, but the crash site was never located, and we may never know what really happened.

The loss of this aircraft caused me to reflect upon an unusual flying assignment during my tour of duty in Southeast Asia in 1967. I was serving as a Marine attack pilot at Chu Lai, Vietnam, flying almost daily attack missions against the Viet Cong who were trying to overrun South Vietnam.

I don't remember having any personal contact with Major Harold Joseph Alwan. We were both fairly new in the squadron and our collateral duties were not associated. He was a maintenance specialist and I was working as a briefing officer. All Marine pilots have assigned duties other than flying.

Helicopters were constantly in the air on supply and troop movement flights. When flying into dangerous areas, the pilots often requested attack aircraft as escorts. They felt that the show of an aggressive presence caused the enemy to be a bit more selective as to which aircraft they fired upon. In other words, the helicopter pilots felt a little safer.

This was February 1967 and the war was in full swing. We were flying around the clock and our maintenance staff made every effort to keep our aircraft in flying condition. Repairs had been made on one of the squadron aircraft, but a test flight was required before it could be released for normally scheduled combat missions. Since Major Alwan was qualified both as an attack pilot and maintenance test pilot, a plan was made to have him fly a helo escort mission and complete the required test flight.

On this flight something went terribly wrong. He and his aircraft simply disappeared. There had been no indication of a problem and no distress calls had been heard. The sad news spread quickly through the base at Chu Lai, but combat operations continued without interruption.

My squadron operations officer summoned me to his office and informed me that a search had been planned to look for the major's aircraft. The experts, after studying the wind, ocean currents, and possible crash location, decided to launch an aircraft on a search mission. I had been chosen to fly this questionable flight.

No attack pilot that I knew of had received any training relating to this type of search. My briefing was very vague, something like, "Just go out there, descend to just above the water, and look for anything unusual."

I was to climb to altitude as I proceeded out over the South China Sea. Upon reaching a point that was 100 miles from the airfield a descent was made to just above the water.

The range of the radio and navigational equipment on my aircraft was just over 100 miles under normal conditions. As I descended both were lost due to the curvature of the earth and my low altitude. I can report that flying a single-seat, single-engine aircraft at low altitude 100 miles out to sea is very intimidating. Most people would find it difficult to comprehend the immensity of an ocean. The water was a deep blue color and there was absolutely no evidence of any other ship or aircraft.

After leveling at a very low altitude, I began to fly somewhat of a square pattern. I saw absolutely nothing unusual. Even though uncomfortable, I made every effort to find some hint of Major Alwan or his aircraft. I remember thinking what a shame it would be if he happened to be nearby in a rubber raft and I flew right over him without making visual contact.

This search was continued until I reached bingo fuel, meaning that minimum fuel remained to safely return to base, at which time I advanced the thrust lever, started a climb, and turned toward my home base. As I climbed through about ten or twelve thousand feet, I heard voices over my radio. I was surprised at the relief I felt.

My debriefing consisted of a squadron officer asking if I had seen anything. My only comment had to be, "I saw absolutely nothing." That flight caused me to form a bond with Major Alwan.

I will always wonder what happened to the major. The war continued even though his family grieved. The war was what it was, and most pilots soon put this loss into the back of their minds. We were totally engaged in the effort to put bombs on target and to guard against making some fatal mistake.

My next combat mission was scheduled for that night. I flew it.

MARINE ATTACK MISSION

1966

The successful completion of any airborne mission, whether training, combat, or commercial, requires the pilot to repeatedly accomplish a certain set of procedures. Repetition, repetition, repetition is a big factor in a flight that ends with the passengers, crew, and aircraft safe and able to fly again.

As a freshman in high school my football coach sent me into my very first game. I was surprised that during the real game we did exactly what we had done in practice. I had expected the actual game to be totally different, maybe even magical. I had that very same feeling when I strapped into that fully loaded attack aircraft for my first combat mission.

I went through the familiar brief and preflight steps, climbed into the cockpit, and had the normal interaction with the ground crew. This sequence of events tended to make me feel comfortable and confident but in fact this flight would be drastically different. My aircraft was loaded with real bombs and the enemy would be returning fire with real bullets. There were people out there who were trained and determined to destroy my aircraft and kill me. Conversely, I also had been trained to cause as much damage as possible. I was at war.

I began this story with the intent of documenting the steps that we pilots routinely performed in the process of flying a combat mission. The following is a somewhat chronological listing of the duties and activities involved in completing a flight in the Vietnam War.

Sometime during the day, just as had been done in all previous training squadrons, the flight schedule was published. Since all pilots were equally qualified, the scheduling officer could assign any of us to any mission. After learning of their next flying event, the pilots made every effort to prepare themselves.

At the appointed time they trudged through the sand, which was mud during the rainy season, to the briefing facility. At that time a modified trailer from an over-the-road truck served as the briefing room. A pilot who had studied all available information would brief the combat crew as to the target location, weather conditions, and the expected enemy resistance. All pilots listened intently, made mental notes but realized that no one knew whether the provided information was fresh or accurate.

Briefing complete, the pilots made their way to the squadron area and suited up for flight. In full flight gear, the aircraft logbook was checked for proper maintenance, fuel load, and armament. They signed for their birds indicating that they were now responsible.

The pilots who were scheduled to fly together sat down to brief as to how this flight was to be conducted. The flight leader reminded the other pilots of their call sign, position in the flight, join-up procedures after takeoff, radio frequencies, and emergency procedures. A similar briefing was conducted for every flight of a pilot's career.

The aircraft and weapons were preflighted carefully even though the ground crew had previously done the very same checks. These maintenance and ordinance men were not offended, since safety was a very important factor. Rarely was anything found out of place—these young Marines were well trained and took pride in their work.

Upon completing the external checks, the pilot climbed the ladder and with the help of a plane captain, settled into the cockpit. This rather complicated procedure consisted of strapping into the seat, which contained a parachute and survival gear, attaching the headphones, and G-suit. The G-suit was an inflatable garment that covered the large muscles in the lower body. As high-g maneuvers were performed, this suit would inflate and put pressure on our lower abdomen, thighs, and calves to prevent blood from pooling. If enough blood leaves the upper body, specifically the brain, the pilot will black out.

Once strapped in, the plane captain retreated, and the ground crew removed the ladder. The pilot then performed the pre-start checklist. This memorized check started on the left and ended on the right side of the cockpit. Every switch, instrument, and control were checked to ensure that they were in the proper position or showed the proper reading.

During engine start the ground crew was always very attentive, ensuring that the start sequence was normal. During this entire sequence the plane was being supplied with external electrical power, and a machine that would provide high pressure air for engine start was standing at the ready. When his checks were complete, the pilot looked outside and made a circular motion with a gloved hand which was the signal for the ground crew to supply the starting air.

The engine began to rotate. At the proper RPM (the gauge read in percent of maximum RPM) the igniters were energized, and the throttle was moved to introduce fuel. The "light-off" could be heard as a low-level explosion, felt as a slight shudder, and seen as the exhaust gas temperature needle (EGT) began to rise. The pilot monitored the instruments, and as the engine reached idle speed, he gave the signal for the ground crew to disconnect the external power sources, air and electric. At this point in time, this lone pilot and his aircraft were an entity—the battle was on.

The pilot and plane captain exchanged a series of hand signals designed to check various flight controls, lights, and systems. Checks complete and wheel chocks removed, the aircraft was now ready to taxi. The pilot added power and released the brakes which allowed the aircraft to move forward. Almost immediately, the brakes were applied aggressively, causing the nose to dip, to ensure that the they were functional.

Just before leaving the fight line, the flight leader would make a radio call: "Oxwood Flight, Check In". In response, the other flight members, if they were ready, would reply, "Two's up", "Three's up" and, "Four's up." The flight would then taxi single file to the active runway. Upon departing the parking area, the canopies were closed allowing the pilot to feel the cool conditioned air. It felt wonderful. Flight suits by this time were sweat-soaked, due to the hot and humid conditions. The cockpits of the aircraft were the only artificially cooled spaces on the entire Marine Air Base.

One at a time, the aircraft were taxied into the takeoff position, the engines were tested at full power, the instruments were checked, and the brakes were released. Upon getting airborne the landing gear and flaps were retracted. After accomplishing a circling join-up, the flight proceeded in formation toward the target. Many times, the home base could be easily seen during the actual attack. This war was happening right in our own backyard.

The flight leader always had the duty of making all the radio calls to the controlling agencies. On a normal flight he would talk to ground control, tower, departure control, a forward air controller (FAC), approach control, tower, and finally ground control. The FACs were usually airborne in small single-engine aircraft. Most of their aircraft had the top of the wing painted white for contrast as they flew over the forests and rice paddies. They were easy to spot as the flight approached.

The pilots had been briefed as to the general expectations of the mission. Upon making radio contact with the FAC, he would spout a wealth of valuable information concerning this specific target. The flight was advised as to the elevation of the target, best run-in heading, reported defensive fire, and clues to help visually find the target. These guys were very good at what they did and very brave to fly low and slow over known enemy positions.

By the time the flight arrived over the target, each pilot had formed a good mental picture as to the true nature of the target and required method of attack. The lead would position the flight so that an organized attack could be accomplished. At this point the flight would break up, allowing the pilots to make individual attacks. In order to maintain proper separation and pattern integrity, a series of radio calls were made. The calls during the attack would be something like: "One in, hot", meaning the lead was diving toward the target and intended to drop bombs, "One off, safe", off the target, bombs switches off, "Two in, hot", "Two off, safe, "Three in, hot", "Three off, safe." The pattern, sort of a tilted circle, was flown until all bombs had been delivered.

After their last attack run the pilots joined up in formation for the flight back to base. As the flight departed the target area, the FAC would make a flyover to check the effectiveness of the attack. His bomb damage assessment (BDA) was relayed via radio as the flight headed for home.

On days when the weather was good these attack missions became quite routine. However, they could become very demanding due to other factors such as terrain and weather. I remember attacking a target where the only possible run-in heading was directly toward the mountainside. After releasing our bombs, because of the rising terrain, we were much closer to the ground than normal. On one of my passes, as I was desperately trying to get the nose of my aircraft pointed skyward, I felt I could discern individual leaves on the bamboo plants. I don't know after all these years if that is an embellishment or not. I do know that there was a moment of wondering if my jet and I would become a permanent part of the landscape.

On another flight I can remember pressing an attack under an overcast sky. The base of the clouds was lower than our normal 7,000-foot pattern altitude. All normal procedures had to be disregarded as we attempted to drop bombs under the clouds. The Marines on the ground needed our support. We had to improvise in order to get our bombs on target.

Upon arriving at the home base, it was normal to make visual approaches. Should the weather conditions prevent this type of approach and landing, individual instrument approaches were flown. After landing, the aircraft were either taxied back to the flight line or to the refueling area. At times, "hot" refueling was used to top off the tanks for the next flight. The pilot would maneuver his jet to an area where men with fuel hoses were waiting on moveable platforms. The canopy remained closed as the fuel hose was attached to the airborne refueling probe. The aircraft tanks could be filled in only a few minutes.

Upon shut down, the next order of business was to make the proper entries into the aircraft logbook. The takeoff and landing times along with any malfunctions were logged. The short debriefing was the last official duty of a combat mission.

The pilots repeated this entire series of events on every flight. They were young and strong, but always aware that these flights were actual combat missions. Many young people were dying. I feel that I was fortunate to have survived.

LOW PASS

NAS Cubi Point
Philippines

In 1966 the Vietnam war was raging. I had been "in country" for several months flying combat missions almost daily. My squadron, VMA-211, a Marine attack squadron, was ordered from the war zone to Iwakuni, Japan for continued training and to take on new pilots. Aviators, whether private, commercial, or military, never stop training. Flying skills are a fleeting commodity and must be constantly reinforced.

Upon arrival in Japan, the squadron pilots immediately began flying locally, while becoming acquainted with the replacement pilots who were arriving from the States. Within a few days five pilots, including myself, flew aircraft to Naha, Okinawa for bombing practice.

During this short deployment a Marine Forward Air Controller team was conducting training out of the naval air station at Cubi Point in the Philippines. They requested real pilots in real airplanes to be a part of this activity. Another pilot and I flew our aircraft to "Cubi" to hopefully make their training more realistic.

The FAC team had positioned themselves on a hilltop only 20 miles or so from the air base. After making radio contact, these Marines made every effort to give us pilots enough information to locate simulated targets that they had selected. Map coordinates, terrain features, and visual clues were used in the process. As the pilots of single-seat aircraft, we had our hands full. We were cramped in a very compact cockpit, traveling at rather high speed, trying to find the target, and at the same time keep the aircraft airborne. It was a demanding yet educational exercise for both the FAC team and the pilots.

The official part of one of these training sessions had been completed when the Marine radio operator asked if I would make a low pass by the team's position. I was a young attack pilot, and most likely a little dumb, flying a cool military jet. A request like this was like offering candy to a child. Following their verbal instructions, I was able to visually locate their position. My A-4 was maneuvered to a point from which a safe but very close pass could be made.

The little jet was humming as I passed at eye level by their position. To my surprise, I saw thirteen or fourteen Marines lined up and bending over with their trousers and underwear around their ankles. They were positioned so that their naked butts pointed directly at me. As I zoomed by the radio operator radioed "Nice pass." I do not remember my exact reply, but it should have been something like "Too much information." I had been mooned.

The armed forces of the United States were actively engaged in an extremely serious war effort. These were desperate times. Many young people were losing their lives but there always seemed to be room for a little humor. These young Marines would soon be plying their skills in this furious conflict and yet enjoyed a bit of a joke.

To the best of my knowledge I never met any of these guys in person. Despite that, I felt that I already knew them rather intimately. I would very much like to hear the stories of their lives. I fear that some of them did not return home safely. Hopefully, most of them are now gray-haired grandfathers somewhere in this great country.

"STANDBY, STANDBY"

Vietnam
Early 1966

Vietnam was a place of intense warfare. During the daylight hours the United States and South Vietnam forces were in almost complete control. The situation reversed under the cover of darkness, when the enemy's pipeline of supplies, food, ammunition, fuel, weapons, etc. came to life.

The Ho Chi Minh Trail began in North Vietnam, proceeded through the mountains of Laos, then branched off into several arteries, all of which continued into South Vietnam. Everything possible was done to disrupt this flow of supplies that were the lifeline for the Viet Cong, whose goal was to overrun South Vietnam.

One of the major branches of this route entered South Vietnam in the jungle to the northwest of Chu Lai, where I was based as a Marine attack pilot. Around the clock, my Marine Air Group launched heavily armed aircraft in an effort to disrupt this flow of men and supplies.

This supply route proved to be a difficult target. It was regularly bombed but rarely did the pilots see any evidence that this was an active route. During the daylight hours the enemy did an exceptional job of hiding themselves and their equipment. After nightfall this seemingly unused road became a beehive of activity. Road repair crews, truck convoys, bicycles, and foot traffic emerged from hiding to make the trail useable or to continue their journey to the south.

During the day, bombing attacks on this trail were relatively routine in that the pilots were able to maintain visual contact with the ground. Occasionally, low clouds made it difficult to put bombs on target. Night attacks, with flares illuminating the area, were much more difficult. It became evident that a safer and more effective way to attack this supply route needed to be devised.

On a strategic mountain top, the Marines Corps deployed a unit that operated a radar system which could effectively be used to attack this target. The TPQ-10 radar system was capable of directing aircraft to a position from which bombs could be delivered accurately during the hours of darkness and in any weather condition.

During a portion of my year in Vietnam, I worked as a briefing officer for my Marine Air Group (MAG-14). My normal workday began well before daylight and lasted until the last scheduled attack flight had been briefed. Working at this job for long hours prevented me from flying missions during daylight hours.

I would arrive at the briefing facility and study the classified messages sent by higher authority. These messages contained hopefully helpful information about the assigned targets for that day. The pilots, before their missions, would report to the briefing room to learn as much as possible about their assigned mission. One after the other, they listened to what I had to say, made notes, and proceeded to the flight line and their aircraft.

Within the next hour, these pilots would be engaged in life-threatening combat. Without any show of fear or anxiety, these guys listened to my meager information, and then proceeded to their warplanes to fly into the face of danger. To a man, they donned their flight gear, manned their aircraft, and proceeded into battle as if it were a normal job. I loved this bunch of tough, sometimes profane, dedicated guys. They were Marines.

Even with having to report to my briefing job well before daylight, I was also frequently assigned a mission at some time during the night. On a regular basis, all Marines were expected to work long hours with a lack of rest. Night after night I launched into the darkness, no matter the weather, realizing that my state of fatigue was a factor in my performance. A recent check of my logbook showed that during one stretch of seven days I flew eight of these missions.

The night in question was dark, and light rain was falling on occasion as I preflighted and manned my jet. These conditions caused reduced visibility, and as always, the moisture made the metal runway slippery. My assigned aircraft was loaded with as many bombs as the A-4 Skyhawk could be expected to get airborne.

When I reflect upon my time in Vietnam I usually think of darkness.

In my mind the moon was almost never present and there were very few lights on the ground. Once my aircraft entered the low clouds, I was completely alone, in the dark, and flying totally on instruments.

Holy Cow! Only about three years earlier I had taken my first flight as a student pilot, during which the airsick bag was put into full use. Now, the Marine Corps considered me to be a fully qualified attack pilot. Even though occasionally a seed of doubt crept into my mind, all assigned flights were accepted. This was what was expected of all Marine pilots.

I had never felt more alone. As far as I knew, I was piloting the only aircraft that was actively pursuing the war effort in this little country halfway around the world.

The TPQ-10 controllers picked me up on radar, and directed me to climb to a specific altitude, heading, and airspeed. I was given verbal commands that would put my aircraft in the right place at the right time. Everything was going as planned, even though I was flying in the clouds and on instruments.

As my aircraft approached the drop zone, the controller instructed me to arm my bombs. I moved all the bomb switches to the armed position, which made the bomb release button on the control column "hot." The plan was to drop my entire bomb load by pressing that button with my right thumb.

As my aircraft proceeded toward the drop point, my controller gave me the warning of "Standby, Standby." In only a few seconds his next words would be "Mark, Mark" which was the command to release the bombs. Just before receiving the "Mark, Mark" voice command, I adjusted my right hand on the control stick and somehow touched the bomb release button.

Thousands of pounds of high explosives immediately departed my aircraft, armed themselves, and fell toward the earth. There was only a slight pause before the controller asked, "Did you already drop?" I had to admit that the bombs were away.

I had accidentally dropped the entire bomb load slightly short of the intended drop point. The drop zone was fairly large since we were flying at night, at 15,000 feet, and under instrument conditions.

I received radar vectors back toward my home airfield. Some clouds and rain were still in the area. A ground-controlled approach enabled me to find the runway and make a normal landing. My concern increased as I taxied my aircraft toward the flight line and my parking spot. Would my blunder attract the attention of the entire Marine Corps? Fearing the worst, my flight was met by only the normal line and maintenance personnel.

Trudging through the wet sand and darkness back toward my "hootch" (my living quarters), I stopped momentarily at the outdoor movie theater. The rain had subsided enough to allow a movie to be in progress. Although wet, our housing area was calm and peaceful. After watching the movie and relaxing for only a few minutes, someone approached, tapped me on the shoulder and asked, "Did you release your bombs early on a TPQ-10 mission?" Willing to accept any outcome, I admitted that I was the culprit.

I had made the mistake and was determined to take whatever came as a result. Exhausted, I went to my nearby quarters and crawled between my damp sheets knowing that in only a few hours the next day's attack pilots would be expecting their normal target briefing. Their briefing officer would have to be me.

This incident was completely dropped. I never heard a word from any of my superior officers. This was a war in progress and evidently a drop of only a few seconds early could be ignored.

Even after all these years, 49 at this writing, I cringe when the thought of this mission passes through my mind. All Marine pilots do their best to be perfect. I always tried to fly my missions to the best of my ability but on this dark night I fell short. To the best of my knowledge there were no ill effects. The war effort moved on.

Lock On

Back Door Dinner
Vietnam

On several occasions during my tour of duty in Vietnam, the war came to a standstill. All aggressive activity was halted. Some sort of high-level negotiations were taking place and the pause became a sign of sincerity. The pilots, however, did not get a day off in that we flew various training and observation missions.

On one of these truce days, my assignment was to play the role of a hostile aircraft that was attempting to attack the Da Nang Marine Air Base. I was instructed to fly toward Hainan Island, China and then turn toward the airbase in a simulated attack. My aircraft was unarmed since this flight was planned as a training exercise. The purpose of this operation was to have the radar operators and Air Force pilots attempt to locate and intercept my aircraft.

The ground-based radar operators, Air Force pilots, and I were all on the same radio frequency. I made a radio call informing everyone that I had turned toward the airbase and therefore the practice exercise had begun.

There was a lively radio exchange between the controllers and the Air Force pilots. Every effort was made to put the defending aircraft into a position to intercept my aircraft.

As I was streaking toward Da Nang at full speed, I could hear the entire conversation as the radar operators relayed my location, speed, and altitude to the pilots that were attempting to make the intercept. One of the Air Force pilots finally exclaimed that he had acquired my image on his radar, "Lock on." He requested permission to fire. His radio transmissions seemed to indicate that he was armed and willing to fire. He knew without a doubt that I was flying a U.S. Marine Corps aircraft and that this was a training mission.

This sorry SOB continued to ask, even plead, that he be allowed to fire. He seemed willing and eager to fire on another known United States warplane. He kept saying, "I have a lock on, request permission to fire."

As I write this story it seems almost impossible that this could have happened. Would any sane pilot request permission to fire on a known friendly? Permission was NOT granted, and the exercise ended with my returning safely to my base. I never had any personal contact with that pilot, but his actions permanently influenced my attitude toward Air Force pilots.

The Vietnam War was not a pleasant time in any of our lives. All United States pilots were engaged regularly in possibly mortal combat. However, when not flying, the Air Force pilots lived in air-conditioned housing with no fear of enemy attack. Marine Corps pilots lived in sweltering tent-like structures, ate inferior food, and on occasion came under enemy mortar attack.

On numerous occasions, we Marine pilots flew with muddy boots and wet flight suits. On one occasion, my wingman Sully and I were flying a bombing mission during which he lost his radio. The weather at our base was poor with low clouds and rain. As per normal under such conditions we were ordered to divert to an Air Force base in Thailand. It happened to be a "muddy boot and wet flight suit day."

The weather did not improve. We were required to remain overnight. BOQ rooms were assigned, and we were given directions as to where we could find food. Upon showing up for dinner at the base Officer's Club, we observed well-dressed couples being escorted to their tables. We were denied entry due to our attire. Food was made available, but we had to order through the back door and eat outside.

When I started writing this story, I had no idea as to the emotions that would be brought to the surface. We were warriors fighting for our country, yet we were turned away. We were served, but as some sort of lower class. That day, my wingman and I had risked our lives trying to put bombs on target but were denied service in a United States service club.

My wingman and friend, Sully, was later killed flying a single-plane night mission.

This story of an Air Force pilot begging to be allowed to shoot down a friendly, and being turned away from their club, is not intended to be a condemnation of the Air Force and their pilots. I have known and respected pilots from all branches of the military. However, my treatment on these occasions leaves a bit of a bad taste in my mouth. It should be noted that the food served through the back door was better than the regular fare at our home base.

The missions flown by the Air Force pilots were as dangerous as our Marine Corps missions. They shouldered the risks but lived a much better lifestyle. We were engaged in the same conflict against the same enemy—they lived in comfort, we lived in rather primitive conditions.

For What it's Worth

Vietnam
1966

Marine attack pilots are trained to fly into the face of danger in order to inflict the maximum damage upon the enemy. These pilots are also assigned responsibilities in addition to their airborne mission. These duties encompassed every phase of operating and maintaining the very complicated machines that were being launched into combat.

"Briefing Officer" was a job that was added during wartime and I served in this capacity for several months. Well before the sun made its appearance in the eastern sky, the briefing officers received and analyzed secret messages that arrived via teletype. These messages contained the latest information concerning location, description, and possible defenses for that day's assigned targets. Hopefully, my briefing would give the pilots an indication as to what they could expect as they pressed their attacks.

One morning, a strange message arrived along with the secret target information. I remember that it was headed, "For what it's worth." A flight of two F-4 Phantom jets had been flying at about 4,000 feet in a westerly direction between the Chu Lai and Da Nang air bases. A saucer-shaped object, which appeared to have port holes and streamers trailing behind, was observed flying along with them. All four of the crew members confirmed this sighting. The flight leader changed direction several times, which the strange craft easily matched. After a short period of time this "thing" accelerated rapidly and disappeared.

The fact that this incident was mentioned in a secret dispatch gave it some credibility. I could furnish no further insight but passed this information on to the pilots. They did not seem to be impressed or concerned. There were no reports of additional sightings.

For what it's worth.

I Dumped on Tokyo

1966

United States Marine attack aircraft had been in Vietnam for a little over a year. Day after day we flew the McDonald Douglas A-4 Skyhawk to the limit. The runway was made of aluminum matting that became very rough and slippery as the underlying sand and clay settled at different rates. During and after a rain, a taxiing aircraft could cause water to squirt up through the cracks, sometimes as high as a foot or two. I flew many times in muddy boots with my flight suit wet up to my knees.

On hot days and when heavily loaded, the jet blast from our mighty little airplanes would blow up sand and dust as we crossed the end of the runway struggling for altitude.

The cockpit instrument consoles became covered with a heavy layer of red dust. I remember leading a two-plane flight back to Chu Lai after a bombing mission. I chose to "horse around" a bit by flying very low and fast near some sort of hilltop fortification. The Marine occupants could easily be seen casually waving as we roared by only a few yards away. These guys were mostly teenagers but trained warriors. Any attacking enemy would be in for the fight of their lives.

Turning toward home base, I deliberately flew inverted momentarily but maintained level flight which required some negative Gs. Mistake. All kinds of debris, dirt, sand and who knows what came from every crack and cranny and rained down upon me. I would never do that again.

Our young but talented technicians, working mostly in sweltering tents, did an excellent job of keeping these mistreated jets flyable. Some maintenance procedures could be done on the flight-line, some in the tent hangars, but the major overhauls were done outside of Vietnam. The nearest facility that could perform this maintenance was at Naval Air Station Atsugi near Tokyo, Japan.

An aircraft in our squadron had reached the programmed flight time limitations and was scheduled for a major overhaul. It had served well in Vietnam, but now needed to be in Japan to undergo this necessary procedure.

I was chosen to fly that plane north to Atsugi. This assignment would have been a major endeavor if we were back in the States— probably not even allowed. Since we were in Vietnam, our leaders simply told us to "get it done."

Relocating this aircraft required two long over-water flights, Vietnam to the Philippine Islands and then to Iwakuni, Japan. Navigational aids and radio communications would be available for only about the first and last 120 miles of these long flights.

The date of departure arrived, and I strapped in, got that dirty little jet airborne, and turned east out over the South China Sea. The squadron flight operations officer assured me that the Philippine authorities were aware of my flight and would be expecting me.

I tracked the course that would start me toward Naval Air Station Cubi Point, located to the west of Manila. The navigational signal from Chu Lai was lost at a little over 100 miles. It would be about 600 miles, all over water, before I would be able to receive navigational information or make radio contact with the Philippine Air Traffic Control. This questionable flying was in an A-4 that was nearing the end of its service life before requiring major overhaul. I just did it, never considering it to be unsafe.

Everything worked out. As I approached the Philippines my navigational instruments came to life. A needle began to spin and eventually pointed steadily in one direction. I was well north of my intended course, but within range of the navigation facility at Cubi Point.

I made a radio call to the Philippine Air Traffic Control, but it was obvious that they had no idea who I was or where my flight had originated. I attempted to explain but soon gave up, partially due to the language barrier. Not knowing what to do, I informed them that I was switching to the Cubi Point Approach Control frequency and thanked them for their assistance.

Approach control welcomed me into their area as if I was a local flight. They acknowledged radar contact and gave me directions to enter their airport control area. I was cleared to land and did so without incident. My lonely crossing from Vietnam to the Philippines was over and there had been no problems.

The years have taken away the details of my stay at Cubi Point. I cannot remember if I stayed overnight or just refueled and continued. The interesting thing to me, however, was that no one questioned my point of departure, my destination, the aircraft ownership, or my authority to be flying this combat aircraft around Southeast Asia. I was a Marine first lieutenant with no official written orders, flying a Marine warplane through several independent Asian countries. My fuel tanks were always filled without question or cost and I was allowed to go on my way.

My next recollection is of meeting a Marine colonel while I was planning my flight from Cubi Point to Marine Corps Air Station Iwakuni in Japan. In casual conversation it was determined that we shared the same destination. I suggested that we fly as a two-plane formation and he readily agreed. We discussed the flight and he decided that I would fly as his wingman. I was happy with this arrangement. At least I would not be flying alone on this long over water flight.

The takeoff was normal, and I settled into a comfortable loose position on his wing. Our planned course was to the northwest, but my Colonel leader turned to the southeast—exactly the opposite direction. I waited a reasonable amount of time hoping he would realize his mistake, but he seemed to be satisfied with this course. I finally radioed "Sir, check your course." He did not respond to my call but simply started a slow turn back to the correct direction. He never mentioned this incident and I certainly didn't bring it up.

I remember staying overnight at Iwakuni, getting a good meal and a good night's sleep on clean sheets. After being in Vietnam, I had learned to appreciate the small things.

The leg to Atsugi was planned to take about an hour but the plane had been fueled for a much longer flight. I didn't consider this to be a problem. It was a beautiful clear day and the short flight was a kick. The flight route gave me an excellent view of Mount Fuji located about 60 miles to the southwest of Atsugi, my destination.

Upon my arrival over Atsugi, the excess fuel on board put the aircraft well above the maximum landing weight. I used this opportunity to fly a long leisurely sightseeing circuit over the sprawling city of Tokyo. This circuit completed, and still too heavy, I started another trip over the city. Growing bored with this game I opened the fuel dump valve in order to quickly bring my weight down below the maximum landing weight. It never crossed my mind that this action would be offensive to anyone. Well, obviously the Japanese did not appreciate my streaming jet fuel into the air over their largest city.

The fuel dumping quickly brought the aircraft within the legal landing weight. My landing request was acknowledged and approved. The landing was uneventful, and directions were given to taxi to the maintenance facility.

As I was accomplishing my shut-down procedures an official looking pickup arrived at my aircraft. Immediately upon deplaning, the driver informed me that the base commander wanted to see me "right now." After a short ride I was ushered into the commander's office. He asked, "Did you dump fuel over Tokyo"? I admitted to the dastardly deed.

I informed him that I had just arrived from Vietnam and was accustomed to doing almost anything with my aircraft, including dumping fuel to expedite a landing. He informed me that there was a C-130 outside on the ramp with the engines running. He forcefully instructed me to board that aircraft.

Picking up my travel bag, I made a dash for the aircraft's open door. I initially assumed that the aircraft was on a scheduled flight. I could have been wrong in that there were no other passengers and very little cargo. Could this base commander have quickly staged this flight to get this dumb A-4 pilot out of town before the Japanese authorities came looking for him?

This incident was never again mentioned. I, however, was forever very selective as where I chose to "take a dump."

B-57 Canberra

Vietnam
1966

On a dark and rainy night, an Air Force B-57 Canberra crashed into the South China Sea, about twenty miles southeast of the Da Nang Marine air base. There seemed to be very little known as to why this aircraft ended up in the ocean. To the best of my knowledge, there had been no indication from the two-person crew, that they or their aircraft were experiencing problems. They just seemed to have flown into the water.

This story has some similarities to my being launched in search of Major Alwan. There were at least one hundred A-4 pilots stationed at our base, but I had been selected to fly two missions in search of downed pilots.

The rain and clouds were gone as the sun peeked over the horizon the next morning. The request for a search plane had filtered down through the ranks to my squadron. A search mission was to be staged from the Marine air base at Chu Lai. I was called to our flight operations office and told that I would be the pilot of this one-plane search. There seemed to be no special reason that I was selected. Maybe, I was just available—the next pilot on the list.

The briefing officer relayed all of the known information concerning the missing aircraft. I was instructed to fly to a specific location, descend, and do a low-level search. No one had any idea as to what I would hope to see. I was told, "Just go out there and see if you see anything."

I carried no weapons. As per normal, my A-4 Skyhawk aircraft was preflighted, taxied to the runway, and flown into the beautiful, seemingly peaceful sky. The wind was calm, the sun was shining, and the sea was flat.

Within only a few minutes I arrived at the briefed location. There are no landmarks in the ocean. Descending to just above the water, I began the search. Nothing. Nothing. Nothing. Suddenly, I was certain that I saw a deployed parachute just below the surface. I applied full power and started a steep climbing turn. This maneuver was an attempt to keep this object in sight. It disappeared.

Remaining on station, the ocean was scanned for any indication that there could have been survivors. No further evidence was observed. Upon my return to base during my debriefing, I relayed my belief that I had observed what looked like a deployed parachute. I was never made aware of any further information as to the fate of these young pilots. Their names, hometowns, backgrounds, or surviving families were never known to me.

Did I actually see a deployed parachute? I feel that the sighting was real, but the truth will never be known. In any case, this sighting would not have changed the outcome. These young pilots were lost in this conflict so far from their homes. They were real people, but they were now nonexistent.

The war raged on.

UNEXPECTED REUNION

1966

Glenda and I have known one another for a long time. We attended the same high school and started dating during the tenth grade. Upon graduation she found employment with the Metropolitan Life Insurance Company in Memphis, Tennessee, while I started college at the University of Tennessee at Martin – Martin Branch at the time, playing football to pay my way.

During the football season, she attended as many games as possible, sometimes traveling with my parents. After the season on most weekends, I traveled back to my childhood farm to help with the work and, of course, to see Glenda. I loved that girl. Toward the end of my college career we decided to make our relationship permanent by getting married. We tied the knot and were as happy as could be, but as with most newlyweds, soon realized that we knew so very little. No one had told us that married life required considerable effort.

Soon after my graduation from college, we made our way to Pensacola, Florida, where I was to begin flight training. Upon successfully completing this program, the presentation of my "Wings of Gold" indicated that I could now be called a Naval Aviator. My first orders were to a Marine attack squadron at Marine Corps Air Station Cherry Point, in Havelock, North Carolina.

I continued my flight training (pilots never stop training) and was eventually deemed a combat-ready attack pilot. The Vietnam war was heating up and nearly all my squadron mates received orders to participate in that conflict, including myself.

With orders in hand, I was given leave to prepare for the upcoming year of absence from my family. A pregnant Glenda and our young daughter Kelly were moved into a modest duplex very near my parents' farm, and only a few miles from where her parents lived. I was satisfied that Glenda would have a strong support team during the time that I would be away.

At the Memphis, Tennessee airport, as we waited for the boarding process to begin, Glenda and I looked at each other, having no idea how to act. When I stepped onto that aircraft, we knew that we were parting for at least a year and maybe forever. I was on my way to participate in the war in Vietnam, and she was on her way to engage in the difficult task of taking care of our young daughter and giving birth to our son. We both would be severely challenged.

As the months passed, she made good on her promise of producing a healthy baby boy, and I worked hard at flying the combat missions to the best of my ability. There was no email in those days; we therefore communicated by regular mail. A letter usually took eight to ten days to reach its destination. She held our little family together, while I tried to stay alive.

People of higher authority made decisions as to the use of equipment and personnel in the war effort. I had been "in country" flying missions nearly every day and fully expected to continue this process until my twelve-month deployment requirement was completed. To my total surprise, my squadron was ordered to relocate to Japan for training and to take on new pilots. We were informed that we would be in that country for as much as six weeks.

I was lonesome, stressed, and felt deep down that I would not survive the year. The plan for Glenda to visit during the time I would be in Japan was the most important thing in my life. I did not care how much it would cost or the difficulties it would cause. I needed her more than I can express. She agreed to make the trip.

The squadron arrived at the Marine air base at Iwakuni and plans were in place for Glenda to soon join me. We squadron pilots immediately started flying training flights and I began to count the days until her arrival. Glenda and I have discussed our memories of this event. It has been more than fifty years and the details have faded. She does not remember the airline that she flew or when or where she bought her tickets. She does remember that she had no worries concerning our young daughter and our newborn son. Our parents gladly agreed to care for our children while she was away. In fact, they were reluctant to give them up upon her return.

Her trip required an overnight layover in Honolulu. She was surprised when she was directed to a bus that was to take the passengers to a hotel. She was given a room key and told the time to board the bus to the airport the next morning. Her flight to Tokyo was uneventful, but there was some confusion concerning her luggage transfer for the flight to Hiroshima. It all worked out, and we had a joyful reunion at this unfamiliar Japanese airport.

What an unbelievable feeling to once again see her face-to-face. My time in the combat zone of Vietnam had made me wonder if we would ever meet again. The train ride to Iwakuni, where I had rented a small Japanese-style house, was used as a time of getting reacquainted.

Several other pilot's wives had also arrived for a visit, and we quickly became friends with two couples. We ate, explored, and traveled together. What a glorious time in our lives. Experiencing a different culture, enjoying new friends, and having each other created some wonderful memories.

Our little house was located down a small alley in a totally Japanese neighborhood. Only a few feet from our front door was a three-foot concrete block wall. The house just over this wall had an open floor plan, therefore we would see most of the family's daily living activities. We could easily see them cooking, cleaning, eating, and napping. They were very friendly even though we could not communicate verbally. As we were moving out, we had a few simple items that we had not used, which we casually offered to this family. We were surprised when they soon presented us with gifts that were well beyond the value of our meager offerings.

The back side of that rental house had a narrow walkway which gave way to a rice paddy. We learned that to furnish fertilizer for the rice, the members of the farm family took care of their bathroom duties in the paddy. In our house, the floors were covered with woven mats and the main bathroom fixture was a trough in the floor. It was made of porcelain and flushed but had to be straddled and required squatting.

Our only personal mode of transportation was an old bicycle which I rode back and forth to my squadron area on the Marine base. I flew training missions during this time. I remember making my way back home after a night flight on that old bike. The streets were dark which required a slow and careful ride. All other travel was either by train or taxi. The normal fare for a taxi ride was eighty yen, about fifty cents.

In an effort to get a feel for Japan we decided to take the train to a small fishing village for an overnight stay. Upon arrival, we could not find even one person who could speak English, and we spoke no Japanese. We still had a wonderful time.

We found a hotel which was totally Japanese. We did not know how to act. The gracious Japanese ladies did their best to make us feel comfortable. They showed us to our room and then the bath area. Our bed was a futon on the floor. A vase of flowers was on a table, and I chose to place them near our pillows. On two occasions while we were out of our room, the flowers were moved back to the table.

We seemed to be the only guests. The bath, with its pool of hot water, was a mystery. We finally chose to disrobe, soak, and relax. We were not interrupted, but we wondered if we were being watched. The staff probably had a good laugh, but we had a good time.

With the two other couples, we visited a park that featured a large Tori. This huge, ornate, red structure had been built in the water of a calm bay. This park was on a small island which was inhabited by a large group of monkeys. I bought a small bag of peanuts to pass out to these cute animals. I had passed, one by one, a few of these goodies to the gentle little inhabitants. Suddenly, a very large and aggressive male banged into my leg and forcefully grabbed the peanut bag from my hand. This made me angry. I reacted with an aggressive move toward this bully. He sat about five feet away, looked me in the eye, and his attitude seemed to say, "Yes, I took your peanuts. So, what are you going to do about it?" He had hate in his eyes. He was lucky that I did not have a shotgun at that moment.

This place was a famous tourist destination. Glenda had been challenged by the Japanese tradition of shared bathroom facilities. In this park, there was a toilet building that had doors which were clearly labeled "Men" and "Women." She had a smile on her face. As we stepped through the separate doors, I looked to my right, and she looked to her left--we were face to face. Only a short wall divided the two facilities. Her dream of total privacy was dashed. She got the job done and we carried on.

Realizing that this visit was an important episode in our lives, I felt that we needed to have our own camera. I chose an expensive, about $45, Pentax to document this unique adventure. I know, I know, that was too much to pay, but the possibility of taking some meaningful pictures made me do it. As the sun descended toward the horizon, our little group traveled by taxi to a recommended restaurant. We were well into the meal when I realized that my camera was missing. It had been left in the taxi. I was totally depressed. My expensive camera was gone along with the photos I had taken that day.

Suddenly, the taxi driver burst into the restaurant, holding my camera over his head while aggressively looking for our group. He seemed to take great joy in being able to return it. Of course, we made an effort to reward him. We felt that the camera would not have been returned in most United States cities. This little display of honesty instilled in me a positive attitude toward the Japanese people.

All good things eventually come to an end. Neither Glenda nor I remember anything about her departure, air travel, or her arrival back in Tennessee. Once again, we parted ways, not knowing if we would ever meet again.

I did not die, and she had done a great job of keeping the home fires burning. Months later we again met face to face at the Memphis, Tennessee airport. There was a certain amount of awkwardness. What would our future hold? There was no way of knowing, but at that moment, we did not worry. We had endured and would endure.

Glenda and Darrel, Japan 1966

INCOMING

Vietnam
1966

The United States Armed Forces were involved in a serious war. The following is an attempt to put into words my experience as a Marine, on a night in Vietnam many years ago. A military base large enough to contain an eight-thousand-foot runway is a big target. The enemy had been trained to use mortars supplied by some third-party country to cause as much damage as possible to personnel and equipment on our base.

Many years later, I realized that in my heart there was no hatred felt toward the enemy soldier. On attack missions, after the last bomb had been released and as the flight joined in formation, the forward air controller would verbally give us a bomb damage assessment. This report would often include the number of structures and fortifications that had been destroyed but at times included the number of observed KBA (Killed by Air). When KBA was included in the BDA I felt no remorse. They, like I, were simply the tip of the spear intended to enforce the decisions that had been made by our political leaders. We had been convinced to put ourselves in harm's way for our country, and our superior's sometimes faulty decisions.

Thirty or more years after the war ended, I revisited Vietnam. During quiet times, as we approached the country on a cruise ship, I stood at the railing staring into the ocean trying to sort through my personal feelings. Upon stepping ashore only a few miles from Hanoi, I found the people to be warm and friendly. They seemed to hold no ill feelings, and in fact, did not even want to discuss that long-ago conflict.

It seemed that to them, the war was a thing of the past and they were eager to embrace the future.

Our living accommodations during the war were very basic. These hastily built structures consisted of a plywood platform about three feet above the sand, a corrugated metal roof, and liftable side flaps. These movable sides were the only means of controlling the temperature inside our hootches. Six officers were assigned to each unit. Our beds were folding cots topped with foam or air mattresses that we had obtained from Japan. The Marine Corps furnished the cots, but mattresses and sheets were the responsibility of the occupant. Dampness became a way of life.

A beautiful white sand beach was located only about 50 yards from this homely abode. Since we worked long hours, there was very little leisure time, but on occasion I strolled this beach. Today people enjoy expensive but relaxing vacations at resorts that are built at such locations. We were engaged in an ugly conflict, therefore this beautiful setting held very little glamour.

On a regular basis Hueys, a popular Marine helicopter, flying to and from combat operations, traveled along this strip of white sand. The distinctive sound of that engine and rotor has stayed with me. Even now, I can visualize the strong young Marines sitting in the doorways with their arms casually draped over an automatic weapon. The noise from these machines became the sound of the war and my involvement in it. Years later, even today at times, the sound of a Huey makes the hair on my arms stand up.

There was always the possibility of a rocket or mortar attack on our base, although this happened rather infrequently. Bomb shelters were built at various locations throughout the housing area. One of these shelters, that could accommodate as many as 15 to 20 men, was located just outside of our hooch. This shelter was simply a sand-bagged pit with a heavy-duty roof piled several layers deep with these same sandbags.

The evening was warm, and the humidity was high. Some of my fellow pilots and I were sitting around in our underwear enjoying a bit of peace and quiet. Some read books, others wrote letters, and one was making a taped message that he intended to mail home. He was using a small reel-to-reel tape recorder that was the cutting edge of technology in those days.

Whomp! Everyone paused and looked up from whatever they were doing. Whomp! Someone said, "That's outgoing." Whomp! Someone else said, "I think it's incoming." Then as a mortar shell exploded nearby, someone shouted, "Holy shit, that *is* incoming." The sound of bare feet pounding on plywood and the subsequent noises of the attack were recorded on the recording machine that the owner had left running in his hasty exit. Most of us scurried to safety in the nearby bomb shelter. Not Bob.

He was in his bunk trying to get some sleep. According to the story that was told, he said, "They will never hit this f--king house." As the mortar rounds came closer and closer, he changed his mind and tried to protect himself by lying face-down on the floor.

A mortar shell hit a tree branch and exploded about three feet above our metal roof. The shrapnel punched as many as a hundred holes in our roof and did some damage inside. I lost my inflatable mattress and Bob was hit by pieces of shrapnel in the back of each of his upper thighs. His wounds were not serious, but he was sore for a few days after the foreign material had been extracted. He was later presented with a Purple Heart medal which was acknowledgment that he had been combat wounded. He called this medal his "Dumb Shit" award. Should that mortar round have missed that tree branch and entered our hooch before exploding he could have been killed. I feel he was a lucky man.

A few days later he expended a considerable amount of energy building his own bomb shelter, just outside his sleeping area. Bob had learned his lesson, and therefore decided to bury a 55-gallon barrel for protection in case of another mortar attack. His project was nearing completion when he decided to make a test run. He was well over six feet tall and his long legs would not allow him to take cover inside the barrel. Crouching as low as possible the whole upper half of his body was still fully exposed. All of his effort had been a total waste.

When it was realized that we were under attack, I bolted from our hooch and dove into the nearby bomb shelter. I came to rest shoulder to shoulder with an officer who worked in administration. His entire body was shaking. He was a Marine but almost never, actually never, received enemy fire while at his desk as he went about his normal duties. I do not consider this a point of bravery or arrogance, but this mortar attack was nothing more than a nuisance for me. I took shelter but never felt that I would be harmed. This attitude was probably foolish in that the folks who were manning that mortar had every intention of killing Marines and possibly destroying aircraft and machinery.

I survived that attack and my year of exposure to danger in that small country located halfway around the world. I came home and moved on with my life thinking that the whole experience had been put to rest. Many years later it became evident that this war was still a part of me and probably had a big effect on my life.

My involvement in this conflict has mentally been a mixed bag. Excitement; in that I used my training to test myself and my aircraft. Sadness; some fellow pilots did not survive. They were strong, educated, and dedicated young men. Regret; due to my actions and those of my fellow pilots, innocent people most likely lost their lives. Memories; the events of this intense year of combat are etched in my mind but my attempt to tell the stories has been healing.

THE GENERAL

Lower and Slower
Vietnam

On occasion, high ranking officers came to our Marine Air Group and requested to fly combat missions. These officers, because of their rank, were always allowed to fly.

Serving as an air group briefing officer, I was in the position to brief and observe these pilots. They were scheduled through individual squadrons, therefore usually walked into the briefing facility unannounced.

On a daily basis these men were occupied with making decisions concerning the big picture and did not have the opportunity to fly on a regular basis. On more than one occasion, I had concerns that these officers had not flown enough to be current or proficient in the aircraft.

I held the job of briefing officer, but also flew combat missions on a regular basis. On a few occasions during my tour of duty, the U.S. military observed "truce" days on which all offensive action was halted. It was assumed that some sort of high-level negotiations were taking place. We pilots flew training and observation flights, but our aircraft were unarmed. On one of these days, I was scheduled to fly with a general whose name has long been forgotten.

Considering his rank, the general had obviously been a successful Marine Corps officer. I had no idea where he was stationed or what his normal responsibilities entailed. We were to fly north along the coast toward the DMZ, the zone between North and South Vietnam where no military action was allowed, to look for enemy activity. Of course, the general was the flight leader since I was a lowly lieutenant. My intent was to give him my full support from my position as his wingman.

The takeoff and departure were normal, and I joined him in a loose formation as we headed up the coast. The cloud bases gradually decreased. To stay clear of these clouds the general descended slowly but also flew slower and slower.

As we began to go in and out of the clouds, I tucked into a much tighter wing position. His wingtip was only a few feet from my canopy. The general finally realized that due to the deteriorating weather, continuing our mission was not a good idea. We were now flying at less than a thousand feet and the airspeed was steadily decreasing. He made a rather quick turn to the left and as I tried to match this turn my stick shaker activated. The stick shaker is a safety device that warns of an impending stall.

Any aircraft requires airflow over the wing surface in order to produce lift. As the aircraft slows, at some point the air flow becomes less than required. This lack of airspeed and loss of lift is known as a stall.

We were now at a low altitude, in the clouds, and nearing stall speed. I did my best to maintain my position, but the general did not initiate a recovery. I soon concluded that for my own safety, I had only one option and that was to leave the flight. I leveled my wings, applied full power, and made a radio transmission that I was leaving the flight and returning to base.

We returned to base separately and made safe landings. This was my first and only time to fly with a general or depart a flight. There was no way to know if my flight leader would pursue some sort of action against me. Fortunately, the general did not write a derogatory report and I never saw or heard of him again.

It would be interesting to know more about this man and the life he lived before and after that flight. Our paths crossed only once, on that dark and rainy day long ago.

THE MARINE CORPS

My Belief

I *am* a Marine. If you were once a Marine, you are always a Marine. The haircut, the culture, and the expectations live forever within your being.

Marines have fought with honor in many conflicts around the world. They have stood their ground, advanced on command, and served with pride. They have also died in great numbers for this country.

I was recently touring a state park in South Dakota and noticed an older man, slightly stooped, who wore a cap that had embroidered on it the word "Marines." I tapped him on the shoulder and announced that I too was a Marine. We both simultaneously said, "Semper Fi." "Semper Fidelis" is a Latin phrase that means "always faithful." This phrase has become the very heart of the Marine Corps.

Marines are not without fear. They are human beings, who dearly love life, and do not wish to die. However, when backed into a corner or ordered to move forward, they will lay their lives on the line for their country and the guys to their left and right. Marines will fight.

This may sound silly but even today at 78 years of age I would attempt to fly an attack aircraft into combat if the Marine Corps asked.

I was deployed to Vietnam for a year and flew many combat missions. I certainly felt fear at times. I worried that I would perish and never see my family again. Living conditions were very basic and at times I wished to be away from that bad situation.

I and all of my fellow pilots flew their assigned missions, day after day, even though any flight could have claimed our lives.

In this book I have attempted to tell stories of my life. I have come to realize that I was and am a part of a great and honorable organization. I truly appreciate the fact that, I *am* a Marine.

Under Arrest

Vietnam
Late 1966

In 1966 the limited military action in Vietnam that had begun ten years earlier had now escalated into an all-out war. We attack pilots were flying missions around the clock from the aluminum runway at Chu Lai. All branches of the United States military were involved in the fighting.

On this hot and humid day, I was part of a four-plane flight that had been assigned the mission of bombing the Ho Chi Minh trail in Laos. This trail was the main supply route for the Viet Cong that were trying to take over South Vietnam. Everything possible was being done to slow the flow of goods and manpower along this trail.

All seemed normal as we taxied our fully loaded A-4 Skyhawk aircraft to the active runway. Upon completing the required cockpit checks, each pilot visually inspected the exterior of the other planes in the flight. Satisfied that we were as ready as possible, we individually taxied into the narrow takeoff position.

As the aircraft ahead of me started its takeoff roll, I assumed the takeoff position. After running the engine up to full power, the instruments were checked, and the brakes were released. The acceleration may have seemed a bit slow, but the day was warm, and my aircraft was loaded to the maximum.

The aircraft gradually gained speed along the aluminum matting runway with its many humps and bumps. Almost all military aircraft maneuvers require a certain scan pattern. Airspeed and lineup were my main concern during the takeoff roll. On two airspeed checks the needle had not moved and I was still well below the speed required for takeoff.

The lack of acceleration suddenly demanded my full attention. At this speed it would never fly. My options were few and the course of action had to be decided upon in only a few seconds.

All Navy and Marine runways have some sort of arresting gear installed and all tactical aircraft are equipped with tailhooks. The idea of tailhooks and arresting gear came from the fact that the Navy had long been launching and recovering warplanes from the decks of aircraft carriers. Carrier landings are a part of every Naval Aviator's training.

The decision to abort that takeoff had to be made quickly. Up until this moment every takeoff during my Marine flying career had resulted in the aircraft becoming airborne and the mission being completed with a safe landing. When it was obvious that my A-4 Skyhawk was not going to fly, I had to switch from a flying to a stopping mind set. I was traveling at over 100 knots and fully loaded with bombs and fuel. Even if the brakes had been fully applied the aircraft would have departed the end of the runway and been destroyed. I quickly pulled the power to idle and dropped the "hook."

Luck was with me. The tailhook engaged the wire and the aircraft came to a smooth but quick stop. I opened the canopy, shut down the engine, unhooked my harness, and gathered my personal gear. The emergency crew soon arrived and attached a ladder enabling me to deplane. I felt the abort had been handled as per my training. I calmly climbed down the ladder and suddenly my feet touched solid ground. At that moment my knees started to shake, and my hands soon joined in with enthusiasm.

Everything had worked as advertised. Had the hook failed to engage the wire, I would have had only one remaining option. The A-4 ejection seat was designed with zero-zero capabilities. The pilot could safely eject on the ground, at zero altitude, while sitting still. I am very happy that these capabilities were not put to the test. Should I have been required to eject, the aircraft would have been destroyed. Would that well-designed ejection seat have delivered me to safety? No one will ever know. The fuel and possibly some of the bombs would have exploded.

A pilot who witnessed my takeoff run and abort reported that a 20-foot flame was coming from the tailpipe, which is not normal. There was no vibration or noise that indicated that there was a problem. I inspected that aircraft the next day and discovered several pea-sized metal pieces in the tail pipe. The engine had experienced a major malfunction and that aircraft was not going to fly.

I was a lucky young pilot to have successfully completed that arrested stop. I like to say that I was put "Under Arrest" and was happy that it happened. This incident happened in a combat environment. I was never interviewed or even asked to write a report. I flew my next combat mission the next morning.

The war roared on.

Uneasy Return

Vietnam

Tom, my leader on this two-plane bombing mission, and I made normal landings and taxied toward the squadron parking area. We had departed the Chu Lai Marine air base in our A-4 Skyhawk warplanes less than an hour before, fully loaded with bombs.

After takeoff, I had joined on his wing as we proceeded toward our target area, only about 30 miles northwest of our home base. We had attempted to put "bombs on target" as directed by an airborne FAC, forward air controller.

Upon making initial radio contact, this brave pilot, who was flying near the target area in a small aircraft, immediately began to give us a stream of information. How to identify his aircraft, the general description of our target and its general location, its altitude above sea level, the best probable attack heading, the enemy fire that we could expect, and his intention of "marking" the spot where he felt the first bombs would do the most damage.

After acquiring visual contact with the FAC, he fired a rocket from his fragile little aircraft into the target area and cleared us to attack with live bombs. Anyone near this marked point should have been very concerned. War. Tom signaled for me to take the normal nose-to-tail separation and we made individual runs until all our bombs had been dropped. The FAC adjusted the aim point after each bomb exploded.

Tom Lacour was a tall thin Marine who grew up somewhere in the state of New York. He was a very relaxed and competent pilot, seemingly unfazed by the war that was raging all around. He was a "cool dude" in today's vernacular.

Barrels filled with sand were stacked between the squadron aircraft parking spots. The intent was that if one aircraft should happen to be damaged by mortar or rocket fire, the next one would possibly be unharmed. Tom and I were directed to our separate parking spots.

As I made the turn into my space, a group of senior officers gathered nearby was obvious. I had never had anyone except the normal ground personnel meet my plane. My first thought was, "Holy Cow, how have I screwed up now?" With considerable apprehension, I shut down the engine, completed the normal check list, gathered my personal gear, and in sweat-soaked flight suit climbed from the cockpit.

In the back of my mind, I feared that my flying career was hanging in the balance. As I descended the ladder, I noticed that the squadron commander and the group commander had smiles on their faces. As my feet touched the aluminum matting surface, these officers approached me with extended hands which I gladly shook. It had been determined that I had flown the 20,000th combat mission from this Marine air base. Pictures were taken and a news release was created. Even the *Covington Leader,* the newspaper for Tipton County, Tennessee, my birthplace, carried the story.

I did nothing special. I feel that if Tom had parked in that spot, he would have been the pilot of this memorable event—who knows?

Tom and I were lucky enough to survive that terrible war in Vietnam. Unfortunately, some 50,000 of our strong young men and women did not come home alive.

We both later served as advanced jet training instructors at Beeville, Texas. We and our families, on occasion, would drive 50 miles to a small Mexican restaurant in Refugio, Texas. This small establishment set our standards for this type of food. In my mind, that is still the best Mexican food that I have ever tasted.

After leaving the Marine Corps, both Tom and I secured jobs as commercial pilots for major airlines. He eventually made his home on the Island of Kauai, and for eight years I served as a pilot for Northwest Airlines in Honolulu. During those years we met only once.

War creates relationships that are intense at the time but tend to weaken. I wonder if Tom and I will ever meet again? My last knowledge of him indicated that he was living a peaceful life in Hawaii and still struggling to correct his horrible slice on the golf course.

Tom, no matter what the future holds, our paths crossed while dealing with stressful circumstances. We were lucky to have survived and I wish you a happy and peaceful life.

Black Sheep

"Feet Wet"
1967

During combat operations, warplanes are often launched from aircraft carriers to strike targets that are on land. The pilots, upon crossing the coastline, make a "feet dry" radio call which means that the flight is over land and proceeding toward the target. Returning, upon crossing that same beach, a "feet wet" call indicates the attack has been completed and the flight is now over water and headed toward the ship.

My twelve-month deployment to Vietnam as a Marine attack pilot was drawing to a close and I was still alive. The past eleven months had been lonesome, hot, cold, exciting, scary, demanding, exhausting, boring, frustrating, and rewarding. I was ready for this combat tour to be over.

This year of combat flying had given me the opportunity to use my training and my aircraft to the maximum. I had a certain amount of pride in my accomplishments and a huge respect for my aircraft, the McDonnell-Douglas A-4 Skyhawk. It had proven itself to be a sturdy, dependable, and versatile attack aircraft. I was proud to have been a Scooter pilot.

Arriving in the war zone, my mindset was that I would probably not live through the year. I simply accepted every assigned mission and flew them to the best of my ability without considering the possible disastrous outcome.

The days seemed to pass slowly but finally it was late in my tour and somehow, I was still alive and healthy. I continued to fly all assigned missions, but the thought of surviving was starting to creep into my mind. I remember thinking "Holy Cow! I have been here nearly a year.

I've got to be careful not to make some dumb mistake and kill myself."

During the process of extended combat operations, equipment and personnel are routinely moved into and out of the war zone. Therefore, it was not unusual that the Marine Corps made the decision to rotate VMA-214, a Marine attack squadron, and its aircraft from Chu Lai, Vietnam to El Toro Marine Corps Air Station in California. It also made sense to have pilots who had fulfilled their tour requirements fly the older A-4C aircraft back home across the Pacific Ocean.

VMF-214 was the most famous Marine Corps squadron of WWII. Its pilots, flying the gull-winged 2,000-hp F4U Corsairs, called "whistling death" by the Japanese, were credited with shooting down 100 enemy planes. As many as 100 more may have been destroyed but could not be officially verified. This squadron was nicknamed the Black Sheep Squadron since it was formed from a group of misfit pilots and commanded by the self-proclaimed bad boy Major Gregory "Pappy" Boyington. The major was a colorful character who personally destroyed 26 Japanese aircraft. The nickname Pappy came from the fact that he was a decade older than the pilots under his command. It is rumored that he always took the aircraft that were in the worst mechanical condition when going into battle. He wanted his pilots to believe that their aircraft were reliable.

Following a dogfight in which the Japanese greatly outnumbered the Americans, Pappy did not return. No one had observed him going down. A Japanese submarine plucked him from the sea and transported him to a prisoner of war camp. Eighteen months later, the war ended, and he was freed from a prison camp located near Tokyo. He received many awards and medals including the Congressional Medal of Honor. Pappy was celebrated as a true American war hero.

I was transferred into VMA-214 to participate in the upcoming Trans-Pacific (Transpac) operation of delivering the squadron's aircraft back to United States soil. I am proud of my short association with this historic squadron. The plan after leaving Vietnam was to fly to Guam, Wake, and Hawaii. The last leg from Hawaii to MCAS El Toro was the longest. All legs, except one, due to their length, required airborne refueling. A week or so before our departure, the planes were configured with long-range fuel tanks.

My fellow pilots and I engaged in what we called "practicing being miserable." With full fuel tanks, we climbed to altitude and flew back and forth along the Vietnam coast making sure all the fuel tanks and transfer equipment functioned properly. After a boring two hours or more and with our tanks nearly empty, we joined with tanker aircraft to sharpen our refueling skills. These long flights were not much fun but very important. If any malfunction had occurred, it was much safer to be near a functional runway rather than far out over the open ocean.

On the morning of our scheduled departure day, we manned our aircraft, completed our normal procedures, and taxied to the runway. Requesting and receiving clearance for takeoff, I added full power, testing this old engine one more time. Most of my departures from this airport had been to the north but today, my last takeoff was to the south.

The instruments indicated that all systems were functioning normally. I released the brakes and felt the acceleration. The runway was rough, but I had become accustomed to this condition during the previous twelve months. Reaching the proper speed, I eased the nose up to takeoff attitude. The little jet lifted off and I retracted the gear and flaps. A left turn, out over the South China Sea, was commenced and as my trusty aircraft roared across the beach I shouted—not out loud, just in my mind— "Black Sheep, Feet Wet--Goodbye, Vietnam."

More pilots were assigned to this Transpac operation than the total number of aircraft. The plan was to share the flying. The pilots not flying on a given leg were to ride as passengers on the C-130 tankers. I was chosen to fly an aircraft the first leg from Chu Lai to Guam.

The route took us over the Philippine Islands where we were scheduled to meet the tankers and take on enough fuel to complete the flight. If for any reason a plane was unable to take on fuel, the pilot could leave the flight and land at the Cubi Point Naval Air Station, an active and strategic military airbase.

The C-130 is a large transport aircraft, powered by four turboprop engines. It had straight wings and a limited top speed. The A-4 is a small single-engine jet with swept wings and has a much faster operating speed. Due to these differences the pilot's undivided attention was required.

The tankers would maintain their highest altitude and accelerate to their maximum speed. We in our smaller jets would descend and reduce speed putting us well below the A-4's optimum speed. Taking on several thousand pounds of fuel brought our jets much closer to stall speed. As fuel was transferred, maintaining our position became increasingly more difficult since the response to control input became sluggish and sloppy. After taking on the extra fuel, full power was required to accelerate and climb back to altitude.

The Marine Corps and Navy use an airborne refueling procedure called "probe and drogue."

The C-130 tanker aircraft were fitted with large fuel tanks positioned on their main cargo deck. A pod containing a reel and a hose with a drogue attached was mounted under each wing. With this arrangement, two aircraft could be refueled simultaneously.

The hose and drogue were already trailing from the pods as we approached the tanker. Using our normal aircraft flight controls, we carefully flew our aircraft's fixed probe into the drogue basket. This basket was approximately 20 inches in diameter and looked very much like a large badminton shuttlecock.

Several white bands were painted on the hose near the pod. After a successful hookup, a certain number of these bands had to be "pushed" back into the pod by flying slightly forward. This maneuver allowed fuel to begin transferring. The entire process took only a few minutes but demanded the pilot's total concentration.

Our uneventful landings at Andersen Air Force Base, on the very northern end of Guam, marked the successful completion of the first leg. As pilots, we had no further duties for the day. Most of us ate dinner, found a bed, and tried to get some rest, hoping to be fresh for whatever was in store for us the next day.

At that time, there was no way of knowing that Guam would be a part of my future. After leaving the Marines, I became a pilot for Northwest Airlines. Toward the end of my career, I served as the Chief Pilot for the airlines' Honolulu-based pilots.

Northwest Airlines also based about 40 pilots and five aircraft in Guam to service routes to and from Japan. The Honolulu Chief Pilot's job came with the added responsibility of tending to the needs of the pilots in Guam. I traveled there many times, accompanied by my wife Glenda on occasion, and had some great golf matches. This small base was staffed with some outstanding young pilots and they ran a great small airline. I loved and respected them and their families.

I was never to know the details, but evidently some of my Marine pilot friends did a bit of celebrating that evening at the Guam Officers Club. Our commanding officer was made aware of this activity and he was not happy. The next morning the operations officer informed me that I would be flying this leg from Guam to Wake. As it turned out, I flew an aircraft every leg, all the way to California. The flight that second day was relatively short and airborne refueling was not required. The flight must have been routine since I have no recollection of the details.

Wake Island is a horseshoe-shaped atoll that is only a few feet above sea level. The runway is on one side of the island and the buildings and living quarters are on the other. Only hours after Pearl Harbor was attacked on 7 Dec 1941, the Japanese attempted to invade and take control of Wake Island. The inhabitants, consisting of about 500 Marines and 1220 civilian employees, put up a heroic defense. The Japanese were handed their first defeat of the war.

A detachment of Marine Fighter Squadron VMF-211 was stationed there with twelve fighter aircraft. Eight were destroyed during the initial attack. The remaining four were soon shot down but not before inflicting heavy damage on the Japanese forces. During my tour in Vietnam, I was attached to this famous squadron for several months.

After massive reinforcements, the second invasion attempt by the Japanese was successful, but they suffered the loss of eight to nine hundred men, several aircraft, and three large ships. The Americans suffered approximately one hundred and fifty killed. This island remained under Japanese control for the duration of the war.

During our short visit, a young sailor obtained a carpool vehicle and gave several of us pilots a tour of the island. We visited some of the coastal batteries. The big guns were still in place but very rusty and derelict.

The startup, taxi, and takeoff were normal as we departed this small island in the middle of the Pacific Ocean. Our trip that day required only one refueling session to top off our tanks en route to the Marine air base in Hawaii.

We met the tankers far out over the ocean but still had enough fuel onboard to return to Wake should that become necessary. After this refueling, our tanks held enough fuel to complete the flight and land with a comfortable reserve.

The flight had gone well until being turned into a "gaggle" by our flight leader, a major. Gaggle, as defined by the T-34 Association manual, is an undisciplined group of aircraft milling about in roughly the same piece of sky, sometimes attempting to impersonate a formation.

The major, at some stage of his career, had been based at the Kaneohe Marine Corps Air Station on the island of Oahu. He was familiar with the area and airport and therefore felt very confident and comfortable. The other three pilots in our four-ship flight had absolutely no experience in Hawaii.

Upon establishing radio contact, the major informed the controller that he wanted to bring his "boys" home from the war in style. He requested and received approval to descend the flight to just above the water. More than one hundred miles from Kaneohe, we were flying at about three hundred feet. Jet engines consume much more fuel at low altitude. His decision caused the flight to arrive at our destination with less fuel than planned. If for any reason the landing had been delayed our fuel level could have become critically low.

The skies were clear, the winds were light, and the major chose to make a visual approach. He signaled for the three of us to join him in close formation. Concentrating on maintaining our position in the formation, we could not turn our heads to look, but our peripheral vision told us that we were flying very near a green vertical mountainside. These vertical cliffs are a feature of the terrain on the eastern side of the island of Oahu. There was no real danger, but it certainly made us feel uncomfortable.

At this point our formation was far from perfect and got worse as our leader made a power reduction. We were in a turn, near mountains, trying to adjust to a power reduction, and in unfamiliar surroundings. The flight quickly degenerated into a "gaggle". The major wanted to show us off as professionals, but we looked like a bunch of beginners. Embarrassing.

I stepped on American soil for the first time in almost 12 months. It really felt good. Hawaii, at that moment, was the most beautiful and fragrant place that I had ever visited. Glenda and I would later live in the Hawaiian Islands for eight years.

We pilots found a room at the BOQ and prepared for a night in Honolulu. We had been welcomed upon our arrival by Todd Eikenberry, a former squadron mate in VMA-332 at Cherry Point, North Carolina. He was now based in Hawaii and graciously allowed us the use of his car for the evening.

The flight from Hawaii to California is one of the longest overwater flights in the world, about 2,550 miles. In order to complete this flight safely, we had to take on fuel three times. The first was far out to sea but with enough fuel remaining to return to Hawaii if necessary. Having full tanks, we could take on more fuel even further out but again with enough fuel to return. These two refueling sessions were accomplished without any problems.

The third refueling was off the coast of California. The tankers departed the Marine Corps Air Station and proceeded out over the ocean to meet us as we approached from the west. We made the rendezvous and with this fueling our "gas" worries would be over.

Unfortunately, here comes the major. As the leader of the flight, he was responsible for communicating with the tanker crew. He instructed them to give each aircraft in the flight only two thousand pounds of fuel. This amount was enough to get us to the airfield but with very little reserve.

The tanker crew questioned him, but he stuck by his decision. I considered asking for more, but I did not. We had been cramped in these tiny cockpits for over five hours. It would have been a relief to put our fuel worries behind us for good. Why not three thousand pounds or more?

The major was still not finished. Upon arrival at the airport area, he again stated that he intended to bring his "boys" home properly. He ordered us into that same tight formation and led us into the airport traffic pattern.

After passing the approach end of the runway the major performed his "break". In this maneuver, the pilot turns sharply away from the formation and pulls the throttle to idle. As the aircraft decelerates, he establishes the landing configuration by extending the landing gear and flaps. He then maneuvers to a position from which a visual circling approach can be made.

Maintaining our position in the formation, we were unaware of the fog bank that existed halfway down the runway. Suddenly there were three jets in the clouds, near the ground, and in a steep turn. We all managed to fly our aircraft out of the clouds and make safe visual landings.

There had been a recent rain, which left standing water in places on the runway. Applying the brakes, (the A-4 was not equipped with anti-skid), I experienced hydroplaning while crossing a puddle, causing one of my wheels to stop rotating. Upon coming in contact with dry concrete the tire popped like a balloon.

I had flown combat missions in Vietnam, under all conditions, for an entire year and had never blown a tire. Embarrassing. There was no real excuse for blowing that tire, but contributing factors could have been fatigue, since we had been in the air almost six hours, as well as my frustration with the major. This was my last flight in the A-4 Skyhawk aircraft.

I consider myself fortunate to have taken part in the relocation of these airplanes from a war zone back to the United States. I do not remember having any concern for my safety, but if one of us had gone into the water that pilot would have been in big trouble. Locating and recovering a downed pilot would have been very difficult. We had flown these single-engine aircraft nearly 8,000 miles, almost all entirely over open water.

This trip was a great adventure. During my airline career I flew across the Pacific many times. However, on each occasion the aircraft was equipped with a minimum of three well-maintained engines. Reflecting upon my experience of flying a single-engine aircraft across the Pacific—I have come to the conclusion that if offered the opportunity to do it again—I would decline.

Beeville, Texas

It Happened So Fast
Student to Instructor

I survived my tour of duty in Vietnam as a Marine Attack Pilot—what now?

The return to my family, which had grown by one, was a trying but joyous event. Darrel Jr. had been born soon after my departure and was ten months old when I met him for the first time.

I was shocked and hurt (but what could be expected?) when Kelly, our daughter at three years of age, hid under the kitchen table and asked, "Who is that man?" After this cool reception, she warmed to me quickly, but I feel that my absence for an entire year permanently changed our relationship.

We spent a few weeks trying to get me back into life as a normal person. I initially thought that the war had no effect on me. Years later, I realized that I had also been permanently changed. Even at 74 years of age, as I write this story, I am still not completely certain as to how the Vietnam experience affected my life. I don't think of it daily, but I am sure the effects are still there.

I was a young pilot eager to ply my trade and prove myself worthy as a Marine Aviator. I don't think I have ever given Glenda enough credit as she was left alone to produce another offspring and manage this little family. My life was at risk on many occasions, but I did not fully understand that she also was in the line of fire every day.

I can't remember the details but evidently the movers came to our little duplex near Atoka, Tennessee, loaded our meager household effects, and delivered them to Beeville, Texas. I had been assigned to this naval air station as an instructor pilot in the advanced jet training command. How could it happen so fast? It seemed only a short time ago that I had checked in as a student for this very phase of training. I was apprehensive as a student and as an instructor.

I had completed this phase of training and had been assigned to an active duty Marine attack squadron. The whole thing had come full circle quicker than could be imagined. I was now teaching student pilots the skills that they would need as they moved on to become operational pilots. Most of these young pilots would soon be locked in combat in Southeast Asia.

We rented a small house on the east side of the small Texas town of Beeville. The front of the house faced a street that looked very much like a street in any suburb at that time. Out the back, past a small paved street, was an open valley of several acres that the city maintained. This open area would become one of the vivid memories of our stay in south Texas.

The war in Vietnam was still in full swing and young Navy and Marine pilots were needed. I settled into a demanding work schedule that allowed only one day off each weekend-- Saturday one week and Sunday the next.

A few times, to help relieve the stress, I went fishing on Lake Mathis about twenty-five miles from our home. Even though I was away from home working most of the time, Glenda encouraged me to take a break. On one occasion she agreed to accompany me, just to see what I was up to. I showed her how to bait the hook and then the proper presentation. On final count her catch was double mine. Life is not fair.

The Special Services department on the base had fishing boats that could be checked out on a daily basis. The attendant and I rigged the wiring system in such a way that would allow the boat trailer brake and taillights to work when attached to our 1964 VW Bug. On one occasion after dark, assuming complete legality, I departed the airfield and headed west toward home. Suddenly, flashing lights appeared in my rear-view mirror. The boat trailer lights had failed. The compassionate officer helped me repair the wiring and allowed me to proceed.

To provide a bit of recreation for base personnel, the Navy had leased land from a local rancher for use as a dove hunting area. Since Glenda was now an expert at catching Texas catfish, I asked her to accompany me on a dove hunting trip to one of these hunting areas. She had practiced with my 20-gauge shotgun and was now capable of handling it safely and with confidence. The hunt was on.

Darrel F. Smith

I positioned her under a large tree that stood alone in the middle of the field. The doves, sometimes in flocks, came to this seeded plot. I picked a spot that was about one hundred yards away and out of sight.

The sky was clear, and the wind was calm, I saw no doves. Within only a few minutes Glenda fired a shot from beneath her tree. Her shots continued with regularity. I was puzzled since I had seen absolutely no doves. The shooting persisted.

Concerned as to what was going on, I walked back to her tree. I had trained her how to handle the shotgun but had forgotten to teach her how to identify a dove. There had been a flock of sparrows flying in and around the tree and she was doing her best to bag one. These birds were lucky that her marksmanship left a bit to be desired. The sparrows survived, and we had a good laugh. She was such a good trooper.

The alert was sounded. A hurricane in the Gulf of Mexico was making its way toward Houston and our base at Beeville, about 70 miles inland. In order to protect the aircraft, instructors and students formed two-man teams to fly the squadron aircraft to safety. These teams were also charged with getting as much training done as possible.

My student and I flew our assigned aircraft clear of the storm, but Glenda and the kids were left to fend for themselves. After the hurricane made landfall the winds subsided somewhat but the rains came and the water began to rise. Glenda remembers that about sixteen inches fell within a few hours.

Tom McGee, a fellow instructor in my squadron, lived two doors down the street. He and his wife Anne contacted Glenda and informed her that the neighborhood was being evacuated. The large valley behind our house was already full and the water was still rising. Another neighbor, the local furniture store owner, was rescuing people along our street. He was kind enough to put these folks up for the night in his downtown store.

Glenda remembers wading with our young children through a foot of water to his waiting vehicle. She and the kids spent the night in the store that was above the flood plain. It was an uncomfortable night, but they were safe and dry. The water came within only a few inches of flooding our house. We sustained no damage and of course during the whole episode I was in some BOQ room hundreds of miles away.

I knew, without a doubt, that if I remained in the Marine Corps, a second year in Vietnam was in my future. I also felt that my year in the war zone had fulfilled my duty. I chose to leave the Corps and began applying to the airlines for employment as a pilot.

I know. I know. The idea of dealing with passengers and never making more than a 30-degree angle of bank turn was a little hard to swallow. I put my Marine attack pilot attitude aside and hoped that some airline would feel that I could be an asset.

One of my applications was eventually accepted by Northwest Airlines and I soon began an entirely new career as an airline pilot. I can truthfully say that without Glenda's help and support I would not have achieved this level of success.

A New Career

Northwest Airlines
1968

What to do? What to do?

My year in Vietnam had been long and had caused me to miss that portion of my daughter's life. Two months after my deployment to that far away country our son had been born. He was ten months old when I met him for the first time.

During my tour as an instructor pilot in the advanced jet training command in Beeville, Texas, I came to realize that I had become a product of the United States Marine Corps. I did not want to leave that organization but knew without a doubt that I would soon be sent back to the war in Vietnam. This would mean that I would miss two years of my children's early life and there was no guarantee that I would survive. I felt that I had fulfilled my obligation to the Corps.

My training as a military pilot had instilled in me some skills that could possibly be marketable. I applied to many airlines and had several interviews including one with Northwest Airlines, based in Minneapolis, Minnesota. My knowledge of this small airline was limited but they offered me a job and I accepted. A few days later Continental Airlines offered me a pilot position. I had already accepted the Northwest job and as a man of my word, the Continental offer was rejected. Over the years my decision to fly for Northwest turned out to be the better choice. There had been no skill on my part, just plain good luck.

Even though my Marine Corps experience had been tremendously educational, I was very ignorant as to how the civilian aviation world worked. Jet engines in those days left a trail of dark exhaust smoke. Upon arriving in the Minneapolis area as we drove along highway 494 near the airport, we could see a constant stream of Northwest 727 and 707 aircraft blasting into the sky. These aircraft were much bigger than anything that I had flown. I was excited, yet intimidated. Could I, a simple attack pilot, ever become a part of a crew that flew these huge aircraft?

We found a small rental house in Cottage Grove about ten miles to the southeast of the airport. We settled in and my training with Northwest soon began. We were excited, however the saying, "They can fire me but I ain't quittin'" again popped into my mind.

As newly hired airline pilots we were subjected to a full year of probation. During that year the company had the authority to dismiss us for any reason. The pay was very low, about five hundred dollars a month, therefore our family of four had to pinch pennies to survive.

New houses were under construction near our rental home. A fellow probational pilot got the contract to clean the windows in one of these developments. Glenda and I both washed windows for a short time. I don't remember how much money we made but any amount of cash was welcomed.

This new endeavor began in the fall and we enjoyed the moderate weather. A lady we met encouraged us to get out and see the north woods and lakes before winter. We took her advice and tried to enjoy the fall colors in a few small state parks. There was no way for us to know how harsh winter in Minnesota could become.

One day, after class, as I was driving toward home in our 1964 VW Bug, a few flakes of snow were observed blowing across the road. This was exciting. We had never experienced a winter in the north. Within a few days our mailbox was completely covered, and we soon learned that winter was something to be endured, not so much enjoyed.

Winter set in with a vengeance. We were amazed and excited. That winter I jumped through all the hoops and successfully completed the required ground school. After being released to line flying, I began my airline career by flying as a flight engineer, second officer, on the Boeing 727. This meager beginning set us on course toward experiencing some of the wonders of this world.

Upon reflection, we were almost completely ignorant about Minneapolis and the state of Minnesota. We simply worked hard, did our best, and hoped it would all work out.

I was lucky enough to complete thirty years in the employment of Northwest Airlines. We had many setbacks but also many great adventures. We have lived an interesting and eventful life.

WAYNE

A Friend for Life

Twenty-four men from varied flying backgrounds gathered at Northwest Airlines headquarters on the eighth day of September,1968. We had all been offered jobs as pilots for this airline but would be required to endure a full year of probation during which the company could dismiss us for any reason. During this year we would be paid only a meager wage. I did not know what to expect and had no way of knowing the flying skill levels of my fellow classmates.

As we gathered for our first classroom session, I took a seat at the back of the room. Even though I had earned my wings as a Naval Aviator and endured a year of combat operations, my confidence level was not very high. As had been my normal mode of operation, I kept a low profile and kept my mouth shut as much as possible.

It so happened that sitting to my left was Wayne J. Anderson, who had grown up in Minnesota, graduated from St. Olaf College, and learned to fly in the Air Force. Wayne was a friendly guy and after a few weeks asked me to join him on a trip to his parents' cabin on Kabekona Lake in northern Minnesota.

On our drive north Wayne informed me that we would be passing through an Indian reservation. Indian reservations were a new concept to me, and I was concerned that we might come under attack. There was no reason to fear and we had a great few days breathing the cool fresh air and viewing the beautiful lake. This experience was beyond anything that I could have dreamed. During my youth there was always more work on the farm than could be accomplished, there was therefore very little time or money for leisure activities.

Several years later, the Anderson and Smith families were spending a few days at the lake. On this trip Wayne and I planned to install a new roof on the cabin. The day was hot, and the work was hard, but we managed to get the job done. After the last nail had been nailed, we descended the ladders and stood admiring our work. Suddenly, Wayne's wife Anne, started laughing and seemed unable to stop. She had noticed that by sitting and sliding about on the abrasive shingles I had destroyed the seat of my trousers. My bare butt was exposed.

The entire class completed that stressful year of probation and began working as crew members for the airline. The flying was nothing like my military experience, but I worked hard at trying to fit in. We could now be called "Airline Pilots."

At some point Wayne suggested that Glenda and I should consider living in Northfield, Minnesota. This small town featured St. Olaf College which Wayne and Anne had attended and Carlton College, both highly regarded small schools.

A realtor that Wayne knew found a simple little house that the owner was willing to sell to us on a contract for deed with no money down. We had no money to put down, therefore this seemed to be a good deal. This was the first of many, many houses we would own during our lifetime.

Our little home, located at 908 Greenvale Avenue, was not fancy but served us well. It had two small apartments in the walkout basement which we rented to St. Olaf students. At that stage of our lives the meager rental income was welcomed. We gradually upgraded our housing as we moved to a small farm about two miles north of town, and after about eight years, back to town to a house near the golf course.

We remained friends with the Andersons and enjoyed many wonderful adventures. They introduced us to The Boundary Waters Canoe Wilderness. This 1.1-million-acre jewel is located in northeastern Minnesota. It is recognized as a destination for canoeing, camping, and fishing. More people visit this area than any other National Wilderness Area.

Wayne and I settled into a pattern of taking a few days each year and using them to create some sort of adventure. Minnesota is known as the land of 10,000 lakes, most of which are located in the northern part of the state. We along with other friends started going "up north" for the opening of the fishing season. We gradually expanded our horizons.

Wayne became associated with a company that bought and sold private aircraft. An aircraft had been sold to a small air taxi service that operated from Kodiak Island, Alaska. He and I delivered the aircraft by flying along the Alcan Highway to Anchorage. The new owner met us at the airport, took possession of the plane, and with us on board flew it back to Kodiak.

We were expected to stay overnight in the rather small home of the aircraft's new owner. His young daughters were moved from their bedroom to mats in the master bedroom to accommodate the strangers from the lower 48. The girls seemed to think that this was the normal thing to do.

The owner was determined to entertain us during our stay on Kodiak Island. The plan was to take a sightseeing trip around the island in his float plane and then go fishing. The weather was terrible. Every few minutes our host would look at the lake and shake his head indicating that we should not try to fly. He finally said, "Let's go for it." The weather looked the same to me.

The island with its rugged coastline was beautiful as we spent an hour or so sightseeing. A large herd of elk was spotted grazing on a grassy mountain side. We were now ready for the fishing part of the day. A smooth landing was made as the pontoons touched down on the smooth surface near the mouth of a small river. Our pilot and guide steered the craft toward a rocky beach. As we traveled up this remote waterway, salmon were constantly jumping into the air. The plane was beached and since I was in the back seat it took me a few minutes to get out the door. Our pilot had a fish on his line before my feet hit the ground. In my mind this was not fishing, this was catching.

After living in the ocean for several years, salmon make their way back to their home stream to spawn. They struggle against the current, attempt to avoid the bears, complete the spawning process, and then die. Upon again becoming airborne we flew along a rather small spawning stream. We observed untold thousands of large dead fish along the edge of the water.

Wayne and I traveled by canoe to a remote lake in northern Minnesota. The fishing had been great, and we were making good time down a flowing stream toward camp. We rounded a bend and there standing broadside in this small river was the biggest moose I had ever seen. As we appeared it raised its head, looked our way, the hair on his back stood up. The canoe was brought to a stop only a few feet from this huge animal. We had heard stories of angry moose charging canoes and people. We back paddled with extreme urgency to a spot about 20 yards from our new friend. This magnificent animal stood his ground and continued to look our way. We said stupid things like, "Hello, mister moose" and "Could you allow us to pass?" We pounded on the side of the canoe and finally with what we considered contempt showing in his eyes he slowly moved out of the stream. We passed within 15 feet and with a sigh of relief continued on our way.

On another trip on a nice day we planned to cross a large lake in a canoe powered by a three-horsepower outboard motor. There seemed to be no threat but about halfway across the wind started to blow and the waves got larger and larger. The canoe would claw its way up a large wave and then fall over the top. The little engine would be suspended completely out of the water. After what seemed like hours, we made our way to safety. Over the years we shared many adventures, including backpacking in Denali park in Alaska where we interacted with 14 grizzly bears.

Wayne and I became best friends. Our families often socialized, and we became as close as brothers. He invited me to sit with the family at his dad's funeral. We were always welcomed at Anne's parents' home in southern Minnesota to watch the blacked-out Vikings home football games. I had never had a male friend and I truly enjoyed our relationship.

Due to the twists and turns of life, Wayne and I now live in different parts of the country but will forever be friends. Wayne and the Northfield experience were very important in our maturing as a family. Had I not met Wayne our lives would have been completely different.

1979 Darrel and Wayne

IT'S GREEK TO ME

The FAA (Federal Aviation Administration) creates the rules and regulations that govern the operation of commercial airlines. Even though this organization oversees the big picture, the individual airlines are responsible for the major part of the required training and checks.

The pilot seniority system, FAA rules, and negotiated complicated pay formulas make it a necessity for all airlines to maintain large training departments that operate for long hours nearly every day. Should a cockpit position become available, such as when a pilot retires, another pilot would bid for and be awarded that position. This would start a chain of training cycles in that several pilots would move up leaving even more vacancies. Most pilots chose to fly the position that paid the most money.

The work between Northwest Airlines and the Pilots Union (ALPA) stated that all instructors in the training department were required to be active line pilots. My last duty assignment as a Marine was as a flight instructor in the Navy/Marine Corps advanced jet training command at Beeville, Texas. I had enjoyed this experience and elected to try my hand at becoming an instructor for Northwest Airlines.

I was accepted into the training department, and initially served as a second officer (flight engineer) instructor on the Boeing 727. After a year or so I transitioned, due to Northwest hiring more pilots, into the Boeing 707 and soon became an instructor on that aircraft. In those days most of the flight training was being done in simulators rather than in actual aircraft. During the months that I served as an instructor, although observing and evaluating trainees, there was very little time spent as an operational crew member. In order to maintain our personal proficiency, the instructors were rotated back to line flying every third month or so.

I was enjoying a month of flying the line and was airborne on a flight from Miami to Minneapolis when I received a radio message instructing me to contact my training supervisor upon arrival. A message worded like this always made me wonder, "How have I screwed up now?"

After completing my shutdown procedures, I called my supervisor and his words left me speechless. He said, "We need a 707 Second Officer instructor to be transferred to Athens, Greece with dependents for a year. Do you want the job?" Holy Cow, my head was spinning. After sputtering and stuttering, I told him I would give him an answer the next day.

Olympic Airlines, the Greek National Airline, had purchased six Boeing 707 aircraft from Northwest Airlines. As part of the purchase agreement, Northwest had agreed to provide pilots to initially fly the aircraft, and instructors to train the Greek pilots.

Glenda and I had always tried to take advantage of any opportunity for a new adventure. We considered this trip to be a once-in-a-lifetime opportunity. What would we do about school for the kids, the house, and the car? There would be some tough decisions, but we dearly wanted to take this assignment. The details would just have to be worked out. I informed the company that I would be happy to accept this challenge.

I was told that my services were needed in short order. I do not remember how much time I had before departure, but Glenda was left, as has happened so many times, to do all the work. Even though there have been times when she became completely stressed out—she always came through like a champ.

Vasili "Bill" Pitsavas, the local pizza restaurant owner in Northfield, Minnesota, heard that I would be traveling to his motherland. He called one night and asked if he could stop by our house. He arrived with a suitcase nearly full of electrical parts—resistors, capacitors, etc. He asked me to deliver this suitcase to a friend in Greece, telling me there was nothing illegal about this act. He claimed the parts were just in short supply back home. I was dumb enough to agree.

Here I was, going to a new country to report for a new job with all this stuff that could possibly be illegal. The flight from New York to Athens was the most miserable of my life. I dreamed up many unpleasant scenarios that could befall me upon my arrival. All my worry was for naught—I passed through customs and immigration with no trouble. I will never again agree to be a courier.

Bob Cavill, the acting chief pilot, picked me up at the airport and took me to a small hotel that would serve as my temporary home. There were a number of Northwest personnel living there that made my transition comfortable. I was excited to be in Athens.

Anxious to get rid of my electrical stash, I contacted a local Greek man as instructed. He did not seem to be very interested but agreed to meet me at my hotel. He unceremoniously took the suitcase and departed, not even saying thanks. Never again.

According to Greek law, any foreigner was required to obtain a work permit before working within the country. The day after my arrival, I was taken to the proper office to start the process of obtaining mine. After laboring through many forms, I was told to return in a week with two photos.

Within a few days I started flying, without the work permit, but returned a week later with the requested photos. Again, I was told to return in one week. Weekly visits were made to this office, but the permit never came. I worked with no permit the entire time that I was in the country. This was my first brush with Greek inefficiency—at times it was maddening.

One of my first chores was to get fitted for my Olympic Airlines pilot uniform. This uniform had a definite European flair, whatever that means. It looked different from airline uniforms in the United States. Many times, I was mistaken for a Greek pilot due to my mustache and that uniform. Passengers would approach and attempt to start a conversation in their native language. Somehow, I found it difficult to communicate since I knew only about three or four Greek words.

My job as a second officer instructor consisted of riding along on regular passenger flights and observing the trainee operate the aircraft systems. They were far from perfect; therefore, extreme vigilance was required to prevent any damaging mistakes. These flights shuttled back and forth from Athens to the Greek Islands and sometimes to London or Rome.

Glenda had wrapped up the details and we had decided on a day for her and the kids to make their appearance in Athens. We needed a place to live. I can't remember how it was located, but I found a two-bedroom apartment in a three-story home in a community not too far from the airport. Without knowing it, I had picked Glyfada which was one of the nicer communities in the Athens metropolitan area.

Our landlord, a retired Greek army general, and his wife, Sofia, lived on the top floor. He had a picture of two very attractive topless women on his desk. One of our kids, about 6 or 7 years old at the time, asked him who they were. With a big belly laugh he said they were his "sisters."

Even at their young age they both rolled their eyes in disbelief. In this country the lower floor of a multi-story building is the least desirable unit—that is where we lived.

The apartment was unfurnished. In Greece unfurnished means just that. There was no furniture, kitchen appliances, or even light fixtures. My airline friends suggested the bargain part of town and that is where I purchased everything to furnish our new little home. This stuff was cheap but functional—we would just have to make do.

We settled into some sort of rhythm. I flew often but was home nearly every night. During the day, while I was away, Glenda and her pilot wife friends started going to the beach. Most days they would pack up the kids and possibly a lunch for some fun in the sun at the beach. I got the impression that a glass or two of wine may have been consumed. It was a good life.

Greek customs were different and at times required that we make some minor adjustment. When we ate out, we usually had the entire restaurant to ourselves. The locals dined much later. If we relaxed and stayed longer than normal a few folks would begin to arrive. It was normal for them to go out for dinner at 9 p.m. or later. It was common to hear music and partying well past midnight.

There were no lines in Greece. Lines had long been replaced with wedges. At the post office, grocery store, bus stop, and any other place where a line could be expected, there was a wedge. One person would be at the wedge point getting service and the rest would be jockeying for position. There was a lot of body contact.

I remember Glenda exiting the post office, after attempting a simple transaction, crying. She had finally worked her way to the window and placed her letter and money on the counter. A larger woman shouldered her forcefully out of the way. The clerk calmly waited on the bully.

I was with a trainee on his first trip to London. Our layover was long enough for him to do some exploring. The next day he was excited to tell me about what he had experienced. He and several other people were waiting at a bus stop for a city bus. When it arrived and stopped, the door opened, and a lady stepped aside and told him to please board ahead of her. This simple act amazed him—he had never in his life seen anything like it.

In Greece, inefficiency was the way of life. During our stay we purchased a new Mercedes and took delivery at the factory in Germany. The tale of this sad auto is a story within itself and will be told later. Initially, we truly loved our new little car. We drove it from Germany back to Greece.

Upon crossing the border from Yugoslavia into Greece, we had some money that we wanted to exchange for Greek money. We asked the border agent where this could be accomplished. He pointed to a building nearby but volunteered that any bank in Athens would do the job.

A few days after arriving back in Athens the money was taken to a small bank located near our rental house. I was told that they could not make the exchange but the bank at the airport would be happy to accommodate. The airport bank directed me to a bank downtown. The downtown bank sent me to a bank around the corner. A clerk at that bank sent me upstairs. A clerk pointed toward a man seated at a desk three rows from the front of the room. The man stood up and motioned for me to approach and said, "I can help you." He took my bills, turned them over several times, handed them back and said, "Too small." I never was able to get the money changed. I finally just gave it to someone who planned to drive north into Yugoslavia.

In Greece, when a foreign family that owned an automobile chose to leave the country, even for a few days, the car was required to be locked up in an official impound lot. The country collected a large tax on any auto purchased by a citizen. The impound procedure was intended to prevent foreigners from selling their vehicle to a local, without the tax being collected, and then departing the country permanently.

Planning to go to London for a few days, Glenda and I needed to go through this procedure. We were directed to an office where officials supposedly could handle this transaction. A man took our passports, looked them over carefully and handed them back to us. He said he was unable to do the job but directed us to an office down and across the hallway. The occupant of this office did almost the same thing. He sent us to another office. This third official sent us back to the first official, who completed the procedure in only a few seconds.

After living with the Greek way of doing business for several months, Glenda and I flew to Germany. Upon arrival, I approached a money changer to exchange some U.S. dollars for German marks. Without saying a word, this attractive young lady quickly made the exchange and said, "Thank you". This efficient transaction surprised me. I asked, "Is that it?" She replied, "Of course."

I have been somewhat negative about our stay in Greece. This is misleading in that we had so many great experiences and met so many really nice people. More than 40 years later we still consider these people to be our friends. Sophia and Constance, our landlords, were exceptionally nice. Decades later we stopped by their house. Constance had passed away, Sophia invited us in for tea and a great visit. I think we woke her from an afternoon siesta.

This wonderful adventure came to a dramatic end. The pilot group and Northwest airlines were in contentious discussions as to the terms of our next contract. The proceedings had not gone well. It came down to the wire but ended in ALPA (Airline Pilots Association) calling a strike, which shut down the entire flight operation.

We were caught in the middle. Our little group was initially considered separate from normal flight operations and we continued to do our job—and get paid. The union did not think it was fair for us to remain on the payroll when our fellow pilots were on the street. We were instructed to stop working and return home.

Glenda and the kids departed. A week or so later I drove our Mercedes across Europe to Antwerp, Belgium, for shipment and then made my way back to the States.

The early end of our stay in Greece was a sad occasion for the entire family. We had learned and seen so much but all good things come to an end. Looking back, we consider this adventure one of the greatest of our lives. If offered the opportunity to repeat this adventure, we would eagerly accept.

Glenda on the right, with the other moms at the beach.

"Unlike Any Other"

Our Mercedes
1972

At one time "Unlike Any Other" was the catch phrase used in the sales pitch of the Mercedes automobile company. By using this phrase, they hoped to promote the idea that their product was superior to all other makes. Reflecting upon our experience of owning a Mercedes, we learned that our car was indeed "Unlike Any Other," but not in the way the company intended.

Fancy or luxurious items were never of much interest to me. This could possibly be due to the fact that I could never afford them. I did enjoy and appreciate things that were durable and timeless. If a product promised to give years of great service, I was willing to pay a little extra to own it.

We lived on Greenvale Avenue in Northfield, Minnesota. A staff member of St. Olaf College, a well-respected private school, was a neighbor and owned an older Mercedes car that was powered by a diesel engine. That old car always seemed to start but with a lot of shaking, noise, and smoke. Our friend loved his car and bragged about it at every opportunity.

His pride in this old machine gradually convinced me that he knew what he was talking about. After all, he was a college professor. As time passed, I slowly formed the impression that an automobile built by the Mercedes company in Germany was a quality product that could be expected to deliver years of exceptional service.

A few years later Northwest Airlines offered me the opportunity to transfer to Athens, Greece as a second officer instructor on the Boeing 707 aircraft. Northwest had sold several of these planes to Olympic

Airlines, the Greek national airline. As a part of the sales agreement, Northwest was to provide pilots to initially fly the aircraft and instructors to train the Greek pilots.

This assignment was scheduled to last a full year. Glenda and I eagerly accepted the challenge. My favorable impression of the Mercedes automobile traveled right along with us.

The forty pilots assigned to the Greek operation arrived with their families and got busy trying to find suitable housing for the next year. It soon became apparent that each household would need some sort of family transportation.

Each family had their own idea as to the best way to fulfill this need. A few chose to rent but that option turned out to be very expensive. Most bought poor quality autos from "reputable" local dealers. These beat-up old cars were generally unreliable and frequently refused to start, especially when they were needed the most.

I was introduced to the idea of buying a new Mercedes through an authorized dealership back in the States. The details have been forgotten but by taking delivery in Europe there was a slight discount and a tax savings. Northwest Airlines Credit Union and a Mercedes dealership in Minneapolis made the deal possible.

Olympic Airlines provided direct service from Athens to Frankfurt, Germany, therefore taking delivery at the factory seemed possible and presented the opportunity for yet another adventure. My rationale was that we would have dependable transportation during our year in Greece and then years of reliable service back home. The sale price included shipping by cargo ship back to the east coast of the United States.

The price was more than we could comfortably afford, but the idea of owning a quality, long-lasting machine was too much to resist. We would be the proud owners of a 1972 Mercedes 220 diesel and take delivery at the factory in Sindelfingen, Germany.

On or near the delivery date, our entire family boarded an Olympic Airlines flight that delivered us to Germany. On the agreed upon day and time, we arrived at the factory. We were welcomed with open arms and shown into a beautiful waiting area where we were offered various nonalcoholic beverages and snacks.

Our personal guide soon arrived and explained that we would be escorted on a tour of the factory that had assembled the car we were about to own. The factory was clean, well-lighted, and fitted with the most modern equipment. It was quite impressive. The employees seemed happy and competent. We loved our car before we had even seen it.

After this tour we were taken to the "delivery" room—it was almost like welcoming a new family member—where we were introduced to our new car. During the next hour or so we were told the purpose and function of every switch and light.

These components were described in great detail; "This is the knob that controls the headlights, when you pull the knob the headlights will illuminate, when you push the knob the headlights will be extinguished." Every control was explained in this manner. It seemed as though they thought we had never before seen an automobile.

We tried to keep the "rolling of eyes" in disbelief to a minimum. After what seemed longer than necessary, we were finally presented with the keys and sent on our way. As it turned out the previous hour could have been better spent explaining the road signs that we would encounter upon attempting to depart the factory grounds.

Since we could not speak or read German, we became lost almost immediately. We made several wrong turns just trying to exit the company parking area. However, being fast learners, within a very few minutes we determined that German signs that display the letters "f-a-r-t" inform the driver that by following this sign you could "escape or depart." Pretty smart on our part, don't you think?

This was our first exposure to this part of Europe. The drive across Germany, through the Alps, and across Austria was beyond our imagination. The scenery was so beautiful and different that we felt like we were in an enchanted world.

Our new little car seemed to labor a bit in its effort to climb the steep and winding roads of the German and Austrian Alps. We were so much in love with this new machine and the wonderful scenery that we tended to overlook any faults. The people were friendly, the beer was cold, and the food was great. We could not speak the language, but we were always able to find food, fuel, and a place to sleep.

In that part of the world a little sign, "Zimmer Free", displayed on individual homes was an indication that rooms were available for rent. These accommodations were clean, reasonably priced, and a hearty breakfast was always served. The feather beds and, on occasion, the sound of a nearby rushing stream made our overnights relaxing and unique.

These few days in the Alps were a once-in-a-lifetime experience. Our kids were young, but I feel they grasped the fact that this was something special. We took many photos of the beautiful mountain views. Reviewing those pictures, we now realize that too many featured our new

Mercedes in the foreground. We still loved our new automobile.

The "delivery" person informed us that the car would need a certain service after only a relatively few miles. We walked the streets of Salzburg, Austria and lounged in the waiting room while this required service was being completed.

We had purchased and studied maps that covered the area from Austria, through Yugoslavia, to Greece. Highway One appeared to be the only route that would lead us back "home." Athens seemed an almost impossible goal as we crossed the border into this communist country. We were a bit apprehensive.

Several friends had advised against attempting to drive a car from Germany to Greece. We were uninformed but full of adventure, therefore we boldly drove into the face of the unknown.

In those days this highway was a two-lane road that proceeded southward and passed near the larger cities. We were surprised to be able to easily find overnight accommodations in motels similar to back home. We were further surprised to find that the reception staff in every establishment spoke almost perfect English.

The trip through Yugoslavia took three days during which we traveled through mostly rural countryside. On most farms the house and outbuildings were enclosed in fences made from thin sticks that were tied together vertically. Several times we saw older women going to and from the fields herding flocks of fat geese. We remember seeing only a few, maybe less than ten, modern tractors working in the fields.

On one occasion we chose to take a secondary road that ran parallel to the main highway. We wanted to see how the general population lived. Passing through a very small town we paused near a weathered statue in the central plaza. As I stepped outside to take a picture, a group of young men started yelling and moving our way. We quickly departed. Just outside of town we met a wagon stacked high with loose hay pulled by horses.

The main highway was crowded with large trucks, causing our progress to be rather slow. The two-lane road plus crowded conditions had obviously resulted in many crashes. We observed many wrecked vehicles near the road where they had evidently found their final resting place.

The truck stop that was so familiar to us back home did not exist. The truck drivers stopped at small fueling stations where they could refuel and tend to their basic needs.

Glenda needed a bathroom break. We stopped at one of these

facilities where, upon inquiring, she was directed to a restroom. When she entered there were several wash basins where truckers were shaving and bathing. She assumed that she had entered the wrong facility and again asked for directions.

The men were quite friendly and directed her to a hole in the floor, which had footprints embossed in the concrete on either side, that was in full view of everyone. She chose to decline their offering and later took care of her business in the woods down the road. She shared upon returning to the car that she had not been the first to use the woods as a "rest stop".

We don't feel that there was any real danger but crossing the border into Greece was like taking a heavy weight from our shoulders. Traveling the roads of northern Greece was like coming home. The beautiful views, better highways, and our new "ride" made our drive to Athens a true delight.

We had completed the journey with no major difficulties and now had a beautiful new car at our service and a new adventure under our belts. Life was good.

This good life took a turn for the worst. ALPA was in serious negotiations with Northwest Airlines in the attempt to hammer out a new work agreement. These negotiations did not go well, and a work stoppage was commenced. The pilots went on strike.

The pilots stationed in Greece were caught in the middle. ALPA leadership came to the conclusion that it was not fair for our little group to continue to work and get paid while the rest of the pilots were "on the street." The Greek Airline management told us that if we went on strike we could possibly be sent to jail. The contract with Olympic Airlines was eventually dissolved. The pilots were promised transportation back to the United States but nothing else.

Glenda and the kids flew back to Minnesota and I remained in Greece hoping to get the car on its way to the States. Yes, the car could be shipped as promised, but only from Antwerp, Belgium. There was no other way--the car had to be driven back north.

Making only a few overnight stops, I delivered the car to the shipping dock and secured a ride on an Olympic flight back to Athens. Would our car be lost forever? I was worried.

True to their word, Olympic Airlines provided transportation for me back to the United States.

I don't remember the details, but we got word that our car was available to be picked up at some port on the east coast. To the best of my memory, I made the trip alone to retrieve our beloved Mercedes.

I found the facility where our car had first touched American soil. The delivery staff, in my opinion, had very little or no training in customer service. They simply did not "give a s--t." The car at some time during its journey appeared to have been used as a "break room." The floor and seats were filthy, and the ashtrays were full of cigarette butts. The exterior was even worse and there were scratches in the paint across the trunk. Their attitude? Take it or leave it. Take it up with the insurance company. The car did start, and I drove away with an everlasting bad attitude toward shipping companies and dock workers.

We were so proud of our German auto but were in for a big surprise. This car turned out to be the worst automobile of our lifetime. We have always joked that this car must have been built the Monday morning after Octoberfest. Just about anything that could go wrong, went wrong.

Our bad experience with that car and the Mercedes Company had begun at the dealership in Athens. At the promised time after a normal oil change, I arrived at the maintenance lobby to retrieve the car. The bill was paid but nothing happened. There seemed to be confusion. To make a long story short the dealership had lost our car. After an hour and fifteen minutes of searching it was located. There was no apology, just a palms-up shrug.

On a cold night in Minnesota Glenda and I drove the Mercedes to a movie. We enjoyed the event and with all the other patrons made our way back to our cars. Everyone soon drove away except for us and one other car. That other Mercedes and our car had to be towed and started at a local maintenance facility. All other makes and models had departed with no problems.

We owned that car for 15 months during which it required shop service 62 days. With only 21,000 miles showing on the odometer the engine blew. The piston rings on the front cylinder had failed. Mercedes paid for only half of the repair bill.

Over and over, I would retrieve it from the dealership shop and during the drive home fall in love again. Then, the next morning it would often fail to start. I am convinced that the Mercedes Company does not build a better car but sells them with high end advertising and snob appeal.

The ownership of this car was not a pleasant experience. However, because of it we did experience some great adventures in parts of Europe that would not have been considered otherwise.

Mercedes diesel-powered autos are often used as taxis in Europe. The drivers seem to be very happy with their cars, often bragging about their durability. It is possible that we just happened to get a lemon. However, the company and dealership tried to place the blame in my lap. One salesman, Bloomberg, accused me of using jet fuel in the car after he learned that I was a pilot.

I will probably never own another German automobile. They seem to promise excellence but, in my experience, do not produce. However, Germany does produce excellent beer of which I have absolutely no complaint. I love their beer but not their Benz.

OUR LITTLE FARM

A Place in the Country
1973

Our first experience of owning a home had been a success. Our little house in Northfield, Minnesota located at 908 Greenvale had provided us adequate shelter and a little extra income during the early years of my career with Northwest Airlines. The house had two small apartments in the basement that we rented to St. Olaf College students and others.

We settled into this little house knowing that it was less than perfect. Along the west side there was a large gully that was very difficult to mow. I remember tying a rope to a small lawn mower, shoving it over the edge, and then hauling it, hand over hand, back to the top.

There was no garage. The harsh Minnesota winters made us realize that some sort of cover for our cars would be highly desirable. The snow-shoveling and ice-chipping got to be a real chore.

I don't remember how we came to consider buying the Viking home and land that was located about two miles north of town. No realtor was involved. I do remember that we took a walk in the Carlton College arboretum as we pondered this huge decision. We knew it was the biggest financial decision we had ever made. What the heck, we went for it.

Dick and Bev Viking had purchased the land and served as general contractors for the construction of the house. Originally there were forty acres, but one lot and home had been sold to Joyce and David, who became our friends. The Vikings chose to keep another portion where they built their next home. We never knew exactly how many acres were included in our little farm, but it became our home for many years.

Even before the final sales transaction, the Vikings gave us permission to begin doing some yard work. On a blustery afternoon, as I worked in the back yard, a rather small and fast-moving thunderstorm passed nearby. Along its trailing edge a small funnel cloud formed, touched down, and traveled a short distance along the ground. It lifted and soon disappeared. A Northwest Airlines aircraft flew through the very same area as it vanished with no ill effects. It was later learned that this brief tornado had damaged a mobile home park and claimed the life of a young child.

The purchase was completed, and we settled into life as "gentlemen farmers" on this bit of land in the country. We were proud of our little place in rural Minnesota.

On a lazy but rainy Sunday afternoon, the family gathered in the walkout basement for an afternoon of watching the Minnesota Vikings play football. I had just assumed a comfortable position on the couch when a small stream of water was observed slowly trickling across the tile floor. This small beginning became an all-out battle to keep our basement from flooding. No matter how much mopping we did, the flow continued to increase. The water table had risen above the level of the basement floor.

Standing in the pouring rain, I dug a hole just outside the back door. Guessing at what might be a point below the foundation slab, I used a sledge hammer to knock a hole through the concrete block foundation. As the hammer finally broke through, water, under pressure gushed out. This hole lowered the water level and the flooding stopped. The flow had immediately slowed and soon stopped altogether but the cleanup had just begun. We don't remember who won the football game.

During the Viking house era, Darrel Jr. was a teenager and had shown some interest in hunting. One day we walked to the back of our property, knowing the prospects were slim, with the intent of finding a pheasant. Suddenly a beautiful rooster exploded into the air. In his eagerness to bag this trophy Darrel Jr. emptied his shotgun without even touching a feather. I feel this event plays on his mental attitude, even to this day.

This type of miss is not uncommon. Darrel Jr. and I were pheasant hunting in a standing cornfield with several other friends. As we marched along, several birds had burst from cover and attempted to make their getaway downwind directly over our heads. Making some very difficult shots, I was able to bag several of these birds.

As we were leaving the field, a lone rooster flew from near my feet directly away from me. This was an easy shot. I also emptied my shotgun without touching a feather. I have taken a lot of ribbing about that miss.

I came up with the idea of planting trees on our land. I bought about thirty or forty black walnut trees to plant along the back-property boundary. The whole family was enlisted to help with this project. I put a large cattle-watering tank in the back of my old pickup truck with the idea of giving our freshly planted trees a good drink to get them started.

I rigged some sort of faucet/valve to the outlet of this tank. As I drove along, Kelly was to allow the water to flow to each newly planted tree. Unfortunately, the whole assembly broke, and water spurted nearly everywhere except on the young plants. In my frustration, Kelly caught the brunt of my burst of anger. I have always felt that I was wrong to direct the blame toward her.

Glenda and I visited the trees only once after moving away from that house. In my mind the trees were fifteen feet tall and looked very healthy. I wonder what they look like today, about forty years later.

During our farm experience the general public became interested in conserving carbon fuel. Eldon Hill, Darrell Cloud, Pete Stoley, and others decided to cut firewood to supplement our heating costs. We downed trees in our woodlot and other places, cutting them into logs which we split for use in our fireplaces and wood-burning stoves.

I don't know how much money we saved but we had a great time doing the work. On one foray, as I backed my old truck into position for loading our hard-earned stash of wood, there was a flattened old barn directly in my path. I arrived home with three tires hissing as I had picked up nails from this old structure. The cost of fixing the flats more than offset any money we had saved by cutting our own firewood.

Our little farm was surrounded by larger farms, swampy areas, and a number of small woods. The plentiful food supply and excellent cover made this area a great place for the whitetail deer.

A Marine buddy, Larry R. Gibson, had introduced me to shooting the bow and arrow while we were stationed at a Marine Corps air station in North Carolina. This casual introduction sparked an interest in the sport that would last for many years.

I had hunted deer in several parts of the country. Some success had come my way in that on two occasions a whitetail had been bagged. One afternoon, dressed in my camouflage clothing, I walked about three hundred yards from the house to a small woods. There were lots of tracks, indicating that deer often traveled this area.

Climbing onto a large, low branch, I stood and leaned against the tree trunk and tried to become part of the neighborhood. I waited. The birds flitted about, the insects buzzed, but no deer appeared.

Time began to drag. Suddenly there was a lot of activity in a nearby tree. Squirrels, I assume in some sort of mating ritual, began chasing each other all around my position. They seemed to have their minds on other things and did not notice that I was there. More than once they scurried up and down the full length of my body. I did not see a deer but to have the squirrels climb all over me was a special treat.

Our good friends Darrell and Jeanne Cloud lived on a larger farm about three miles to the west of Northfield, Minnesota. Darrell, also a pilot for Northwest Airlines, and I had met when we flew as part of the same crew.

The families shared many great adventures over the years. I think it was through the Clouds that we came to be the proud owners of Dixie. This short and fat little pony, with saddle included, was suddenly in the stall of our barn. She was pleasant to be around but had a mind of her own. If she decided on a course of action, no amount of tugging or pushing could make her change.

Once, Darrel Jr. had been on a short ride. As the horse and rider approached the barn, Dixie decided to go into her stall. Darrel tried his best to prevent her from entering. The door was narrow, and his feet were caught between the pony and the door frame and were turned backward.

I was angry with this little hard-headed horse. I dragged her out of the stall, climbed aboard and rode her hard. Upon approaching the barn, she was winded but not defeated.

I made a deal to give the horse to a captain with whom I had flown. He arrived pulling a trailer that the horse didn't want to ride in. We worked hard but finally got it loaded. The captain thanked me and was about to leave. The saddle was very nice, and I asked if he would like to buy it.

Airline Captains have a reputation of being tight with their money. He was noncommittal. I suggested $30 since I had made him a present of the horse. He hesitated and then offered me $15. On the airline, his salary was three times mine. I picked up the saddle and threw it into the trailer and said, "It's free, now get the hell out of here."

We truly enjoyed the years that we lived in the country. We began considering a move to town when the kids were about to go off to college. My airline career required that I be on the road about half of the time. The harsh winters of Minnesota were a bit too much for Glenda to handle all alone.

There were no regrets or sadness—we just moved on.

NIKKO, JAPAN

Glenda and I were in Tokyo accompanied by our frequent traveling partners, Darrell and Jeanne Cloud. We were trying to experience as much as time and money would allow.

When we asked for suggestions from a travel agency lady, we were amazed when she turned to her computer, made several keystrokes, and then started touching the screen. We had never seen a computer that would respond to screen touching. She took several minutes but finally suggested that we visit Nikko, a resort town in the mountains. After about two hours on a bullet train, we were far from the hustle and bustle of the big city. As we stepped off the train, we found the mountain air to be cool and refreshing.

After getting settled in a Japanese-style hotel, we visited a public bath where the males and females went their separate ways to strip naked, soak in a very hot pool, soap-up, and rinse off. At times during the process we were required to sit on a short three-legged wooden stool which was a bit awkward. Quite an interesting experience. This hot bath put us into the proper mood for a peaceful night's sleep.

After an exceptional breakfast, we were ready to explore the area. Studying the tourist information, we had learned that there was an old and famous shrine on the very top of a nearby hill. We wandered toward that hill but found no trail or stairway that seemed to lead up the mountain.

During our travels around the world, we have found (we feel that other Americans have learned the same) that when you don't speak the language, the locals will be more likely to understand if you speak loudly, slowly, and in broken English, while gesturing wildly with your hands. Not.

We were momentarily disoriented as we stood and looked in every direction. A man who appeared to be Japanese approached, and I asked him, "How to find stairs to top of hill to big shrine?" I vigorously made stair-climbing motions with my hands and pointed toward the top of the hill. He paused, smiled a bit and said, "I don't know, man. I just arrived yesterday from New York."

We eventually found the trail to the shrine. This little side trip was a success and I learned that everyone who looks like a local may not be one. This experience also led me to modify my approach when speaking with locals.

Isn't life fascinating? I feel it is okay to make a slight fool of yourself if you can also laugh at yourself.

North to Alaska

September 1983

I grew up on a small farm in Tennessee where every family member worked toward keeping the operation going. Some of my assigned jobs were boring and at times I helped pass the time by doing a bit of daydreaming. I remember thinking about hunting, sports, and sometimes even girls--those mysterious creatures that sent fear into my heart. I also dreamed of traveling to interesting places, but Alaska was too remote to even consider.

My duties as an airline pilot had me returning to my home base seated on a Northwest aircraft as a deadheading crew member. My mind again wandered, and travel popped into that empty space. I was scheduled for ten days free of duty and wondered if Glenda and I could take a driving trip? Where would we go, Northern Minnesota, Wisconsin, how about Alaska?

We had, because of necessity, lived a simple life. We lived in a conservative house and drove conservative cars. Years earlier, during the first national fuel crisis, we had purchased a used Oldsmobile that was equipped with an eight-cylinder engine. Even though it had low miles, it sat on a used car lot unsold because people were concerned about the amount of fuel that this type of engine would consume. I made an offer of $1500 which was quickly accepted.

That old Olds proved to be a great "ride" but it was becoming a bit "long of tooth." This is an old horse trader's expression. As a horse grows older its gums tend to recede which makes the teeth appear longer. This machine was definitely showing its age.

Should a car that old with one hundred and fifty thousand miles showing on the odometer even be considered as a possible mode of transport from our home in Minnesota to the last frontier? Many people would have been very doubtful.

After arriving in Minneapolis and hurrying home to Northfield, I suggested to Glenda that we make the drive. Within a few hours we departed with the air conditioner totally disabled, for points north. Cool air would have been nice for the first day or so, but the temperature dropped steadily.

The first day was hot and windy as we drove to the northwest. Minot, North Dakota was chosen as our first overnight destination. The hotel featured a small casino and Glenda proceeded to lose twenty dollars at a Blackjack table. Our hope had been that she would win enough money to pay for the trip. We could only mourn our loss.

The next night after driving through miles and miles of grain farms, we found shelter in Calgary, Alberta. The surrounding countryside was a mix of ranching, farming, and oil drilling activity. We were excited since this area was completely foreign to us.

Day after day we made our way toward Alaska and Anchorage. The mountains and vegetation were beautiful beyond description. We loved it. It became a game to search for the next gas station, eat at the local cafes and bars, enjoy the views, and marvel at our being there.

At one eating and drinking establishment, a patron was doing his best to persuade a female friend to go home with him. He bought beers and asked, almost begged, her to be his partner for the evening. She was reluctant. He was persistent. Bottom line--she chose not to go with him because, "When the fire burns down in the stove, the dogs will eat my supper."

A day or two later we were in a similar type saloon. The local men were standing at the bar with their favorite beverages in hand. Several women were gathered in a group near the far end of that bar. To us, it seemed that one of the ladies was trying to get the attention of a certain male. She went to the restroom on two occasions and each time as she passed her target, she gave him a firm whack on the backside. He never acknowledged her.

This drive had been beyond our wildest expectation. The scenery, wildlife, and rather harsh surroundings made for a wonderful new experience. Our old car had performed perfectly. The motor had operated smoothly, and it did not use any oil. We felt that it would have taken us all the way back home if we had so chosen. Our interaction with the locals was an important factor in our enjoyment.

We rolled into Anchorage at about two in the afternoon. As we were making our way toward our hotel, we saw a sign, "We Buy Cars." We stopped. I asked, "Would you be interested in buying our car?" He responded, "Well, yes. Would you take four hundred dollars for it?" As if offended, I responded, "Oh man, I feel it is worth at least six hundred." He countered, "Okay, five hundred." I replied, "Sold."

This exchange took less than one minute. I loved that old car and it had served us well. We always drove it with respect and serviced it on schedule. A young man who worked at the car lot gave us a ride to the hotel in our old and beloved car. His departure was at maximum power with tires squealing. My heart ached. He obviously did not know, or care, that for a long time that old car had been a part of our family.

After a night between clean sheets, a Northwest DC-10 delivered us back to the lower 48. We could only smile as we knew that we had just completed yet another memorable adventure.

Should the opportunity arise, we would gladly repeat that long and enjoyable drive.

ON TWO WHEELS

Motorcycles

My first motor-powered two-wheeler was a Vespa scooter that I had noticed at a service station with a "For Sale" sign on it. We were able to come up with the two hundred dollars and purchased that little red machine. That scooter was perfect for the two-mile commute to my squadron area. Glenda could now use our little VW bug to come and go as she pleased.

That little scooter served us well for several years but was sold as we left the Marine Corps to join Northwest Airlines. Off and on over the years I bought, rode, and sold several small motorcycles. The tendency was to upgrade to a larger bike on each new purchase. Driving through Faribault, Minnesota I noticed a Honda CX 500 sitting in a yard with a "For Sale" sign attached.

This bike just didn't sell. It sat in the same spot for several weeks and I finally stopped to have a look. Long story short, I bought it. This motorcycle was the biggest to that point and capable of operating safely on the freeways. Its biggest fault was the after-market fairing. This shield did the job of protecting the riders from the wind but seemed to be mounted just a bit crooked. The bike had the tendency to turn right during all riding conditions. This flaw was no problem while riding day to day near home. However, it was a pain on extended rides. After a day of freeway driving, I would be exhausted. The constant, although slight, pressure that was required caused muscle cramps in my arm and shoulder.

Itching for an adventure, a plan slowly developed in my mind. I wanted to do some road trips and Glenda reluctantly agreed to go along.

It was October and the Minnesota weather could be turning cold at any time. We made the decision to take the motorcycle to Florida.

Several days before we were to depart, Darrell and Jeanne Cloud came to our house for dinner. We shared our plans for our cross-country trip. Almost immediately, Darrell asked, "When are you leaving?" When we told him that we were leaving on Wednesday he replied, "Wait till Thursday and we will go with you."

That was the beginning of nearly three years of touring the United States on motorcycles. It evolved into what we called our "Perimeter Tour" in that we attempted to circle the entire country while staying as close as possible to the border or coastline.

Leaving Minnesota on a beautiful crisp fall morning, we headed south with the intent of joining the gulf coast at Pensacola, Florida. Our experience level was fairly low, but we were having a good time and learning fast. It seemed to us that we were slightly ahead of the major increase in cross-country motorcycling. Wherever we stopped people would gather, stand around, look at the bikes, and ask questions. We were a bit unusual.

Riding through traffic in St. Louis we became momentarily separated. Glenda and I were in the lead and decided to pull to the side of the road and wait. Waiting longer than expected we began to worry. Darrell and Jeanne finally showed up but with some mildly bad news.

We never learned the details, but a passing car had given them a little bump. They did not go down but did receive some minor damage to one of their saddlebags. We paused for a while, discussed our options and then pressed on.

After two days of riding about 400 miles each day we arrived at my childhood farm near Atoka, Tennessee. We stayed overnight with my parents. We were fed well, observed cotton in the fields, and reflected upon my early humble lifestyle. Darrell Cloud even strapped on a cotton sack and pretended to pick cotton.

Scott, the Cloud's son, was flying in the Navy and was stationed in Pensacola, Florida. He and his family lived in a small house but all of us were able to find a place to sleep. We slept in beds, on couches, and on the floor. It was great fun.

The fact that my bike was pulling to the right was wearing on my mind and body. I remember that Darrell Cloud checked the local newspaper and found a 1982 Honda Gold Wing that was listed for sale. We drove to the owner's house that was near the beach, the bike looked great except for one small detail. The salty air had etched away the chrome in a few places on the engine.

The bike was bought without a mechanical check or test ride. It proved to be very reliable and comfortable. We simply loaded it up and headed for points west. That bike was ridden for many, many trouble-free miles and all over the United States.

I paid $3500 for the bike and sold it years later for about $2500. Today, more than thirty years later a very similar bike can be bought for about $2500 and most are reliable and functional rides. What a machine.

We headed west along the coast and settled into somewhat of a pattern. On our days off, we spent as many days as possible riding and exploring the countryside and cities near the edge of the country. We found safe places to store the bikes at the end of each ride. Most of the time we found storage facilities which would rent us a unit large enough for our two machines. What an experience.

This adventure took place about thirty years ago. It would be hopeless to attempt to remember the details because of the passage of time and the length of the trip. We kept the bikes out on the road for about three years. Nearly every state was visited, and we covered about 35,000 miles. We saw and experienced so much. Reflecting on that ride, the idea of doing it again comes to mind. Wishful thinking. My old body could not stand the wear and tear.

An attempt will be made to tell of happenings along the way. These little tidbits will be written in no particular order. I will write them as they pop into my mind.

We rode in all kinds of weather. In New Orleans we endured a torrential downpour one night. It was impossible to see, so we pulled to the side of the street and stopped. I put my foot down and found that the water was ankle deep. There was no place to hide, we just sat there and hoped not to drown.

On one occasion we had split up but made a plan to join up again in Mobile, Alabama. Glenda and I were already in place, but the Clouds were riding in from Pensacola. It was cold, very cold for that part of the country. A miserable day for them. It took several hours before they felt warm again.

We never made advanced room reservations. One day we rode late and ended up in Sanderson, Texas, population 834, which was *not* a tourist destination. The only rooms we could find were strange, old, and probably dirty. The furniture was old and shabby. There was a pot belly stove with a stove pipe that went through the ceiling. A concrete vault-like thing had at one time been used as a shower. It contained an overstuffed chair on our visit. We had a great laugh and were happy to be on our way the next morning.

The California deserts presented a special type of experience. One of our worst days was riding through Death Valley on a very windy day. This wind, from our right front, blasted us with hot desert sand. I leaned as far forward as possible and used my left hand to protect my eyes. I was wearing a full-face helmet but still needed more protection. Glenda turned her face away from the brutal wind and put her head on my back. We road several hours with the bikes leaning heavily into the wind.

We arrived in Las Vegas after this ordeal and looked for a room. There was some sort of special event going on and the hotels were full. We found some really poor rooms in the outskirts and spent an uncomfortable night. The wind continued and when we got up the next morning there was a four-inch-high sand dune just inside our door. A small crack under the door had allowed wind and sand to enter.

Everything had gone as expected and we arrived in Tucson, Arizona well before dark and in good health. As we frequently did, we probably had a beer or a glass of wine to clear our throats of road dust. I have no idea how this layover evolved but the girls decided to dye the guys hair. We were old enough to have gray hair showing and they decided to fix that problem. The dark dye got scattered all around the room and some even got on our hair. The process and the finished product caused a tremendous amount of laughter--Jeanne wet her pants.

We stopped for a rest and to enjoy the view along Highway One in California. I looked out to sea and saw the blow of a whale. This was a first for me and I watched and watched for another. No more evidence of whales was observed.

I was awarded a bid as Captain on the Boeing 757 and my training was to be done in Seattle at the Boeing facilities. Our bike was in San Diego. Our normal foursome plus Al and Vera Haugen, who had joined the group, made a plan to ride to Seattle where the bikes could be used as transportation during this period of training. The ride along the coasts of California, Oregon, and Washington was beautiful and one of our favorite trips.

We were in the New York Adirondack Mountains at a small but nice motel. Some of us were outside when we observed something strange in the dark sky. Wanting Glenda to see this strange sight I ran to our motel room and pounded on the door to get her attention. I pounded on the wrong door which caused a good round of laughter. I took a bit of kidding for my wrongdoing. The strange sight was a rocket that had been launched in California.

We were on our last ride on that motorcycle. We were traveling alone and had spent the night in a motel in Texarkana, Arkansas. It rained. We sat an entire day practicing being bored. The forecast indicated that the rain was ending, and the skies looked a bit brighter. I said to Glenda, "Let's go for it." We did. That ride to Memphis was also one of our worst. This rain was not your average rain. Wind, water, and cool temperatures made us miserable. No matter how hard I tried to keep it out, the wind went up my sleeves and under my clothing. We had parked our car at the airport when we flew out to begin this trip. Glenda was happy to drive as I made the last dash for home.

I had never been so cold. My body was uncontrollably shaking. My clothing was quickly removed, and I climbed into a bathtub of warm water. Surely, recovery would be almost instantaneous. Wrong. Evidently my core temperature had dropped, and the shaking continued for some time.

We had traveled for several years and thousands of miles on two wheels, but this would be our last cross-country ride. What an experience. Some say that we were lucky. Our riding days were over. Maybe it was time.

Darrel F. Smith

MOUNT RAINIER

A Challenge
1984

They stood in the snow at twelve thousand, five hundred feet, nose to nose, shouting angrily. Our climbing team had attempted to find a route around the right side of a huge vertical wall of ice. After struggling to a viewpoint, it was obvious that this direction was out of the question. The crumbled blue glacial ice was too steep and dangerous to even attempt.

Returning to the center of the ice wall and looking to our left, we saw a series of crevasses, large cracks in the ice, with walls of the same blue glacial ice. These crevasses were close together and so deep that I couldn't see the bottom, probably because I was afraid to go near their edges. The angry exchange was taking place between the two experienced climbers in our team of four, both having climbed Mt. Rainier three times.

One declared that we had made a good effort, but we would have to come back another day to attempt the summit. He felt it was too dangerous for us to continue. The other had shouted, "Bullshit. We have worked our butts off and we sure as hell are not turning back." Having no climbing experience, my friend Curt Bryan and I had no clue as to which to believe. The heated disagreement continued for some time.

This adventure began when I received a call from Curt Bryan, a classmate in our initial training class as pilots for Northwest Airlines. He had been a Navy pilot, loved the outdoors, and was in great physical condition. He had been part of a four-man team that planned to climb Mt Rainier. Their expedition was to begin only two days from the day that I had received his call. One of the proposed climbers had to cancel, therefore I was invited to join the group as a replacement.

I borrowed an ice axe and crampons, metal devices with large teeth, designed to be strapped to boots for walking on ice or snow, from a lawyer friend who had done a little mountain climbing. Not knowing what was needed, I crammed nearly all my camping gear into a large bag. I was aboard the next flight to Seattle.

Curt and his wife, Sandy, graciously allowed me the use of their guest bedroom. He and I covered their family room floor with our climbing gear. We spent hours trying to decide what to include as we packed our backpacks. That evening an experienced member of our group came for a visit to give us "first timers" some words of wisdom and basic training. The next day in our climb, we would be required to rope up as we started up the Inter Glacier. Knots, ropes, and procedures were the topics covered in this session. We climbed the Bryans' stone fireplace.

The next morning four climbers, one wife, and all the gear were squeezed into a large station wagon for the 50-mile drive to our jumping-off point. Arriving at the White River campground, we unloaded the car, strapped on our backpacks and, without ceremony, headed up the Glacier Basin Trail. This trail was not difficult, winding along the White River and through some old growth timber. After a leisurely lunch, we arrived at the foot of the Inter Glacier.

It was time for another lesson. The experienced climbers took a few minutes to teach Curt and me the technique for self-arrest. Should a climber fall and start to slide off the mountain, he was to turn onto his stomach, spread his legs and dig the point of his ice axe into the ice and snow. This lesson took about 15 minutes. We were now trained mountaineers. We roped up and attacked the glacier.

As we made our way up this vast field of ice and snow, eventually Mother Nature made her call to each of us. The wife, who was going only to the first camp, announced that she needed to take a pee. Only ice and snow were visible for what seemed to be miles. One of the guys sort of stammered that we would look the other way. I was surprised when she replied, "Well, you can do as you please but if you have never seen one of these things—maybe it is time." She then dropped her trousers and got the job done.

Our goal that first day was to make our way to Camp Schurman near Steamboat Prow, a large rock shaped like the bow of a ship. The camp, located at about ten thousand feet, was roughly halfway up the mountain. It consisted of a Rangers hut, a toilet, and enough relatively level ground for maybe 10 or 12 tents. The plan was to arrive early enough to set up the tents, prepare a meal, and try to get as much sleep as possible. After we got the stove going, we mixed several totally different freeze-dried meals, creating a gourmet delight.

Since I was the last member to join the group, I was totally in the dark as to the planned sleeping arrangements. As the light gradually began to fade, the climber who had his wife along approached me and said, "You will be sleeping with us tonight." I did not know what to expect. I crawled into the tent and situated myself on the extreme side of the bed made from unzipped sleeping bags. I did not move. Soon the couple arrived—she stripped down to her bra and panties. He slipped under cover on the far side and she took the place between us. I did not sleep—what if I rolled over and threw my leg or arm across this woman? I stayed on my back with my arms tightly clamped across my chest. I desperately needed sleep but felt that I got very little. I didn't want this guy to be beating on me in the middle of the night halfway up a mountain.

Long before daylight, we shouldered our much smaller packs and with headlamps illuminating the way, started up this formidable mountain. As we walked out of camp, several strings of lights could be seen snaking their way upward. These groups that had started climbing earlier were well ahead of us.

The initial pace was steady but slowed significantly as we ran into the first of many crevasses that we would encounter. Glaciers are massive rivers of ice that are always on the move. This movement creates huge horizontal cracks, sometimes wide and sometimes narrow but always deep. We were required to travel left and right as we made our way through this dangerous maze. At times we would walk on the lower edge of a crevasse with the gaping mouth of the next only a few feet below. A fall here would cause serious injury if not death. I was terrified.

On several occasions, we were required to use snow bridges, natural bridges of ice and snow of unknown strength, to cross these monster crevasses. A climber would approach the end of the bridge, sit down, dig in his feet, and force his ice axe handle deep into the ice and snow. The rope was then wrapped around the handle. Once established in his best position he would yell, "On belay." Another climber positioned himself just short of the bridge. When he gets up enough courage he yells, "Climbing" and carefully walks across. The man on belay feeds out the rope as he goes. This procedure was repeated until the entire team was safely across. Our leader insisted that we yell so that everyone had no doubt as to what was going on. Fatigue and lack of oxygen caused sluggish reactions both physically and mentally. We could not afford a mistake.

We struggled upward through various snow and ice conditions. The surface ice would thaw during the day and then freeze again at night. It could be like crushed ice or smooth and hard. At one location, a large area was covered with bowl-like depressions about three feet across.

The eastern sky began to show some light with not a cloud in sight. Our leaders had insisted that we start climbing very early. We needed to reach the summit with enough daylight remaining for our trip back down to camp and then out to the car. As the sun warmed the surface, the ice would melt, making it much more difficult to make progress. This day would prove to be sunny and very warm; short sleeves and sweating were in order.

Shortly after an unbelievably beautiful sunrise, we approached the ice wall. Glacier ice can sometimes pull away from the ice above creating a wall, known as a bergschrund, like the one we were facing. Our experienced climbers were still trying to come to an agreement as to our next move--were we going up or back down this mountain? They finally decided that we would attempt to go up, but cautiously.

They studied the series of crevasses to our left and decided on a route out of our spot of concern. We would carefully walk a narrow ridge between two of those menacing cracks in the ice. Our walkway was about three feet wide and slightly rounded. On either side was a vertical drop of unknown depth. Should a climber go over the edge, the man immediately behind him was instructed to jump off the opposite side. Once things stabilized, with a man off either side, a plan could be made as to how to retrieve them. The reasoning was that with our footing and state of fatigue we would otherwise be pulled over the edge one by one. I was shaking in my boots.

Our precarious walk to safety went without a hitch. The remaining climb to the summit was a matter of putting one foot ahead of the other. As we approached the summit, several teams of climbers had funneled into a single path, which was well worn and easy to walk. Approximately one hour before reaching the crater rim, one of the experienced climbers began to show symptoms of altitude sickness. He had a severe headache and was mentally confused.

There were twenty or more climbers on the crater rim as we arrived. The day remained almost perfect and the view was exceptional, Seattle was easily visible. Looking to the south, Mt. Adams, Mt. Hood, and the still smoking Mt. St. Helens were in plain view.

It would have been nice to rest or even take a nap, but we needed to get to a lower altitude. Our sick buddy was not getting any better. We paused only a few minutes before commencing our long descent. The ailing climber was tied in as the first man on the rope, the lead, to give him something to keep his mind occupied. This arrangement did not work. He kept attempting to lead us the wrong direction. Someone else took the lead and we hurried down the mountain as best we could.

I am happy to report that after getting to a lower level, the sick friend made a full recovery. The descent to camp was uneventful. We did run low on water and did not take the time to melt snow.

Arriving at Camp Schurman, we organized our backpacks, stocked up on water and ate a meal. The trek down the glacier and out to the car was still a major chore. The rocky but short trail from camp up Steamboat Prow to the Inter Glacier was our first challenge.

The glacier in places was smooth and free of obstacles. We were taught the art of glissading. Still roped up, we sat single file with our ice axes held behind with points down. We slid on our butts using the axes as brakes. The wife was on the rope just ahead of me. When she stood up after a long run the entire seat of her wool trousers was missing. Her cheeks were quite rosy.

This was one of the most physically demanding days of my life. We arrived at the parking lot and I could see the car only a hundred yards away. I did not feel I had the strength to get there.

Many times, during the remaining years of my flying career with Northwest Airlines, I observed Mt. Rainier from the air. It is truly an awesome mountain, and, at times, I found it hard to believe that I had once stood on its summit. I will remember this climb as one of the greatest adventures of my life.

ONE STEP, THEN ANOTHER

1984
Running *is* a Mind Game

The pain in my left knee had become abundantly noticeable as I passed the nine-mile marker and there was no indication that it would let up. My calf and thigh muscles seemed on the verge of cramping, but I pressed on. Finishing my first marathon was foremost in my mind—at this point, quitting was not an option.

Hours later, the hill ahead, six miles from the finish line, was small but steep. To this tired and stressed runner, it looked like a mountain as I struggled onward.

A grain of doubt lifted its ugly head somewhere deep within my being as the pain and exhaustion mounted. Failure now would be a terrible blow after investing so much time and effort into the preparation. My mind told my body to keep putting one foot in front of the other, hang in there, and don't quit.

I don't recall when the idea of maintaining some sort of physical fitness by running came into my mind. Eventually a weak effort at jogging was attempted. I remember being slightly embarrassed when I informed a shoe salesperson that I wanted to buy "running shoes." My athletic endeavors up to this point had required a stocky and strong body. My inherited body had served me well during my high school and college football careers but was ill-suited for long-distance running.

Going about my duties as a pilot for Northwest Airlines, I met several people who were runners. Their stories aroused my interest. I had no dreams of achieving any major success but had enough curiosity to give it a try. My first attempts were painful and disappointing. How could these people run mile after mile and seem to enjoy the experience?

I knew nothing of the sport but started jogging for short distances several times a week. Without even realizing it, my jogs became longer and longer. I became more deeply involved even to the point of subscribing to the "Runner's World" magazine, which featured stories that were interesting and inspirational.

In a hotel room on a layover, I finished reading a book about an unlikely man who had entered and completed a marathon. He had been very overweight, depressed, and emotionally was at the lowest point of his life. He decided to depart this world by running at full speed until his heart failed. Well, he ran as hard as possible, but his body rebelled and quit before his heart failed.

Due to this extreme exertion his body produced a flood of endorphins that gave him the greatest "high" of his life. He was a changed man. He started working out, eating properly, and began dreaming of a new life. His efforts eventually enabled him to complete a marathon.

As the book was finished with tears in my eyes, I stood and declared, "By golly, if he could do it, I can do it." A promise was made to train for and run 26.2 miles, a marathon.

This promise was kept a secret since I felt that friends and family would laugh at this unrealistic goal. How could this old guy with his stocky body even dream of running such a long distance? I quietly plodded onward.

The days, weeks, and months passed as I struggled through miles and miles along the graveled roads just north of Northfield, Minnesota. Many times, I turned a corner knowing that it was exactly one mile to the next. It seemed so far, how could I ever run that distance?

Glenda and I were very good friends with Darrell and Jeanne Cloud who lived a few miles west of Northfield on a small farm. Darrell had been in the Air Force but now, like me, was a pilot for Northwest Airlines. It so happened that he had also developed an interest in running.

Over dinner, and possibly a glass or two of wine, we made a pact to run and hopefully complete Grandma's Marathon along the shores of Lake Superior in northern Minnesota. We never ran together, he was a much better athlete and therefore ran much faster. However, we often discussed our successes and failures as we attempted to follow our training schedules.

We gradually increased the length of our training runs and eventually felt we could almost be called real runners. I arrived in Honolulu from Tokyo for a layover on a typical day in paradise. The sun was shining, and the temperature was in the low 80s. As per my training schedule, I pulled on my running shoes with the intent of completing a casual six-mile training run.

Only about three blocks from the hotel a severe pain developed in my left knee. I tried to run through this discomfort as I had done many times with other small bodily aches and pains. I simply could not shake it off. My pace slowed and eventually all I could do was walk slowly back to the hotel. The pain did not subside, and my depression increased with every step.

Grandma's race was only two weeks away and my knee continued to rebel. All training was stopped. I was afraid that my chances of running the race were slipping away.

Even though my body was questionable, the Clouds and the Smiths went through the motions. We drove to Duluth and, with some difficulty, found accommodations in the southern outskirts. We were lucky to find a suite with two bedrooms built on some sort of platform, somewhat like a mushroom. There was a stairway of about 15 steps that led to our front door.

Well before race time, Glenda and Jeanne delivered the two Darrels to near the starting line, which was a short distance to the southwest of Two Harbors, Minnesota, on the north shore of Lake Superior. There were thousands of skinny, long-legged people already gathered. In this crowd, I felt totally out of place. Why did I ever dream of attempting a 26.2-mile run? Mentally, the pain in my knee seemed to make itself known.

We were signaled that the race had begun. The mass of people slowly started to move toward Duluth and Grandma's Bar, our destination that was miles and miles down the road. The elite runners had a mile or two under their belts before we crossed the start line.

Darrell and I stood together waiting for the race to begin. Initially we walked, then shuffled, and finally settled into a slow jog. Within a very few minutes, I lost sight of Mr. Cloud and never saw him again during the entire race. He was well ahead of me.

There were thousands of runners. It was therefore a surprise that I interacted with a relatively small number of people. I would slowly plod along but finally pass Miss Big Bloomers—after a short while she would pass me. Very early in the race I chatted with a man from Minneapolis. I saw him many times as we made our way along the course.

I remember running behind a lady who appeared to have recently lost a lot of weight. Her birthday suit had not adjusted to this major change, but she was making her way along the route, giving it her best effort. With no disrespect intended, I thought, "I should be able to finish ahead of her." This turned out to be much easier said than done. As we passed the seventeen-mile marker I finally was able to leave this woman in my dust for good. She was a real runner and showed extreme determination.

My knee continued to hurt but I pressed on. The last part of the race was completed with me in some sort of daze. I lost the concept of miles and time until a spectator yelled, "Only two miles to go." Two miles seemed like such a long way. Doubt again made a brief appearance. Could I make it? Could I make it?

Suddenly, I saw a very large clock. I stumbled over the finish line as this clock displayed four hours and twelve seconds.

Someone threw a T-shirt, a skimpy reward for so much effort, over my shoulder as I came face to face with Glenda. I remember saying to her, "You have no idea the length of a marathon." I was exhausted, and it took several minutes before the world again came into focus.

Darrell and I were very proud that we had been able to complete this marathon. We were so sore we could hardly climb the steps to our elevated bedrooms. What a great adventure.

This was the pinnacle of my running career. It took years for my knee to return to a healthy normal. I jogged off and on for a few years but never again got into good enough shape to run a marathon.

Years later, I was living in Hawaii and became aware of the Honolulu Marathon that attracted thousands of mostly Japanese participants. My airline duties did not allow me to train but I dreamed of taking part. I applied for and was accepted as a participant. I did not run even one mile non-stop in my training.

Two hours before race time I called a taxi for the three-mile ride to the start line. The taxi never arrived; therefore, I slowly walked through the darkness and humidity to the area where the thousands of runners were gathered for the race.

My intent was to walk the entire course. As the race began everyone started running. They shamed me into doing the same but after six miles I could take no more. A pattern of walk a little, jog a little was put into effect. I drank a lot of water and continued my run-walk struggle until crossing the finish line in about six hours.

The day was very hot and humid even for Honolulu. Many of those tall, skinny, and muscular participants gave up and simply walked away. Public address systems were hurriedly set up along the route to inform the runners of the extreme conditions. It was a horrible day for an endurance run.

I was able to struggle through the unfavorable conditions and cross the finish line. The next morning the Honolulu Star published the times of every finisher. I discovered that I had finished ahead of about six thousand people, mostly older Japanese housewives.

I look back with pride upon the two marathons that were completed. During that time running became an important part of my life. I got to the point of feeling guilty if a day passed without my running. I remember getting up well before daylight and running eight or so miles during a snowstorm.

All in all, running had a positive influence on my life. It gave me a bit of pride knowing that I could pull on my shoes and run ten miles or more on any given day. I do not regret any of those long runs along the lonely graveled roads in Minnesota. It was a passing moment but for that short period of time in my mind, I almost thought of myself as a runner.

A note:

On an earlier layover in Honolulu, during a training run, I passed an elderly lady as we started up the hill on the backside of Diamond Head. She seemed to be struggling and as I passed, I said, "Good morning, ma'am." The heat and humidity took their toll as this hill seemed to never end. About three quarters of the way up that monster the "old woman" overtook and passed me. Without any show of pride or arrogance, as she passed, she said, "Good morning, sir." Damn. Again, I was put into my proper slot.

THE COOLIE HAT

Overlooking Mainland China

We loved to travel. Glenda and I, accompanied by friends Darrell and Jeanne Cloud, were enjoying yet another adventure, as we had been visiting Hong Kong for several days. A travel agent suggested that we take a train ride to the Chinese border. China at that time was basically a closed country. We chose to attempt this endeavor.

The view from the train was a treat. We traveled through small villages and near many small farms where people worked in their rice paddies. This trip gave us an idea as to how the people in the countryside lived.

As the train made its way northward, we were befriended by a young Chinese man. He was pleasant, helpful, and willingly shared his knowledge. Long story short, he was a taxi driver trying to find customers for a tour of the area at the end of the train ride. We resisted. He persisted. We agreed.

We visited very old villages, small farming towns, and public markets. Our driver was intelligent, friendly, and very familiar with the area. He also had a great sense of humor. As a pig farm came into view, Darrell Cloud attempted to find and ready his camera to capture the sight. He was too slow. The tour leader told Darrell that he could name that picture, "past the pig farm photo."

At the end of our local tour our driver delivered us to a hill-top vantage point where we could look over the border into China. Our casual observation indicated that the folks in that country were doing exactly what the people in Hong Kong were doing. In fact, everything looked the same.

As we stood and pondered the scene, a vendor lady approached in an attempt to sell her supply of Coolie hats. These were the conical hats that the Asian farm workers wore daily. She chose to pick on me. I told her, immediately, that this hat was of no interest to me.

She was very persistent. She was amazed that I was not willing to buy one of her hats for twelve U.S. dollars. I truly did not want this product and told her so. She would not take no for an answer. She begged and pleaded but gradually started to lower her price. She told me that her children would go to bed hungry if I refused to buy that hat.

My traveling companions stood around and enjoyed the exchange. I refused, and she persisted, as this back and forth discussion continued for several minutes. She was on the verge of tears since her kids would go hungry. Finally, reluctantly, she lowered the price to five U.S. Dollars, even though her kids would suffer. I agreed.

I produced the money and took possession of my new hat. She immediately turned her attention to the other Darrell in our group. She asked him to buy one of her hats. He asked, "How much?" I was shocked, and hurt, when she said, "Two dollars, U.S."

This little story is just a small example of the joys of traveling the world. Over the years, as we have moved from house to house, that hat has hung in many closets and garages. It may yet be in our home or in storage, but we don't know where.

I still feel guilty, since the hat lady's final price to me did not allow her kids an adequate evening meal. However, I feel that they grew up well-fed and maybe even came to be employed as coolie hat salespersons at the border.

Lolo Pass

Splish Splash
A Refreshing Dip
Montana

Northwest Airlines had for years served the not-so-big towns across the northwestern tier of the United States, from Minneapolis to Seattle. This service consisted of a single aircraft, the Boeing 727 during my initial years, leaving Minneapolis and making its way through the mountain stations to Seattle. These flights would call at Fargo, Jamestown, Billings, Bozeman, Butte, Missoula, Spokane, and finally Seattle.

At times the mountain flying was modified in an attempt to be more efficient and to offer our customers the best possible service. One of these experimental flight routings had a flight arriving late in the evening in Missoula, Montana. The rules regarding crew rest made it illegal for the incoming crew to fly that aircraft out the next morning. This crew would therefore have the next full day free of duty.

Since Glenda and I always tried to take advantage of any opportunity for an adventure, we decided that she would accompany me on one of these flights into Missoula. During the day off we would be able to explore that part of Montana. Our flight arrived on schedule and we made our way to the hotel and soon hit the hay.

The next day dawned clear with the forecast indicating that the temperature would reach into the low 90s, a bit warm for the mountains. We were up early, had a nice breakfast and headed out in our rental car. Another small adventure was underway.

We studied the maps and decided to visit the National Buffalo

Range that is located only a few miles to the north of Missoula. We saw numerous buffaloes in the distance and the scenery was very nice. Heading to the south, we drove through the narrow pass along the river to the east of town. The name Missoula came from the Indian word that called this area "the valley of ambush" due to the many conflicts between the local Indian tribes and the Plains tribes.

We gradually made our way back through town in a southwesterly direction. At the small village of Lolo, we happened to find Highway 12 that led up and over the Lolo Pass. The famous Lewis and Clark expedition had traveled this route on their historic journey to the Pacific Ocean.

The temperature was well above normal as we followed the Lochsa River. After driving over the pass we came to an unpaved parking area near the stream, just off the main road. We parked the car and waded, with pant legs rolled up, to a large rock in the stream. The sun was warm, and we relaxed on our watery perch, soaking up the beauty of the day and the surroundings.

We were young and full of mischief. I came up with the idea that it would be fun for Glenda to go for a swim. I tried to convince her to remove her clothing and take a refreshing skinny dip near our rock even though the cars were passing on a regular basis along the highway only about 50 yards away. She was very reluctant.

My pleadings were falling on deaf ears. Back home, her car was a wreck and definitely needed to be replaced. I told her that if she would do this daring deed, I would buy her another car. She finally slipped out of her clothing and carefully, keeping our rock and me between her and the highway, submerged her naked body into the deeper part of the stream.

I, hereby, would like to state that this event was not for my benefit alone. Obviously, I had already seen her in the nude. I just felt that her being naked in this stream just off the highway could be considered a memorable event.

As the cool clear water came up to her chin there was a tremendous roar from the road. As mentioned earlier, it was a warm day. A group of ten or twelve Hell's Angels type guys brought their Iron Horses to a dusty stop in "our" parking area. They shut down their loud engines and, fully clothed, charged into the water. Glenda, totally naked, was suddenly surrounded by these bearded boisterous bikers.

I quickly took off my shirt and passed it to her. She put it on, fastened all available buttons and quietly sneaked back onto the rock. I remember that she aggressively tucked my shirt to ensure that no part of her body would be exposed to this wild group.

Early the next morning our trusty Boeing 727 dutifully carried the crew, passengers, and Glenda into the clear blue skies. A bit of ground fog made our departure interesting.

We drove along this route a few years ago and looked for the exact spot where this event had taken place. The entire road had been rebuilt and we were therefore unsuccessful.

I am confident that Glenda, except for embarrassment, was never in danger. This minor happening is just another example of some of the adventures that we have experienced in our wonderfully eventful life. A question for you ladies who happen to read this little story. Have you ever gone swimming nude with a motorcycle gang? Glenda has.

Well, of course I bought her another car, a used Honda Accord. She seemed to be pleased.

THORONG LA

1996

Glenda is tough. She tends to underestimate her abilities, but usually completes any task ahead of most of her peers.

Prayer flags, marking the summit of the Thorong La Pass, were visible only a quarter of a mile away. Glenda looked at the flags and then at me with doubt showing on her face and said, "I don't think I can make it." It had been 4 degrees above zero when we started climbing before daylight, 5 hours earlier and 4,000 feet below. The trail was not exceptionally steep; we were able to stand and walk the entire way. The going was slow, however, since every step at 17,000 feet above sea level was a major endeavor. The lack of oxygen limited our movement to a slow-motion pace.

This adventure had started months before, when in casual conversation Marlene Lomas, a fellow employee at Northwest Airlines Honolulu Flight Operations, informed me that she was going trekking in Nepal for the fifth time. After quizzing her about the details, I knew this was something Glenda and I should do, a-once-in-a lifetime adventure.

My best salesmanship was required to convince Glenda that we needed this trip to make our lives complete. After a little foot-dragging, she agreed—what a trooper. She purchased a pair of quality hiking boots and began whipping her body into shape by climbing the hills around Honolulu. Recently, seventeen years later, when we hiked a rocky trail in the Arizona desert, she wore those very same Basque, Skywalk boots.

I contacted Jim and Pat Harrington, the expedition organizers, to sign-on but was told that all slots had been filled. Unwilling to take no for an answer, I sent them a pitiful, whining letter pleading that we be included. I think their distaste at seeing a grown man grovel was too much for them to handle. They agreed to make room for us. Whoopee! We were on our way to 15 days of trekking in the Nepalese Himalayas.

Anticipating a physically demanding adventure, we hiked and climbed in the local hills, attempting to improve our strength and endurance. Our muscles responded, but there was one big problem. We were training at sea level, but our coming hike would be at a much higher altitude, up to nearly 18,000 feet.

Northwest Airlines provided us with a ride to Tokyo and then on to Bangkok, Thailand. On the night flight to Bangkok, a comet was easily visible, its tail extended a great distance across the sky. The next two days were filled with sightseeing, wonderful meals, and arranging transportation to Kathmandu, Nepal. So far, everything was going as planned.

The Thai Airlines flight was uneventful except for a view of Mt. Everest in the distance. Upon clearing customs and immigration, we were greeted by Jim and Pat, the expedition organizers, Phurba, our lead Sherpa, and his wife who was holding their youngest child. Sherpas are people who live in the mountainous regions of Nepal and Tibet and provide expert help for trekkers and mountain climbers. They are also known for their ability to withstand the rigors of living and working in the thin air of the high mountains.

They presented us with Nepalese flower leis and taught us the meaning of the word namaste. We were then loaded into a small van for the trip to the hotel. We experienced wild drivers, a flat tire, and a traffic jam caused by sacred cows taking a nap on a bridge. Namaste is a word of greeting, similar to "good day" back home. It is spoken with praying hands and a slight bow at the waist.

Our hotel was a simple four-story building that furnished our basic needs but very little luxury. For instance, when the shower was used, the spray pattern covered the entire bathroom—toilet, sink, and floor. The bed was much less than comfortable. However, the hotel did have a nice outdoor patio. Picnic tables were situated under large shade trees where cool adult beverages could be ordered and consumed.

When I think of Kathmandu, dogs come to mind. I called this city a "sea of barking dogs." There seemed to be hundreds and hundreds. The barking would gradually slow and then completely stop. Then one dumb dog would bark, and the sea of barking dogs would return. It was difficult to sleep since this happened over and over again.

It took about four days to obtain the proper permits for our trek, during which time we explored the city. Kathmandu is a bustling place with many interesting sights. We witnessed a cremation, holy men in cage-like rooms, monkeys roaming wild, snake charmers, shrines, a trekker losing control of his bowels, and wool being processed near the river.

All trekkers, Sherpas, and supplies were loaded onto a school-bus-like vehicle for the trip to the point where we would start the walking part of our adventure. This trip was hot and windy. The cooking-fuel containers, stored in the center aisle, seemed to be leaking and the fumes were overwhelming. Some of the trekkers experienced headaches and nausea.

The bus experienced a tire problem, causing a delay of approximately one hour in a small village. This pause gave us the opportunity to get some fresh air. As we wandered about town some unacceptable sanitary conditions were noted. For example, a small stream running through town was the water supply for cooking, washing clothes, and drinking. A short distance upstream there was ample evidence that animal and even human waste could easily have contaminated this stream.

After eight or ten hours, the uncomfortable bus ride mercifully came to an end. The bus jolted to a halt in a small village with a name that sounded like "body odor," the end of the road for wheeled vehicles. Our trek was about to begin.

After spending a fitful night in our tents, which had been set up in a dry rice paddy, we witnessed an interesting event. A large group of men, boys, and a few women gathered in the paddy, squatted and faced Phurba, our leader. The negotiating began. All the food, bedding, tables, chairs, tents, fuel, and our personal gear would have to be transported on the backs of porters.

This gathering was the accepted way for the available porters and the expedition leaders to interact. An hour or so later, a number of porters had been hired but not quite enough; a few would have to carry double loads. One woman, wearing a large ring in her nose, became "the egg lady." She carried a large square pack containing enough fresh eggs for the entire trip.

Just at daybreak, a quiet, gentle voice could be heard, "Good morning, sir, good morning, ma'am, bed tea." Hot tea, cream, and sugar were offered by a young Sherpa who was kneeling just outside our tent. We would drag ourselves out of our sleeping bags and enjoy a warm cup. It happened every morning.

Pardon the language, but the next thirty minutes was referred to as a time of "Shoveling Shit" by the trekkers. We shoveled sleeping bags into their carry bags, clothes and personal gear into duffel bags, and ourselves into the outfit of the day. All things shoveled, the results were pushed outside through the tent flap. Our personal porter was always quietly waiting with a simple cotton rope, anxious to get his workday under way. The porters would wrap their rope around the day's load and make a loop. The load was carried on their backs with the loop across their heads where a thin pad was placed for comfort.

Almost immediately after we crawled from our tent, it was taken down and packed for transport to the next overnight campsite. While we enjoyed a leisurely breakfast, the porters were on their way up the trail.

Our party, including the trekkers, Sherpas, and porters, consisted of about sixty people. This number would vary as new porters were hired and others returned to their home villages. There was no way to know for sure, but we felt that our group, on a normal day, stretched over several miles along the trail.

There was no formal beginning of the day's trekking. The porters would depart camp as soon as they could get their loads together. The trekkers would follow at their leisure after a hearty breakfast. The Sherpas would clean up after the meal and bring up the rear, usually overtaking and passing us on the trail. Glenda and I always tried to get an early start—we set a slow but steady pace and would arrive at the next camp or lunch site along with the others.

As the noon hour drew near, we started looking for the blue tarp. Some of the Sherpas would race ahead, spread out a twelve-foot by twelve-foot blue plastic tarp, and prepare lunch. On an average day we dined on cold cuts, bread, and fruit served with some sort of Kool-Aid-like drink. We would kick off our boots, have lunch, lie on the tarp, and sometimes take a nap.

The locals seemed to enjoy watching, they would stand quietly just off the edge of the tarp and take note of our every move. There would, at times, be twenty or more. On one occasion, the tarp was placed in a small field that was completely covered with young marijuana plants.

Lunch break would end as the trekkers saddled up, a few at a time, and headed up the trail. After a few hours of walking through some of the most beautiful scenery on earth, a Sherpa would greet and direct us to our overnight campsite. If the porters had made good time, our tents would be set up and ready. The trekkers would drift into camp and throw their daypacks in front of any unoccupied tent. If the porters were a little late, we would find a comfortable place to sit and relax until the tents were available.

There was no TV, radio, telephones, taverns, or restaurants at our overnight campsites. Our time was occupied with rearranging our personal gear, trying to clean our dusty bodies, and waiting for dinner. Sometimes, a shower could be purchased in these small mountain towns.

Glenda and I once walked a mile in light snow to a private home in pursuit of a shower. We were invited into the kitchen where we stood around a huge open wood-burning stove that had no vent to the outside. The shower room was across a courtyard where five men sat outside at a table in the snow. The showerhead was attached to a garden hose that hung limply from the ceiling. The low volume of water that drizzled from this fixture had been warmed a bit, but it was a struggle to soap up and rinse off. The fee was about 25 cents per person, so I guess we could not expect too much. We then walked the same mile back to camp, still in the snow.

Several days in Kathmandu, and more on the trail, was time enough for almost everyone to have experienced some adverse effect on their gastro-intestinal system. Even though the restaurants in Kathmandu and our Sherpa staff attempted to make the food compatible with our bodies, it was hopeless. It seemed that nearly everyone had problems, causing many cases of trekkers frantically diving behind the nearest bush, hoping for a little privacy. A good portion of the time, these attempts simply did not work. I think we had a view of nearly every trekker's bare butt during the trip—much too much information.

Our unsettled GI tracts motivated one of the trekkers to create a new term, at least to us—HAFE, High Altitude Flatulent Explosion. This term was a very accurate description for one of our frequent symptoms. The condition of our GI tracts was a favorite subject of conversation during meals.

This routine, with some variation, was the way we lived. Day after day we climbed higher and higher, passing through many small towns, each with a series of prayer wheels. A prayer wheel is a cylinder, sometimes as large as a 55-gallon drum, mounted upright with rollers top and bottom, located under a roof. The idea was to give each a spin and say a prayer as you passed. The entire group of wheels would be left spinning as we proceeded into town.

One of our overnight stops was in the village of Tal. A wedding was taking place, which included music and dancing. The bride, carried on the back of her brother, finally arrived. She was covered, head to toe, with clothing and blankets and was carried all around this small town. The chanting and drinking began and continued throughout the night. There were vertical cliffs all around, the echo of the chanting made for a very unusual and mostly sleepless night. The next morning, we observed a party participant departing the village via horseback. He was obviously intoxicated and had a very difficult time mounting and staying onboard.

Manang, a slightly larger town, was located at 12,000 feet above sea level. Our leader chose this spot as a rest and laundry day. Two inches of snow had the tents sagging when we woke up. The day was clear and cold but most of the women washed a few items of clothing by hand. During the day we heard and saw several avalanches across the valley, but they were of no danger to us.

Our trek, well over a hundred miles long, was along the very famous Annapurna Circuit. The Annapurna Mountains are some of the highest and most beautiful in the world. Each day was filled with never-ending extraordinary views that are impossible to describe. The highest point on the entire route was the Thorong La Pass. The focus of our first ten days of walking was on successfully making our way up to and over this formidable obstacle.

Our last night short of this pass was spent in a very small village that was about 14,000 feet above sea level. It was very cold. Glenda and I zipped our sleeping bags together and piled all our clothes on top, but we still slept cold. The goal for the next day was to get over the Thorong La.

Well, of course Glenda made it. We just kept putting one foot in front of the other and suddenly we were at the pass, the highest point of the trip, 17,769 feet above sea level. She never knew that at her moment of doubt, I too felt that I did not have the strength to make the pass. The small group of trekkers that gathered near the prayer flags on the summit was in high spirits, laughing and talking. Not one person was heard to say, "Boy, I would love to do that again."

The snow disappeared almost immediately as we started our descent in a desert-like landscape. Ample sunshine and good visibility allowed us to look onto the Tibetan plateau in the distance. We made our way to Muktinath, the first small town, located about 5000 feet below the pass. I don't remember seeing a single blade of grass in this town but there was a ton of dust. Our camp was in a small walled field which held more than its share of that dust. Local women arrived in camp and displayed their hand-crafted jewelry and trinkets with the hope of making a sale.

The overall trip was taking much longer than we had expected. The layover days in Bangkok and Kathmandu had added at least a week. I felt it was time for me to get back to work and Glenda had developed a sinus infection from the dust and was having difficulty breathing. Considering these factors, we chose to leave the trek in Jomsom, a larger town, which had commercial air service. After being on the trail for 15 days and having successfully negotiated the pass, we considered the adventure complete and a success.

We were flown from Jomsom to Pokhara on a large older Russian helicopter. The luggage was piled on the floor and the passengers sat on benches along the sides, some with no seat belts.

Everest Airlines delivered us back to our starting point in Kathmandu. Immediately after liftoff, the captain of this small aircraft opened a newspaper and read it for the entire flight.

We arrived back in Honolulu, exhausted but pleased. We probably will never visit Nepal again, but we will never forget our experiences in this beautiful country. This was truly a trip of a lifetime.

Miscellaneous Observations:

Donkeys were used to transport cargo to the remote mountain towns. They traveled single file in small groups of ten or twelve, each carrying a bulky load. We were told to always stand on the inside of the trails as they passed. A trekker could possibly be pushed over the edge, possibly to their death.

Our digestive tracts took months to get back to normal. Doctor visits did not seem to help.

We were already at our overnight campsite when our porter arrived with our personal baggage. Someone suggested that I try to carry his load. With the help of several people I got the load up on my back but I could barely walk. Everyone had a good laugh. This porter looked like a 14-year-old kid and his head came only up to Glenda's shoulder. He had carried that load all day.

Female trekkers were expected to wear long skirts, down to their ankles, at all times.

After a few days, Anne, one of our friends, started getting favored treatment from one of the older Sherpas. He went out of his way to make sure she was comfortable. One day, she experienced a sudden "HAFE" attack, which created a rather loud noise. He thought that was the funniest thing he had ever heard. We thought he would never stop laughing.

Care had to be taken not to step into something smelly, if for any reason you departed the main trail. It was common for people to move only a short distance off the trail before doing their business.

During the days spent trekking, we had no knowledge of current events. On the flight from Pokhara to Kathmandu Glenda read in the newspaper, over the captain's shoulder, that Nick Faldo had come from behind to beat Greg Norman in the Masters Golf Tournament. I read that a famous person had died, but I cannot recall the name.

On our trip from Kathmandu to the end of the road, where we would start walking, a man sat on the roof of the bus. He gave the bus driver directions and information by slapping the top of the bus with an open hand--go fast, slow down, it is OK to pass, etc.

Along the trail high in the mountains, someone spotted a Lammergeier on its nest across the valley. This rare bird is a large eagle-like vulture that makes its home in the high mountains of Asia.

At some point along the trail, a Sherpa commented that we were thirty to forty miles from the nearest wheeled vehicle. Even while on the bus we observed roadwork being accomplished by women with baskets.

One of our young Sherpas made his way to Hawaii and then on to California where he became the valet for a very famous movie actor. While in Honolulu, he stayed in our guest bedroom for several nights. He was very impressed with the bathroom—he felt it was too clean to use.

Update:

October is normally the very best time for trekkers to attempt to complete the Annapurna Circuit. The skies are usually clear of clouds and the temperature is moderate. This month in 2014 had begun as advertised. The adventurers were enjoying great weather and their hike was going as planned.

Unfortunately, everyone was totally unaware of, or chose to ignore the warnings, that for a week or longer a typhoon had been making its way across the ocean. After coming ashore, this storm had delivered a lot of rain and caused some flooding, but little damage.

This weather system was dissipating but still contained an extreme amount of moisture. Upon reaching the mountains the air was forced upward. This action with its associated decreasing temperature turned the moisture into snow. The Thorong La pass and the surrounding area received several feet of snow in a very short period of time. There was no warning that this unusual event was about to take place.

The skies went from clear and sunny to gray and angry in a very short time. Everyone was caught off guard. Even the locals had not experienced such an event in their lives. Trekkers from many nations were scattered along the high-altitude trail. The storm quickly turned into a full blizzard. The snow and wind made it impossible for many to find shelter. People were separated from their parties and left to their own resources.

Many people, as many as forty, were unable to find shelter and therefore perished. Many found cover and survived after spending a frightful night thinking that they too would not live.

Our trek in 1996 was blessed with very good weather, despite the two to three-inch snow overnight at Manang. The storm of 2014 was a rude reminder that mountain weather can become desperate at any time. We consider ourselves lucky.

Glenda and Darrel

CAPTAIN SMITH

1997

For three years I had served as the Chief Pilot for the approximately 400 pilots at the Northwest Airlines Honolulu Base. This relatively small group seemed to form a special bond. We had personal contact on a regular basis and in many cases addressed each other by our first names. It seems that I knew, at least by sight, just about every pilot, mechanic, aircraft cleaner, gate agent, and flight attendant that called Honolulu their duty station.

The Chief Pilot's office was naturally the focal point for problems or unusual events that the pilots incurred as they flew their monthly schedules. They were the ones who had to make the hard decisions at night, thousands of miles from land, concerning weather, fuel, disruptive passengers, and numerous other possible happenings. Many, many times these tired souls would tap on my door after parking their huge machines and ask to speak with me a moment. They had been up all night with the responsibility of a very expensive aircraft and more importantly the safety of hundreds of trusting passengers on their shoulders. They sometimes needed a little encouragement and support.

How could I, sitting in my office, understand what they were feeling without flying the line just like them? In order to maintain my proficiency, I made every effort to fly at least one trip each month. I would look at my Chief Pilot's required duties and find a trip that would fit into my available days off. The assigned pilot was contacted and asked if he or she would allow me to fly that trip. That pilot would receive full pay but be allowed to stay at home.

Most pilots were very happy to take a short, paid vacation. Some loved their jobs so much that they did not want to give up their trip—I always respected their wishes. I enjoyed these trips and felt much more knowledgeable when pilots approached me with questions about their experiences.

In Honolulu there were only about three giant steps from the door of the Chief Pilot's office to the door of the flight planning room. On the days of my line trips I arrived early at my office to deal with current events. There always seemed to be something going on. Some days, it was difficult to pull myself from my office to attend to the flight planning process. Sometimes, I felt that my best effort could not be given to this endeavor—thank goodness for good copilots. They seemed to understand and shouldered the load.

This little story is about one of those proficiency flights. I was to serve as the Captain on a Boeing 747 for a trip to Tokyo, remain overnight, and then return to Hawaii. The westbound flight must have been totally uneventful in that I don't remember any details.

Our arrival in Tokyo was on time and we were directed to park on the ramp where we descended large portable stairs to the tarmac. We had to wait momentarily before boarding large buses that transported passengers and crew to the terminal. At the bottom of these stairs, I could look over my shoulder and behold the magnificent machine that had transported my crew and more than 300 souls safely across a huge ocean. I marveled at the fact that this guy from a small farm in the hills of West Tennessee had just been in charge of a transpacific flight.

During the next twenty-four hours, the crew attempted to get the proper nourishment and some rest since our body clocks were totally confused. We needed sleep, but due to jet lag our bodies insisted that we should be awake.

The next afternoon, upon arriving at the airport for our return flight to Honolulu, the cabin crew proceeded to the aircraft and immediately commenced the demanding chores required to make ready for a full load of passengers. Their work was complicated and at times strenuous. There was always stress involved. The pilots leisurely proceeded to the flight planning area where we went through our normal preflight ritual. We completed our duties while exchanging pleasantries with the station personnel and then were transported to the aircraft.

Upon boarding, it was customary for the Captain to approach the lead flight attendant and brief her or him as to what could be expected during the over-night flight, mostly concerning flight time, weather, and expected turbulence. This day, I approached the lead and pulled her aside in order to pass on any pertinent information.

I knew this woman. We had worked together on several of these

Pacific Ocean crossings. She had been flying these trips for years and was a tough lady. She had seen and heard almost everything, knew her job, and took no guff from anyone. I was aware of how hard the cabin crew worked during the seven or more hours of these flights.

I addressed her with a somewhat joking attitude and asked, "Ok, how are we going to handle this?" With a slight frown, she sort of cocked her head to one side and asked, "What do you mean?"

I replied, "Well, my name is Darrel, but I would prefer that you address me as Captain Smith. As commander of this trans-Pacific flight I want you to understand that our job of flying this big aircraft is very stressful, therefore we will be requesting some special attention. These overnight flights can be long and very trying for us. Would you please have one of your flight attendants drop into the cockpit about every fifteen minutes, with our favorite beverages, to ensure that we are awake, and all our needs have been met. I like my coffee with one and a half sugars and just a splash of cream. By the way, would you please serve my steak, medium rare, about one hour after takeoff."

This experienced lead flight attendant quietly listened to my little speech. Her head remained cocked to one side with her eyes locked on mine. She paused for only a moment before speaking. I love her for her quick wit and feisty reply, "First of all, Captain Smith, F--- YOU," as she generously displayed the appropriate hand signal. "Every seat on this aircraft will be filled with a paying passenger's ass and the entire group will be expecting continuous drink service and two full meals during the night. If and when we have time we may or may not offer you guys some coffee. Your meals, should we even remember, will only be served after every flight attendant has had an opportunity to take a meal break." My meek reply was, "Well, okay, I just wanted to make sure we understood each other."

We both had a good laugh. I then proceeded to give her the briefing that she had originally expected. We parted company as friends.

The flight went without a hitch and the cockpit crew had wonderful service, as usual. The proper beverages flowed, and the meals were on time and properly prepared. It always amazed me that the terribly overworked cabin crew could do their stressful jobs, day after day, so efficiently and with a smile. They were definitely the mainstay of our airline. They always stepped forward and did what was required and more. I respect and honor them. Ladies and gentlemen, thank you, you held the airline together.

RANDY AND MARIE

1992

Northwest Airlines had made the decision to base pilots in Hawaii to service routes to Asia and also back to the mainland. I bid for and was awarded a Boeing 747 Captain position at this recently opened base.

Over the years Glenda and I had always tried to take the path that would expose us to new adventures. This assignment would give us the opportunity to explore the Hawaiian Islands and also the Western Pacific.

We enthusiastically began to explore our new place of abode. We acquired trail maps and asked the local hikers to recommend interesting hikes on the Island of Oahu. We had found and enjoyed hiking several trails and were always on the lookout for new ones.

The guidebooks reported that hikers with keen eyes could possibly see the remains of a WWII crashed aircraft along the Aiea Loop trail. We made our way up the winding road that climbed higher and higher into the mountains. The surroundings began to look more and more like a tropical rainforest which was exactly what it was. The parking lot, surrounded by thick, lush vegetation, was wet. We had planned to hike this loop trail in a clockwise direction.

It rains a lot in Hawaii, especially in the mountains. The frequent showers were usually of short duration but sometimes became quite brisk. We had become accustomed to this local weather phenomenon and learned to endure damp clothing on occasion. Imitating the natives, we soon learned to duck into a building, under an umbrella, or behind a big tree until the rain shower subsided.

After plodding along this ever-ascending trail, the almost inevitable shower suddenly developed. We happened to be near a vertical bank that had been formed when the trail had been cut into the hillside. The lush vegetation from above had created a considerable overhang. We pressed our bodies against the bare earthen wall and huddled together against the elements. Our temporary shelter served us well during this short cloud burst, but probably would not have been nearly so effective during a prolonged rain.

The rain had begun very slowly, increased to a downpour, and rapidly decreased. Since we were fairly comfortable, we lingered in our little hideout. We had remained mostly dry and since the rain had decreased to only a mere sprinkle, we considered continuing our hike.

To our surprise a man and woman appeared with little pixie umbrellas chatting gleefully as they made their way down the wet trail in the opposite direction. Our first impression was that they were members of the Little People. Every Hawaiian believes that Menehunes (also known as the Little People) inhabit the deep forests and remote valleys of the Islands. The mythology contends that these people of small stature were the earliest inhabitants of the Sandwich Islands. They were known to be mischievous, love fishing, and enjoy bananas.

We had learned that it was the custom to leave small gifts at the beginning of any trail. It was believed that the Menehunes would accept these offerings and therefore allow the hiker to pass in peace. A popular gift was a small stone wrapped in a Ti (a local plant) leaf placed in the fork of a small tree. It was common to see several of these gifts at or near the beginning of any remote trail.

As this couple approached, we left our shelter and stepped out onto the trail. Introductions were made, and conversation flowed easily. Randy and Marie Powell were from the state of Washington but loved Hawaii and its many interesting hiking trails. Since Randy had worked for a major airline there was a bit of common ground.

We learned that they had ridden a city bus to the nearest bus stop and then made the uphill trek to the trailhead. Upon completing their hike, they planned to take the bus back to town.

Glenda and I suggested that we would be happy to give them a ride back to Honolulu since our route back home would take us very near their hotel. We wanted to complete our planned hike and parted company not knowing whether they would accept our offer of a ride. We did not expect them to be waiting as we finished our hike.

We enjoyed the loop trail hike and we did spot the remains of that long-ago aircraft crash. We also saw a dead half-grown wild pig wedged in the fork of a tree just off the trail. It appeared to weigh about 20-30 pounds but there was no clue as to the meaning of this pig in the tree.

The trail was relatively easy, and after an hour or so, we stepped out of the still damp forest only about 100 yards from our parked car. We were wet to our knees but happy that we had finished the trail.

Much to our surprise, Randy and Marie, the "Menehune" couple, were waiting near our car. Our friendly conversation continued as we gave them the promised ride back to their Waikiki hotel. We parted company but did exchange phone numbers.

We lived in a rented house on Mariners Ridge, high on the mountainside above Hawaii Kai. The house had extra bedrooms. Since the Powell's seemed like nice folks, we invited them to stay with us for the duration of their Island visit. They accepted, and we picked them up at their Waikiki hotel.

This chance meeting was the beginning of a long relationship. During our eight years of living in the Islands, they came for occasional visits. Together we enjoyed some great hikes, good meals, and lively conversations.

Glenda and I soon discovered that they were both artists, each in their own way. Marie was a master of turning local scenes into exceptional pieces of art. Over the years we purchased several of her original paintings, which to this day are proudly displayed in our home. We really and truly expect her to become world famous, which would make our originals worth millions. Randy was also an artist in his ability to matt, frame, and market Marie's work. They were a great team.

On several occasions, we had the opportunity to visit them in Washington State on the Long Beach Peninsula. During a visit to their home on Willapa Bay we hiked a beautiful trail to a historic old lighthouse. This trek was physically demanding but well worth the effort. There were overlooks, just off the trail, that presented exceptional views of the ocean.

It was a warm day as we quietly approached one of these beautiful overlooks. A couple seated on the only available bench was not aware of our arrival. As we walked up behind them the lady suddenly removed her shirt by pulling it over her head. Almost immediately she realized that she was clad in only her bra in full view of four total strangers—an awkward moment.

Hike completed, we returned to their bayside home where we relaxed on their deck, nursing adult beverages. A fire was crackling in the fire pit as the light slowly faded. Marie suggested that Randy share his story of a long ago encounter with an unknown creature.

He seemed reluctant to tell the story. The fire burned down to glowing embers, the darkness settled in, and the drinks achieved their proper effect. There had been a pause in the conversation and Randy began to tell his story.

His home life was not going well, and he felt that he needed to get away. He was working for a major airline and was stressed by the happenings in his personal life. He was at his wits end and wanted to be alone.

His family owned a small camping trailer and had camped and hiked in the woods on numerous occasions, but he had not done any serious backpacking. A friend from work, who was an experienced hiker and mountain climber, suggested that he spend several days backpacking on the Salmon River Trail. This trail started near Welches, Oregon and continued upstream into the Mt. Hood area.

With several days free of duty, he decided to clear his mind by camping and trekking along this trail in the deep forest. His wife and kids delivered him to the trailhead. He inventoried his equipment which included yellow work boots, canteen, dried food, sleeping bag, and a 14 ft x 14 ft piece of plastic to be used as a shelter. He also carried an empty tin can with a few small rocks in it which he hoped would alert the bears that he was in the area. The heavy backpack was shouldered, and he eagerly hiked into the wild, hopefully to come to grips with his present situation. The plan was to hike the twenty miles to the Frog Lake Campground, where the family would pick him up.

The heavy load and the ever-ascending trail made the sweat bead on his forehead and tested the strength of his leg muscles. This was exactly what he needed. Dense Pacific Northwest evergreen trees surrounded him and restricted his lateral visibility.

After two or three hours into the hike he came to a rather severe rock-covered sidehill area, steep to the left with a drop off to the right. He stood studying the trail and observed that after going straight for a bit, it made a sharp hairpin turn. Suddenly, there was the sharp sound of brush breaking and rocks falling. He immediately assumed that a bear was charging. The tin can bear rattle was forgotten as he threw off his pack and looked for a tree to climb. Nothing happened. He saw no movement and heard no further noise. He saddled up and was happy to get on down the trail.

After another hour or so he found the small stream that was his planned campsite. Walking across a log bridge, he spotted a flat area, a good place to set up his shelter. He paused for a moment to take in his surroundings. He did notice that a trail from higher up the hill led directly toward where he planned to erect his makeshift shelter. A considerable amount of work is required when a backpacker sets up a camp for the night. A shelter must be erected, wood has to be collected for a fire, cooking pots and pans are readied, and a source of water must be located.

As Randy went about accomplishing these duties he began to think of dinner. Since he was now a mountain man, he felt it would be cool to catch his meal from the stream. He rigged a fishing pole and fished for about 45 minutes and then gave up. Fish would not be on the menu. The light began to fade, and it was time to get to cooking.

He returned to the campsite, started the fire, and readied his freeze-dried meal. His words: "I can remember I was bent over at the fire and it was almost dark, when the most horrific roar I have ever heard came out of the darkness. It sounded as if something was standing right next to me. I looked to my left and saw only vibrating air. I didn't wet my pants, but it was an option. I tried to keep a clear head, but the fear was overwhelming. I saw nothing. I immediately threw my entire night's supply of wood on the fire and drew my four-inch hunting knife. I was ready. For what? I didn't know. No dinner that night."

The light from the sun was now completely gone. Gradually, the fire burned down and out. It was dark, very dark. He felt that something was out there, much bigger than him, that was also fishing, and he feared that he was the fish.

What to do? Attempting the eight-mile rugged trail in the dark did not seem to be an option. There was no choice. He crawled into his plastic shelter and sat, wide awake, until dawn. No further sounds were heard.

He ate, packed up, and continued on his planned route toward Frog Lake. It felt great to be moving away from this spot, but he felt that "the unknown" was watching. After several hours he came to a forest service road. As he stood trying to decide what to do next, a Forest Service truck came around the bend. With the sight of that truck he made his decision. He wanted out of the woods and accepted a ride to the highway.

In his effort to get home he tried his hand at hitchhiking. He was in luck, a truck driver picked him up and dropped him off at the end of his own driveway. To this day he cannot adequately describe what he heard. He was afraid beyond description.

There was something unusual in the woods on that day so long ago. I feel that this incident affects Randy even unto today. Most of us disregard stories of Big Foot as myth. A few have come face to face and therefore are believers. Randy is a believer. He is a sincere, rational, and grounded man and if he believes that there are ape-like creatures living in our huge forested areas then I also believe it.

Randy recently said:

"I did not see it, but I heard it. In all my years of hiking and climbing, I have never again heard such a sound. It made my eyeballs vibrate and the memory is still vivid in my mind. There have been many reported encounters with Big Foot and some of those accounts are eerily similar to mine."

Many birds could be observed in the wetlands near the Powell's bayside home. I remember hiding in one of their blinds observing the great blue herons. At that time birds and other wildlife were favorite subjects for Marie's paintings.

On another occasion, the Smiths and Powells met in the Colombia River valley for three days of hiking. Randy and Marie made arrangements for us to stay at a resort along the river. During the day, led by Randy, we hiked the steep trails on both sides of the valley. Our leader was like a driven man. We struggled up some very tough trails, the longest being along the south side above a famous waterfall. We made it to the summit which, if I remember correctly, was about 15 miles round trip. Glenda developed a severe pain in her knee but finished like a trooper.

While Glenda and I were still living in Hawaii, a plan was made to climb Mauna Loa on the Big Island. It is the world's highest active volcano and was advertised as being a real challenge. The advertisements were very accurate.

Randy and Marie, Darrell Cloud, and I made plans to climb this mountain. Jeanne Cloud and Glenda delivered us to the starting point with plans to meet us as we descended the other side of this formidable pile of ancient lava. The girls reported having a very relaxing time as we struggled up and over that mountain.

The trail was not steep, but it was relentless. The miles and miles of gradual incline and the ever-increasing altitude took their toll.

The goal that first day was to reach the park service cabin at Red Hill. This cabin offered only bed platforms attached to the walls and a bit of shelter from the elements. I don't remember if there were any sort of mattresses, but I do remember that it was not the Hilton. We dined on freeze-dried food and tried to get some rest.

The trail, marked by cairns, piles of broken hardened lava, made its way through a seemingly never-ending landscape of lava. The entire time we were on the mountain we saw no living thing, including plants and insects. The trail seemed to go on forever. The summit could not be seen therefore it felt as if we were never getting any closer. It was a grueling day.

There was a cabin on the crater rim, where we intended to spend the night. The guidebooks called the final two miles approaching this cabin the zombie walk. What could be so bad? The trail was basically level as it followed the crater rim. I will share that this section of the trail was, in fact, one of the most demanding hikes of my life. We had been climbing all day, the weather was hot and dry, and we were at 14,300 feet above sea level. Brutal.

Marie was just ahead of me as we struggled along the trail toward the cabin. We could see it but at only 200 yards it seemed so far. Two strong young men hurried toward us with the intent of giving us a helping hand. They offered to carry our packs. In my delirium, determined to make it on my own, I adamantly refused their offer. What a dummy.

This cabin was very similar to the one at Red Hill but had a magnificent view into the crater which was much larger than I would have ever imagined. The toilet was positioned across a crevice that seemed to be hundreds of feet deep. As you used this facility the vertical edge of the crater was only four or five feet away.

Just outside the cabin was a water collection tank but the water needed to be filtered. Darrell Cloud worked for some time processing enough drinkable water for the next day's descent.

Exhausted and in an effort to recover, I made myself a cup of clam chowder from a freeze-dried packet. It was the most wonderful chowder that I had ever tasted. I tried the very same chowder after arriving back home and found it to be horrible. It seems that food can taste totally different, depending upon the situation.

The next morning, we were up early trying to get warm and prepare a bit of breakfast. Suddenly from the kitchen area, Randy quietly said, "I am going to need a little help in here." Marie was curled up on the floor holding onto his ankle completely passed out. The altitude, cold air, and harsh living conditions had evidently been a bit too much for her. She made a complete recovery in only a few minutes and had no further problems.

As we backtracked along the zombie walk, the cold air made the many steam vents in the crater a wonderful sight to behold. The hike to meet Glenda and Jeanne was uneventful. It was an anticlimactic end to a world-class adventure.

Soon after my retirement Glenda and I booked passage on an around-the-world cruise. One of the stops was in Auckland, New Zealand. Randy and Marie in years past had applied for and received some sort of citizenship to that country. They had settled into the routine of spending the winter Down Under but returning to Washington State during the summer. They lived in a small town near the Bay of Islands. She worked on her art and they both hiked the beautiful local trails.

We left our ship, rented a car, and traveled to their place for a short visit. We had a pleasant time and chalked up another adventure with the Powell's. During this visit we bought two of Marie's originals which we now have displayed in our home in Rapid City, South Dakota. Our visit to their home in New Zealand was in January of 2000.

We have gotten together only a few times since the New Zealand rendezvous. We once lived in a mobile home for several months in Rapid City. The Powells came to visit and we had a great time exploring the Black Hills. On another occasion Glenda and I made a one-day visit to their art gallery and home from our motorhome that was parked along the Oregon Coast.

Randy and Marie have been friends for a long time. They have been a pleasure to know and have encouraged us to explore this wonderful world that is our home.

Randy and Marie

MY GIRLS

A mile away, the heat waves from the three huge jet engines could be seen but not a sound could be heard as the red-tailed Northwest Airlines DC-10 slowly started its takeoff roll. Every seat was filled with Japanese tourists who had spent a week of sun and fun on the beaches of Hawaii, but now were on their way back home. The roar of the engines finally reached my ears as the aircraft accelerated along the runway toward the speed required for lift off. Finally, the nose of that half-million pound "beast" slowly pointed skyward and the tires lost contact with the pavement. Tears came to my eyes then and even now as I write this story. I was so proud of "My Girls".

Eight years before my retirement as a pilot for Northwest Airlines, the company posted openings for Boeing 747 Captains at the Honolulu pilot base. I bid for and was awarded one of those positions. The first three years of that tour, my wife Glenda and I lived a wonderfully relaxed life enjoying the Islands and the almost perfect weather. When Dick Dodge, the Honolulu Director of Flying, otherwise known as the Chief Pilot, chose to retire or pursue other endeavors, I applied for that position. There were several applicants but to my surprise, I was selected.

Shortly after WWII, Northwest Airlines pioneered commercial flights between the United States and Japan. The 50th anniversary of that event occurred during my tour of duty as the Honolulu Chief Pilot. The company used the event as a point of celebration and image enhancement.

As Chief Pilot, I was aware that there were female pilots based in Hawaii that were qualified for every cockpit crew position on the McDonnell Douglas DC-10. I conceived a plan to launch a flight across the Pacific with an all-female crew, which to the best of my knowledge would be the first in history. In my mind, this flight with its all-female crew would be a great way to celebrate the many years that the Airline had flown the Pacific.

My proposal was presented to the Vice President of Flight Operations who gave his immediate approval. He requested that all planning and arrangements be handled through my office in Honolulu. The project was a go. If handled properly, the company would receive some favorable publicity and the Honolulu-based employees would have a little fun.

The list of female DC-10 pilots was studied carefully. Since all were equally qualified, any one of them could be assigned with full confidence. Our goal was to have an all-female cockpit and main cabin crew. This was accomplished except for one male flight attendant who could not rearrange his schedule. The three female pilots selected were excited and readily agreed to take part in this historic flight. I would gladly publish the names of these women who so smoothly flew that DC-10 off the runway, retracted the landing gear and flaps, and turned westward toward Tokyo, but my memory fails me. They were my heroes, but I cannot remember their names. Senility? Probably.

It is only fitting that the names of these female pilots be part of this story. I contacted Jerry Vierkotter the Honolulu base manager during the time of my tour of duty. He once again came to the rescue.

Sharon Finch, the captain, was the most senior female pilot at the base and had flown other company aircraft at that position. The First Officer, Suzanne Skeeters, was senior enough to be flying captain but chose to fly co-pilot due to family obligations. Eva Akata, of Japanese descent, completed the crew by being assigned to the second officer position. I thought with her ethnic background she would attract considerable media attention, but the main focus was on the captain.

The media was informed as to the date and time of the flight. Several days before the day of departure, television and newspaper reporters began arriving, having traveled from Japan to cover the event.

Sharon, the captain, made her home on an island other than Oahu, possibly Maui or The Big Island. This was normal in that our long-haul flying required a pilot to report for work only two or three times a month. In addition, there were flights between the other main islands and Honolulu on an almost hourly basis; therefore, commuting was not difficult.

The media discovered her home address and showed up on her doorstep on the morning of the flight wanting to see and record her preparations. Normally, on the days that she was scheduled to fly, her husband prepared breakfast as she dressed and packed. When ready, she would seat herself and he would serve the meal. The Japanese reporters were shocked. They insisted that the husband sit down and that she, in uniform, serve him. Obviously, Japanese and United States cultures can be quite different.

The Northwest flight operations building, and the Honolulu Airport Terminal were abuzz the day of departure. Reporters, eager to get the story, were very aggressive and frankly we lost control. Departure time was nearing but they were still in the cockpit, taking pictures and trying to interview the crew. I had to almost physically remove them from the aircraft.

I returned to the cockpit to give the crew a little pep talk. "This has been a madhouse. Now, it's time to get down to business. I want you guys to settle down and start from the beginning. You are professionals and your passengers expect and deserve a safe and comfortable flight. I expect you to complete your normal procedures and fly this baby as if you owned it. Good luck." As I left, I noticed that Suzanne, the copilot, had a picture of her son taped to the window frame.

The flight was completed without a hitch. The story was a big hit in Japan, carried by many TV stations and published in millions of newspapers.

Several years later, my flying career ended with my retirement at the mandatory age of 60. As a bit of celebration, a retirement party was organized. This gathering evolved into a "roast the old chief" event. A number of speakers took the podium to remind everyone of my many blunders and mistakes, some real, some created.

A Marine friend claimed to have read reports from my commanding officer while I was on active duty. He said the reports stated: the only reason enlisted Marines would follow this officer would be out of idle curiosity and this officer is in over his depth in a parking lot puddle.

Another pilot stated that even after 35 years, my knowledge of flying could be summed up in three basic truths: Pull back, the houses get smaller—push forward, the houses get bigger—and do everything possible to keep the pointy end of the aircraft going forward.

Sharon, the captain of that all-female crew, made a short speech expressing her appreciation for my facilitating the flight. She considered it an honor to have taken part. According to her, my greatest concern was that during the flight one of them would leave the cockpit to go to the restroom and they would all go.

I loved "My Girls" and still do.

Note: In the title and in other places in the text I refer to the pilots of this flight as "My Girls." I want to state that this reference is not intended to offend or discredit them in any way. They were trained professional pilots and conducted themselves in that manner. Once all the hoopla settled, they flew that big jet uneventfully across thousands of miles of open water—just another day at the office.

However, in my old age, it still gives me a warm, fatherly feeling to think of them as My Girls.

Smithsonian?

Really?
1999

Glenda's phone rang. Mayan, our granddaughter who was on a short visit to Washington, DC, had made the call. Obviously excited, she was talking so fast it was difficult to understand what she was saying. She was calling from the entrance to the cockpit area of a Northwest Airlines Boeing 747 that was part of a recently opened display at the Air and Space Museum of the Smithsonian Institution. "I found it. I found it. I am standing beside Grampa's uniform."

Tommy Tucker, my trusted co-pilot, and I had just completed a normal layover in the company hotel near the Narita Airport in Japan. We completed our flight planning duties and proceeded to our aircraft. We found the cabin crew and numerous other people working busily to ready this huge aircraft for yet another Pacific crossing.

Takeoffs, departures, approaches, and landings were the fun parts of airline flying. The time between could become hours and hours of checking, logging, and monotony.

Thank goodness the average captain's memory was relatively, maybe *very*, short. Therefore, he could be entertained by the jokes and stories of his fellow pilots even though he had heard them all only a week earlier. Their offerings always seemed fresh, humorous, and interesting.

Our old heavily loaded Boeing 747 was very slow to climb to altitude. The big jet had finally been nursed to the initial cruising altitude, the last few thousand feet showing only 100 to 200 feet per minute climb rate. We were now well out over the Pacific and everything settled into a comfortable let's-get-through-the-night mode.

During the last four and a half years I had served as the Chief Pilot for the approximately four hundred pilots based in Honolulu, Hawaii. I was familiar with most of the folks at this base. Most of the pilots knew that I was approaching my mandatory retirement age of 60 years.

Our old but trusty jet performed perfectly as we rode the jet stream from Tokyo toward the Hawaiian Islands. There had been a period of silence. Tommy turned slowly toward me and asked, "What are you going to do with your uniform after you retire?"

Aroused from a period of extreme alertness, I replied that it would never be used again. He asked, "Would you like to donate it to the Smithsonian?"

Tommy was very good friends with the curator of a new display being developed for the Smithsonian Air and Space Museum. Northwest Airlines had donated to the museum the very first Boeing 747 aircraft, which during its last years of service had been flown regularly between Honolulu and Tokyo. I had served as captain on several Pacific crossings on that very aircraft.

I told him that I would be happy to donate my uniform to the cause. I had no clue as to how this could be done. He gave me a name and address that I put in a place where it could later be found.

Upon retirement, I gathered my entire uniform (hat, jacket, trousers, shirt, tie, belt, shoes, and socks) and sent the lot to the address that Tom had given me. I soon forgot the entire event. A few months later I received a form letter that, if signed, would relinquish any claim to the items that I had mailed. This document was quickly signed and returned.

Long story short, my uniform was used in this new Smithsonian display. Our granddaughter had found it and was excited.

I do find it interesting that I wore that uniform to fly that aircraft across the Pacific several times. There are many, many pilots who have flown the Pacific and that aircraft more than I. Every pilot who flew this magnificent aircraft should be proud to have been part of the history of the Boeing 747.

Please know that I still love Northwest Airlines and consider it one of the best that ever existed. I am proud of my association with that historic airline.

Tommy, thank you for requesting that I donate my uniform to the Smithsonian. I have never visited this display. As I write this little story, years after retiring, I wonder if that old uniform is still in place.

Granddaughter Mayan, with the uniform display at the Smithsonian.

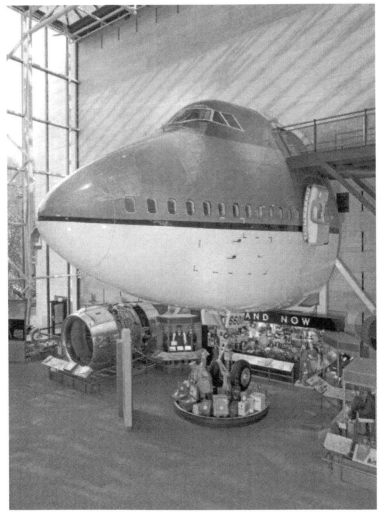

The Northwest Airlines 747 display at the Smithsonian.

AROUND THE WORLD

The Turn of the Century
1999

My career as a pilot for Northwest Airlines was drawing to a close. By law, at that time, all airline pilots were required to retire at the age of 60. A few months before my birthday, Al and Vera Haugen became aware of a very unusual cruise that was being planned. They somehow made the decision to book this adventure and invited Darrell and Jeanne Cloud and Glenda and me to go along.

A group of Canadian businessmen, I suspect after several beers, came up with the idea of launching a cruise that would sail around the world, visiting all seven continents. I applaud their boldness but question their judgement. They somehow were able to secure the good ship *Aegean One* for this optimistic adventure. The plan was to dispatch this small ship and about 450 passengers on a 120-day, around the world odyssey. Only a short time after sailing, the passengers began calling the ship *Aging One*.

Our little group from Minnesota knew nothing of ships and cruising. None of us had experienced even a short cruise. What if we didn't like cruising? Willing to take the chance, we all decided to accept the challenge. I can report that we all learned to enjoy shipboard life. Even though the trip at times seemed to drag a bit, it has remained one of our favorite adventures. This positive experience has motivated us to spend many enjoyable days on other cruise ships.

The decision to make the voyage had been made but how do you pack for a trip that would experience the extremes of all climates? We looked forward to crossing the equator and making a landing in the

Antarctic, but how could we pack the proper clothing for these two extremes and all the weather conditions in between?

The cruise was planned and marketed to begin in Athens, Greece, then proceed westward around the globe. We found out later that the ship and crew, including the captain, had never been outside of the Mediterranean Sea. This "Little Ship That Could" left port with the intention of spending four months sailing the seas of the world.

Glenda and I had chosen to live in Reno, Nevada upon our retirement and had purchased a nice townhouse on the Lake Ridge Golf Course. Kelly and our granddaughter, Mayan, had been living in Phoenix and were looking for a change. Their house had just sold, and we made a plan to have them move into our townhouse. They would be the perfect caretakers. All the required pieces seemed to fall into place. Our long cruise was now a possibility.

We flew from Reno to Seattle and then nonstop to Amsterdam. We decided to visit friends in Switzerland prior to the sailing date. We and the Clouds stayed several days in that beautiful country before returning to Amsterdam. We then flew on KLM (Royal Dutch Airline) to Athens, Greece where our cruise was to begin.

Earlier in my airline career our family had lived in Athens for several months. Northwest Airlines had sold seven Boeing 707 aircraft to Olympic Airlines with the agreement that Northwest pilots and instructors would man the aircraft and prepare the Greek pilots to eventually take over.

We rented an apartment from a retired Greek army general and his wife. During the few days before our sailing we visited Sofia (Constance had passed on). She remembered us and the kids, and we spent a lovely time with her over tea. She was so gracious even though we had interrupted her siesta.

After a bit of confusion with transportation we finally arrived at the dock in Piraeus, the seaport that serves Athens. We could see our little ship (it looked pretty big to us) through a fence but there was no one to brief us as to the boarding procedure. This seemed to become the theme of our entire trip. We knew nothing, but we had no idea that the crew also knew nothing. It was the blind leading the blind.

Somehow, everyone was boarded (it seemed like a miracle to us). Right away there was a strong sewer-type odor that filled the ship. Calls to the front desk did nothing to alleviate this problem. As the sun slowly sank below the horizon and the light started to fade, we weighed anchor. Glenda and I stood on the back deck feeling the slight vibration of the diesel engines as the lights of the port receded into the night. Four months at sea? The moment was rather emotional.

It would be impossible to write of the many ports and adventures. I can only attempt to present a few bits and pieces.

After interesting and educational stops on the islands of Crete and Sicily we docked at Gibraltar. The locals spoke English and the city was clean and well kept. "The Rock" looked exactly like we expected and the cable car trip to the top was exciting. The wind was blowing, and the sea birds put on quite a flying exhibition. From this vantage point we could see the local airport and Spain in the distance. The airport was unusual in that a busy road crossed the runway near its center. All automobile traffic came to a halt to allow the departure or arrival of aircraft.

We chose to walk back down to the city. As we made our way along a winding paved walkway, we encountered the Barbary Apes. No one seems to know how a wild population of these animals came to live in Gibraltar. The ones we interacted with were friendly and polite. Sometime in the not too distant past the government had moved an unruly group of about 45 back to their homeland in Africa.

Another interesting stop was at Madeira, a Portuguese island in the Atlantic. It crossed my mind to just stay on the ship for the day. That would have been a big mistake in that the island was beautiful, the people were friendly, and the food was great. The ship visited thirty-five ports, and all were exciting and interesting in their own way.

Most of the passengers had not transited the Panama Canal; therefore, you can imagine our excitement. We were not informed until the last day that our passage would be during the night. We arrived early and tied up at a very unattractive town. Some of us hired a taxi for the short trip to a duty-free shopping area. The driver insisted the we keep the doors locked, the windows up, and our cameras hidden. We had no trouble but a man and woman who were part of the crew were attacked while walking down the street. She was dragged down an alley and their possessions were taken. The woman was soon released basically unharmed except for a few minor scratches. Within an hour the local police returned everything that had been taken. No serious damage was done but we learned to be a bit more safety conscious.

Well after sundown, we got underway and went through the canal in the darkness. We watched and found it interesting; but we lost a night's sleep. A local woman boarded our ship and gave us great insight into the building and history of this monumental human achievement.

We had never been to South America and we looked forward to the several planned stops. The ship traveled at a slower speed than had been programmed into the itinerary. We were always running late. While trying to make the best forward speed we were late arriving in Callao, the port that serves Lima, Peru. We were allowed only a few hours to explore.

A taxi was hired, and we packed three couples into a small station wagon. All the seats were filled requiring two of the men to ride in a small cargo area. The center of Lima was in a festive mood and the Christmas spirit was in the air. There were decorations and people were out in the streets. A band with dancing girls was marching down a main street. All in all, a delightful two hours. We had to get back to the boat! I was a cargo compartment rider on the return trip. I did not mind but without my realizing it, this cramped position had slowed the blood flow to my legs. I hopped out of the cab, but my legs would not work. There was no feeling and I could barely stand or walk. This condition soon corrected itself and we made our way back to the "Aging One." Although short, our visit to Lima was well worth the effort.

Upon arrival in Ushuaia (the southernmost city in the world), a special part of the trip had been planned. We were flown to Buenos Aires to visit that city and to celebrate the arrival of a new millennium. Glenda and I were excited that we would spend a few nights in a hotel. Our room on the ship was very small and we slept on narrow separate beds. Our hotel accommodations were very much like the ship, a disappointment.

Buenos Aires, Argentina is a beautiful city with many statues and lovely buildings. We saw the sights, toured the city, obtained US dollars from a cash machine, and made a day trip to Uruguay. The highlight of this trip was a short plane ride to see Iguazu Falls. These falls are located near where the countries of Brazil, Argentina, and Paraguay meet. We had never heard of this natural attraction and were surprised to see this most impressive sight. You just have to visit these falls to appreciate their size and beauty.

We boarded small boats and motored around on the river above the falls. One of these tour boats had engine trouble but was towed to safety. Paved trails with guard rails allowed us to walk to see the many different views. We again boarded boats, but this time below the falls. The boat drivers seemed to be almost too aggressive in that they forced their craft into the cascading water.

Arriving back in Ushuaia we had time to explore the city. Many houses had beautiful and colorful flowers in their gardens. With these wonderful days under our belts we sailed south from the world's most southern city. We were told that there are several ways to determine if you have been to the most remote continent. Some people say that by crossing a certain latitude, others feel that when you see the icebergs, and still others believe when you see the penguins you can then truly say that you have been to Antarctica. We crossed that latitude, saw hundreds of icebergs, and viewed untold numbers of penguins. As we set foot on solid ground, we had no doubt that we had achieved our goal.

We provided our own clothing but were issued rubber boots. Outboard-motor-powered boats shuttled the passengers between the ship and the beach. We were told that our landing beach was on Half Moon Island. We were allowed 45 minutes to explore and observe the hundreds of nesting penguins. The adults returning from their fishing trips walked within a few feet of us as they made their way to their nest. They did not seem to mind as we approached their babies. We could easily see the feeding of these plump furry youngsters. A seal was on the beach, but it pretended to not notice us.

Our prescribed time ashore seemed much too short as we approached the boats for the trip back to the ship. We were allowed to board only after we had used brushes to clean the penguin poo from our boots. That evening everyone gathered. We were in a festive mood and the conversation was lively as we were served a bit of champagne in celebration. Yes! We had in fact made a landing in Antarctica.

We departed southern South America for New Zealand. We were at sea for 18 days with only a one-day break. On this day we felt lucky to be able to go ashore on Easter Island. We had heard of, but few had seen the Moai on this remote island. It is still a mystery how the large stone objects were made and moved about the island.

There was a problem, but we were not aware of it. The ship sailed away, and we were told that it was going for fuel. At our expected boarding time there was no ship in sight. We went to a nearby hotel, sat around outside, and listened to a local band. We waited. No one seemed to know what was going on. The ship finally returned at well after midnight and we were allowed to reboard. Years later, some of us were informed that the owners had instructed the ship to return to Greece. The company was having trouble paying its bills and that day had been spent in negotiations. Glenda and I were able to return to our room at around three in the morning.

We were glad to see land in New Zealand after what seemed a long crossing. Glenda and I left the ship, visited friends on the north island, and flew to Melbourne, Australia where we rejoined the boat. We learned that we had not missed much. After a very rough passage to Sydney, the ship was running behind schedule and only four hours were allowed to explore this beautiful city.

The trip continued with more exciting stops: Tasmania, Perth, Bali, Singapore, Seychelle Islands, Mombasa, Kenya, Alexandria, Egypt and Ashdod, Israel.

As the ship made its way across the Mediterranean toward Piraeus we felt a strong mix of emotions. We were happy to be getting home after such a long trip but sad to be leaving our friends after such an unusual and adventuresome trip.

"The Little Ship That Could" had bravely accomplished the task of taking this diverse group of adventurers around the world. There were moments of doubt and discouragement, but also a wealth of joy and adventure. Glenda and I would gladly do it again.

THIS OLD TRUCK

I discovered it abandoned, on the farm of my youth, out beside the tractor shed. My brother Jerry had parked it there years earlier, assuming that this would be its final resting place. This old 1984 Nissan Pickup with 276,000 miles showing on the odometer had faithfully transported him back and forth to work for a very long time.

It looked really bad, primarily because it was really bad. It had flat tires, a junk-filled bed, broken windshield, torn seats with springs showing, and weeds were growing beneath the entire truck and into the engine compartment. A more rational person would have said, "It's dead" and that would have been the end of this story. Not me.

Mable and Venoy, my parents, lived and toiled on this small West Tennessee farm during their entire married life. They had enjoyed fairly good health, but their age was taking its toll. They desperately wanted to remain on the farm and in their home. My sister, brother, and I decided that we would do as much as possible to honor their wish.

Their weakening physical condition made it necessary that someone be in or near the house at all times. I lived in Reno, Nevada and therefore tried to stay at least 10 days during each visit to keep my commutes to a minimum. The job was tedious and at times I would escape for a few minutes in an effort to maintain my sanity. It was during one of these short breaks that I discovered the "Silver Bullet." Our friends EK and Marianne Whiting gave the truck that nickname several years later.

I ignored this old wreck for a while. However, every time I walked anywhere near, it seemed to beg for help. Finally, I asked Jerry if he would give me permission to tinker with it. He surprised me when he answered, "Have at it. As a matter of fact, I will give it to you. I'll bring the title." As he was walking away, he sort of half-turned and said, "I don't remember that it had any major problems. It was running." His comment sparked a glimmer of hope.

My "sanity breaks" now had a purpose and I will admit that they came a little more often. Not being very knowledgeable about auto mechanics, the simple jobs were done first. The tires were aired up, the trash was removed, the grime and grease were wiped away, and the fluid levels were checked. Someone suggested that, considering the age, the vacuum lines should be replaced--I did that.

These simple chores had been completed and now I had to decide whether or not to invest some real money. What the heck, I bought a battery. After pumping the gas pedal a few times, I turned the key with a nervous hand and to my surprise it started. Holy Cow, it was running--not smoothly--but running.

I continued to make small adjustments here and there. It ran better and better and I drove it more and more in the local area. The title was transferred into my name.

Several months later I happened to be near a Nissan dealership, and it was convenient to stop at their service department. I explained that when I adjusted the mirror just right, under certain conditions, a small amount of smoke could be seen coming from the exhaust pipe. I asked the service manager if he had any suggestions. Remember, this truck had 277,000 miles on it and looked pretty shabby. The service manager paused, looked at the truck then back at me, scratched his head and said, "As a matter of fact, I do. Do not adjust the mirror so that the exhaust pipe can be seen." I replied, "Got ya. You are absolutely correct, thank you for your help."

It was time for "This Old Truck" to put up or shut up. I finished my current 10-day tour of duty with my folks and decided to engage in an adventure. With no special preparation I fired up the truck, determined to find out how much life, if any, remained.

I drove about 1800 miles in the next three days. Tennessee has more bordering states than any other and my intent was to visit them all. The route chosen allowed the tires of that old truck to touch: Tennessee, Arkansas, Mississippi, Florida, Alabama, Georgia, South Carolina, North Carolina, Virginia, Kentucky, and Missouri. I also drove through a small portion of Louisiana, just for good measure.

Rolling back into the farmyard, I was completely exhausted. My body and head were aching. The little truck seemed defiant and did not even seem to be breathing hard. I think I heard it say "Ya' want to do it again?" This was the first of many adventures involving that old truck. As it had for my brother, it served me well during the four or five years that

I owned it.

The details have been forgotten but I drove this old Nissan from Tennessee to Reno, Nevada. During this drive I devised a plan to drive this once abandoned old vehicle to every state except Hawaii. In the past I had been accused of attempting some pretty strange adventures. This plan could very well be called another questionable endeavor.

In order to fulfill my plan to drive the truck to 49 states it had to go to Alaska. I had driven the ALCAN Highway enough to know that it was a long hard trip. The idea of driving all that way and then retracing my route seemed a bit too much to do alone. I needed a partner. EK Whiting quickly came to mind. I explained to him that I needed someone to drive an old truck that had about 285,000 miles showing to Alaska. He listened and then paused after I finished talking. He said, "That is one of the most outrageous ideas that I have ever heard. Therefore, I am very interested."

He and Marianne flew into Reno, shopped for food at Costco, fired up the truck, and headed north. They spent around two weeks playing tourist as they made their way toward the "Last Frontier." They even took a side trip so that they could say that they had visited the Canadian Northwest Territories. They experienced no problems.

The phone rang and when I heard EK's voice I held my breath. He said "Darrel, we have a problem. Something is stealing our M&Ms." Somehow a mouse had hitched a ride and had chewed through the bag. The real reason for the call was to ask my advice concerning driving the truck to Prudhoe Bay along the Haul Road. They did that, parked the truck at the airport, and took an Alaskan Airlines flight to Anchorage.

The Haul Road is in actuality the Dalton Highway, a 414-mile unpaved supply route for the Prudhoe Bay oil fields. It can be dusty or muddy depending on the temperature but was covered with ice and occasional snow-covered areas during my drive.

After a few days I arrived in Prudhoe to find the engine compartment drifted full of snow. After liberating that old hunk of metal, it started. I bought a gallon of water for a little over five dollars and left town hoping to reach Cold Foot, the only town with a motel along this road.

The little truck never missed a beat. I plowed through many snow drifts and I saw arctic foxes, owls, caribou, and musk ox. There was a bit of apprehension and I was very glad to pull into the motel parking lot. I drove a little over 1,000 miles on ice and snow before finding dry pavement. This was a real adventure and maybe a bit risky.

On one occasion, Glenda joined me in Tennessee, and we made a whirlwind trip into New England in this battered old truck. We needed to "bag" these states. We took a ferry across Long Island Sound and drove the length of Long Island and through New York City. We had the opportunity to drive beside many luxury cars and past numerous very famous sites. Glenda at times seemed to be embarrassed by our mode of transportation but the little old truck showed no shame.

I love things that last a long time and are reliable. I loved that old truck. With about 325,000 miles showing on the odometer, it was sold for $600. The engine just purred on the test drive and the buyer seemed enthusiastic. I wonder if it continues to serve.

A House with a Motor

The Bus

After a leisurely lunch in a small town in the high meadows of Nevada, we crossed the street and climbed into our new (to us) motorhome, strapped in and turned the key to start the big Cummins diesel engine. Nothing happened. I released the key and sat back in total disbelief. On the second attempt the engine turned over slowly but started.

We trundled on down the road on our "shake down" trip in our motorhome with our little white Toyota pickup in tow. We had gone only a few miles when there was a very loud crashing sound along the left side of the coach. Our insecurities were confirmed. We were out of our league trying to live and travel in a "Bus."

At about six months before my 60th birthday, the mandatory retirement age, we chose to end my career as a Northwest Airlines pilot. We settled in Reno, Nevada and expected to live in our townhouse on the Lake Ridge Golf Course for a long time. We were happy. We were shocked to learn that many of the adventures, and misadventures, of our lives were still in the future. Establishing a sedate and boring lifestyle was far from what happened.

I cannot explain the sequence of events that set us on the course of selling our dream home and buying a motorhome. All at once, the property was on the market. An acquaintance, who had viewed our townhouse through a realtor, stated that there was no way we could demand the price we were asking—it sold within only a few short weeks.

Bob, a golfing buddy, allowed us to live in his condo for a very reasonable price while we tried to figure out the next move in our lives.

We searched, by every available means, in hopes of finding the perfect vehicle for our new adventure. We became aware of a couple that had recently relocated to Reno and had a motorhome for sale. They had retired from rewarding jobs and a small ranch in Texas with plans of traveling North America in a large coach. A company that was involved in unmanned flying vehicles became aware that these two people were now unemployed. They were offered contracts that were just too good to turn down. Their motorhome would not be needed for a long time and they advertised it for sale.

The negotiations began. They wanted to sell, and we wanted to buy. A short time later we agreed upon a price. We thought we paid too much and they thought the price was too low. Both sides worked at getting the bus out of storage and parked in front of their home. He wanted to brief me on all the required maintenance procedures and the operation of this big rig.

It started to snow. It was cold and windy. He made an effort to tell me what I needed to know but I was too miserable to listen. We finally just gave up and he wished me good luck as I drove away with Glenda following in our car. Many small (and large) bits of missed information would have come in handy later.

We parked this beast in a casino RV park and began the rather complicated process of transitioning from living in a townhouse to becoming full-time campers. The biggest question was what to do with all the stuff that we owned that we really didn't need. Glenda was stressed.

The weather was getting colder and at some point, the pipes would freeze. We decided to do a quick trip to familiarize ourselves with the bus. We drove east along the Loneliest Highway to Ely, Nevada. We found a very nice RV park and with some difficulties we got the water, sewer, and electricity hooked up. The first day on the road had been completed. A good night's sleep was anticipated.

Things did not go well. We slipped into the comfortable queen size bed and tried to calm down. We did not immediately fall asleep and soon Glenda began to feel claustrophobic. I feel that this was a psychological reaction to the strange and smaller new living conditions. After dressing quickly, we made a quick exit. Thank goodness the weather was mild as we walked the streets of the RV park. I was worried. That big box had just been bought for a good chunk of money and Glenda could not stand to sleep in it. The "attack" passed, and she was able to live in the motorhome for the next three years without any further problems.

The loud sound from the left side of the coach was a large awning that had not been properly secured. It had broken loose and was thrashing about in the wind. I climbed upon the roof of the coach and gathered the culprit as much as possible. Something was needed to tie it in place. I removed my boot lace and got the job done.

As the plan to live in a motorhome slowly developed, I had envisioned touring the entire country. What could be better than going to the far corners of our nation and having a decent house to come home to each night. Well, it ain't as good as it sounds. It was a pain in the butt to pick up and move to a new location. We expected a stress-free operation but there always seemed to be problems.

We were not alone in the problem department. Our home was very modest. The fancy units cost much more than ours. One day in Arizona we were parked beside a motorhome that the owner casually mentioned cost a million dollars. He and I worked all afternoon trying to solve some sort of water supply problem. Even with dirty knees, a banged head, grimy hands, and a flood of profanities, we were never able to get it to work.

My thoughts as we hit the road were that we would be on the go nearly all the time. As mentioned, it was complicated getting that thing ready to move and then getting it set up again. We never went east of Denver. The on-the-go mode quickly evolved into the squatter mode. A nice area would be chosen, the bus would be set up and we simply squatted there for at least a month before moving again. We did enjoy leisurely exploring those great locations.

We seemed to always have a problem with the coach. The whole bus shook as we traveled down the highway. The tires seemed to be out of balance and none of the several tire shops fixed this problem. We finally learned that the tires on our unit had been recalled. We were set up in Arizona but were told that if we came to Seattle the tires would be removed and replaced at no cost to us.

Our motorhome had only one slide-out, and it leaked. This was an intermittent problem in that it only leaked when it was raining. On the trip to get new tires, the company, whose factory was in Oregon, agreed to fix the leak. While we were involved with these repairs, we were instructed to take the coach to the Cummins engine facility for its last check before the warranty expired. A crack was found in the exhaust manifold and the problem was repaired for no cost. Problems like these and others occupied too much of our time. The company worked on the leak for almost a week and we thought it was fixed. Then there came another rain. It leaked.

Because of the time involved for these repairs, most of that summer was spent on the Oregon coast. On another occasion we parked in Salt Lake City for a month or more and hiked the Wasatch mountains and the valleys to the east of town.

At some time during each summer we returned to Reno for at least a month to see our doctors and dentists.

We spent the winter months in Arizona where we enjoyed the weather and played a little golf. The motorhome parks had many amenities such as golf, swimming pool, and all sorts of group activities.

Glenda finally had had enough. Even though we parked in great places, I tended to be her only friend and I was not even a female. We had no roots. For instance, we once met and socialized with our next-door neighbors. We enjoyed their company and looked forward to visiting with them again. Well before daylight, a 500 horsepower Cummins engine started about 15 feet away. Upon peeking outside in the morning, we discovered that our new friends were gone forever.

As we were beginning the motorhome adventure, we had put money down on a townhouse in Reno. The construction was complete at about the same time that Glenda hit the end of her rope. Three years had been enough. We bought the townhouse, moved in, and put the "bus" up for sale. It sat and sat. Finally, we received an offer that was low, but a deal was made. It was good to hear and see that Cummins push the bus out of our lives. Another small facet of our lives was now closed.

Our House with an Engine

Harmon

At this point in our lives Glenda and I were homeless. We had chosen to sell our lovely townhouse overlooking the eighteenth fairway of the Lake Ridge Golf Course in Reno, Nevada. My wanderlust was the driving force in our decision to buy a forty-foot, diesel-powered motorhome with the intent of exploring the wonderful sights of this great country.

Life threw us somewhat of a cruel curve. Mable and Venoy, my parents, were growing older and they dearly wanted to stay on the old family farm during their last days. My siblings and I decided to do everything within our power to honor their wishes.

Our motorhome was parked in an RV and Golf Resort in Gold Canyon, Arizona. I was spending ten days of each month trying to make my parents as comfortable as possible.

I had struggled through my "tour of duty" and was attempting to make my way back to Arizona. On this particular day the most likely route to get home was to proceed through Minneapolis, since I was attempting to travel on a pass.

The segment from Memphis to Minneapolis had been completed with no complications, but the flight to Phoenix was overbooked. The possibility of getting on board as a standby was questionable. In the last few minutes of the boarding process I was somewhat surprised to hear the gate agent call my name.

I was given a boarding pass and was again surprised that my assigned seat was in the first-class section. It was difficult to subdue a smile since there had been a real possibility of not being boarded at all. I climbed over an already seated passenger in my effort to get to my window seat.

This passenger, whom I immediately recognized, was friendly and helpful. I settled in, fastened my seat belt, and attempted to find some reading material. My seatmate was a famous person and I intended to respect his privacy. In my mind, famous people must surely get tired of the constant attention from the general public.

After only a few minutes, Harmon Killebrew, Hall of Fame baseball player, turned to me and asked, "So, you are going to Phoenix, what will you be doing there?" My three hours of expected boredom disappeared.

After chatting a bit, I asked, "So, have you ever been involved with professional baseball in any way?" As per his personality he simply stated that he had once played for the Minnesota Twins. The flight passed in a flash.

We talked at length about his college career, his time with the Twins, and his present association with that organization. He expressed interest in what it was like being a military and airline pilot. I kidded him as to having a street named after him. He chuckled and said that it was only a short street.

He was comfortable enough to discuss his world-famous teammates. All in all, it was a very memorable three hours. The one sad moment was when he told of being the Twins representative at the funeral of Kirby Puckett. Kirby had been a superstar for the Twins but had died much too young.

In my opinion, Harmon and I, for that moment in time, connected. I enjoyed this brief relationship and feel that he did also. During the flight we discussed an event from the past but could not remember the name of the person involved. As I retrieved my personal items the name came to me. Deplaning just a few people ahead of him, I turned and announced the name to Harmon. He gave me a smile, a thumbs-up, and said, "That's it."

Harmon is gone now but I will always remember this chance meeting and the conversation with this famous but humble man. In my mind he was a great human being. Upon hearing of his passing, Bert Blyleven his former teammate said, "That's what I will miss most about Harmon. Not his playing ability, but his personality and the way he treated people."

THE SHIMMERING TREE

My parents, Venoy and Mable, lived their entire married life on a 160-acre farm in West Tennessee. They were uneducated country folks who did their best to make a living on that small farm.

Three children had arrived but their struggle to survive had only continued. I was the middle child but never realized that such a struggle existed. We always had adequate food, shelter, and clothing. Because of their sacrifice, my sister, brother, and I were able to obtain some sort of education which gave us the hope of living better lives.

They grew older. Venoy's body became weaker and Mable's mind wandered. They needed help. My siblings and I tried to do our best to keep them comfortable in the old farmstead home, but it was a struggle.

Venoy at 94 years old began to breath erratically. I happened to be present and inserted his hearing aids. My love and admiration were spoken but there was no indication that he heard my words.

After his funeral my Mom looked me in the eye and said, "Someone died but I don't know who." She lived another year or so but was mostly in a totally confused mental state. At times she was quite entertaining. She could see and have conversations with people who were not there. She truly believed that a whole family lived in the tree in her front yard. When we walked out to see them, she would say, "Well, I guess they went to the store."

One Sunday afternoon, she was resting in her favorite chair when Mary, a lady who helped care for her, came for a visit. Mary leaned over to give her a kiss and with surprise said, "She's not breathing." We moved her to the couch and as we were fussing over her, she took a deep breath. Mary said, "She's breathing, she's breathing." I said, "She's a tough old girl." Mable opened her eyes and said, "You bet I am, I can beat the shit out of most men." I had never heard her say that word before. Her mind immediately drifted away.

She passed with me near her side. I was more than sixty years old and this old woman had been a part of my entire life. She was not formally educated but was a very wise woman. With a strong hand she had started me on the path of striving to become an honorable person.

My parents were now gone.

The morning after her burial, I drove to the small country cemetery. As per normal at this time of year in Tennessee, it was a warm, calm, and humid day. I walked across the wet grass to my parents' grave site. I had a heavy heart.

I sat on their headstone with my emotions in a state of confusion. My Mom's grave was fresh, and it was difficult to stop looking at it. I mourned.

Collecting myself, I stood, looked about, and said out loud, "Venoy and Mable, if you are okay, please give me a sign."

In the Tennessee early morning stillness there was not even a hint of a breeze. Suddenly, the leaves of a single nearby tree started to shimmer. This vigorous movement lasted for only a few seconds, not one leaf on any other tree moved. A natural happening? Probably. No one will ever know.

I have always taken this phenomenon to be a sign that I should continue to strive for the best life possible. As they taught, I still try to learn as much as possible, work hard, and be fair and honest in my relationships with others. I feel that my parents would be happy.

Years ago, someone told me that coins found on the floor or ground were sent by deceased parents. Although nearly worthless, I always pick them up and treat them as treasures.

I think of my Mom and Dad.

GRAND CANYON

February 2006

The idea of hiking into the Grand Canyon had been in the back of my mind for a long time. The Canyon is remote, obtaining a permit could be difficult, and the trip could possibly be expensive. I simply had not made the effort to plan and complete such an event.

The opportunity to attempt this adventure came about by accident. Glenda and I were in Gold Canyon, Arizona seeking relief from the cold winter in Reno, Nevada. We played golf about once a week with a group of friends and hiked the nearby desert trails quite often. On one of our golf outings Roger Sassar mentioned that he was going to take a walking trip to Phantom Ranch. This government-managed facility is at the bottom of the Grand Canyon and provides shelter, food, and a hot shower to overnight hikers. Reservations and fees are required.

Roger lived in the Mountain Brook community. Their recreation department often sponsored outings and events as a service to the residents. A year earlier this department had applied for a permit that would allow ten people to make the trek down to the Ranch, sleep in a clean bed, and eat two meals.

At the time we lived in a townhome community which was nearby but not part of Mountain Brook. Roger informed me that the sign-up sheet was simply lying on an office counter with no one specifically in charge. He only smiled and shrugged when asked if he thought I should put my name on the list. Pretending to live in the development, I walked into the office and bravely added my name to the list. No one seemed to notice or care.

Realizing that the hike would be physically demanding, I started hiking more often, concentrating on climbing hills. Glenda accompanied me on many of these hikes and we both whipped ourselves into fairly good physical condition.

At about this time an old Marine buddy and his wife invited us to hike to the Havasupai Indian village, which was also at the bottom of the Canyon. We accepted this challenge which was scheduled for about a week after my hike to Phantom Ranch. Without any real planning we had two separate opportunities to hike into this magnificent landmark.

As the date of my hike to Phantom Ranch approached, we made reservations at the famous hotel on the south rim for three nights. The El Tovar Hotel was a bit more expensive but very convenient and historic. With only a short drive, Glenda could drop me at the starting point and the hotel was only about 200 yards from the top of the exit trail.

We checked in, dropped our luggage in our room, and decided to take a walk. After walking only a few feet from the hotel entrance a condor soared very low overhead. We could easily see its white identification tag that was attached to a wing. Condors are considered an endangered species and there is an active program to re-establish a population in the Grand Canyon area. It is believed that there are about 200 California condors now living in the wild. This rare bird can have a wingspan of nearly ten feet. The sighting of this rare bird was a thrill, and this alone made the trip worthwhile.

The evening before the hike was comfortable and relaxed. Glenda and I had a leisurely dinner and went to bed early. Our room was very rustic, but the bed was soft and inviting. The day ahead would be very challenging.

We awoke to sunny skies but brisk temperatures, actually cold, about 25 degrees if my memory is correct. After a nice breakfast Glenda drove me to the trailhead where I planned to meet the other members of our group. I was anxious to get underway in that none of us knew how long it would take to walk down to the Colorado river and the ranch.

Roger had made a plan to hike with a friend, so we waited. That friend never showed so we eventually began our walk. Standing on the rim the cliffs looked too steep to accommodate any sort of trail. I was a bit apprehensive, but the trail was wide, well-maintained, and not very steep. Glenda hung out with the guys and snapped some pictures. She escorted us for the first quarter-mile and took even more pictures.

There are no words that can describe the beauty and grandeur of this magnificent canyon. I have been fortunate to have traveled to many wonderful places in this world. The United States is by far the most varied and beautiful.

As we descended, the temperature began to rise, and our coats were soon removed. The trail was dusty and the water that we had brought along was greatly appreciated. Approximately halfway down there was a rest area with toilet facilities. We took off our packs, loosened our bootlaces, and relaxed on the available benches. Some may have even taken a short nap. This rest stop had no water available.

On several occasions, during the trip down to the Colorado River we observed mule-trains traveling in the opposite direction. The ranch depended on these animals for transporting all needed supplies. The fee we paid for our permits included dinner (steak or stew). All food including our steaks was hauled into the canyon by mule-train.

As we tramped along the dusty trail, the Colorado River became visible far below. Nearing the bottom, as we rounded a turn, we could see a tunnel that was cut through a shear rock cliff. The tunnel led to a very sturdy bridge which we used to cross the river. A dusty half-mile walk delivered us to our destination.

Wow, it was a relief to kick off our boots and relax around the furnished picnic tables. Some of the guys had brought along flasks of their favorite alcoholic beverage. This relaxing time before dinner became a time of telling stories and some seemed a bit larger than life. We talked, laughed, and gathered our strength.

The Ranch, operated by The Park Service, consisted of several stone buildings. Most of these rustic structures were used as sleeping quarters. However, there was one that housed a shower facility. The largest building served as a canteen, dining room, and pub, depending upon the time of day. Our cabin of two rooms contained bunk beds which were furnished with clean sheets and a decent pillow. There was a washbasin and a toilet located in a small closet-like stall. This cabin was equipped with an air conditioner, although due to the cool weather it was not needed.

As the light began to fade, I made my way to the shower room in an effort to rid my body of the days accumulated dust. It felt really nice. All cleaned up and hungry, I joined the guys at the chow hall. I was surprised that my steak was tender and tasty. Remember, that steak had made the trip into the canyon on the back of a mule.

After dinner this room turned into a pub. We sat around, enjoyed a beer, and attempted to sing along as a hiker played a guitar. Most everyone turned in early since we knew that tomorrow would be more difficult than today. I selected the lower bunk and Steve Lackey manned the top. Two times during the night he said, "Darrel, Darrel, would you please hand me my pillow?" Somehow, he had allowed his pillow to drop to the floor.

Suddenly, our bunk house was full of activity. It was still dark, but the hikers were up and attempting to get their gear together. Steve and I struggled out of bed and went to breakfast. We were surprised to find that most hikers were suited up and ready to start their climb back to the south rim along the Bright Angel Trail.

We had a hearty breakfast, took our pre-packed bagged lunch, and quickly filled our canteens. Most of the hikers were already on their way. We donned our packs and headed out of camp, well behind the early birds.

It was dark, but we were able to follow the well-worn trail that led always upward. The sun slowly made its presence known. The dawning of the new day was an exceptional sight. We slowly made our way toward the south rim. There were ten miles and nearly five thousand feet to the nearest cold beer.

Steve and I trudged along together but soon realized that our personal paces were not the same. After a while I slowly began to move ahead. He and several other guys settled into the same pace and hiked together the rest of the day.

About halfway to the rim we took a break at Indian Gardens. This location had a shelter, a corral for the mules, and running water. As we rested in the shade of some very large trees, a female mule deer walked through camp. She seemed to not even notice that we were there.

As I made my way along the trail, I slowly overtook Roger, who had departed camp well ahead of me. We were both getting somewhat tired as we made our way up the ever-ascending trail. I found that my best progress was made when I set a very slow pace that could be maintained. Roger was struggling with some pain in his back and leg. Nearing the south rim, I encouraged him to dump most of his water and allow me to take a few pounds from his pack.

It was great to see Glenda, who had walked a short distance down the trail to meet us. We had made it! After a round of high fives and a few pictures we adjourned to a local pub. The mug of cold beer was perfect for the occasion. Steve and others soon joined us. As we talked Steve turned to me and said, "I feel a little dizzy, if I faint please place me on the floor and elevate my feet." We insisted that he lie down before he passed out. He made a quick recovery and soon seemed to feel completely normal.

This two-day challenge will always be remembered. I was lucky that Roger casually mentioned that he had signed up for this trip. If not for him, it is very likely that I would have never gotten around to walking the canyon. Thanks, Roger.

We spent the next few days in northern Arizona exploring Navaho country. Our next canyon adventure was only a week away. We saw and learned so much. Another adventure had been accomplished.

Canyon Rafting

September 2006

The sounds of the raging rapids were intimidating as our rubber raft seemed to accelerate. We assumed the brace position, I grabbed and held the strap on the back of Glenda's life jacket, vowing to never let go, as she frantically gripped the handholds. We crouched as low as possible in several inches of water and held on with all our strength.

I am a poor swimmer and Glenda is a non-swimmer. Our oarsman had only partial control of our rubber boat as we were thrown into the confusion of the rapids. The muddy, red-colored, angry water seemed more than our raft could possibly survive.

Glenda showed no fear, even though afraid of the water, as she and all other occupants uttered some sort of war-whoop type yell as our boat pitched violently into the rapids. A flood of sediment-loaded water crashed down over the entire boat.

This adventure had begun in Hawaii when a fellow pilot, EK Whiting, and his wife Marianne asked Glenda and me to accompany them and some of his classmates from West Point on a rafting trip down the Colorado River.

He had attended West Point and upon his graduation chose to transfer to the Air Force. During his time at the Academy, he had formed friendships that would last a lifetime. He and his classmates, over the years, had experienced several reunion adventures. I believe EK organized this canyon trip. Glenda and I were honored to be invited and we accepted.

Some of our adventures had included outdoor activities, including camping and sleeping in tents. After our last extended camping trip,

Glenda declared that she would never again sleep on the ground. I agreed to abide by her wishes but out of nowhere, "along came EK and Marianne." Glenda was very reluctant but finally agreed after my pleading.

I believe that she now has done her share of "roughing it" and we both agree that sleeping on the ground is a thing of the past. My body aches even at the thought of tent-living. Our present description of roughing it is the Hampton Inn or an ocean-view cabin on a cruise ship.

As an added attraction we chose to drive the most scenic roads on our trip to Moab, Utah, where we would meet the rest of our group. This drive was a blast and the last 30 miles or so along the Colorado River were spectacular. The Dewey Bridge (1916) was built to accommodate the early settlers who were en route to points west. We parked the car and walked about, reading the historical signs, and visualizing what life was like during the frontier days. The vision of heavily loaded wagons and tough men and women was easy to imagine.

Several years later we traveled this same route in the opposite direction. We were in for a big surprise. I looked forward to again visiting this historic bridge. As we approached, it was obvious that things were different. The cables were still in place but there was no decking. With a strong wind present from the west, a small fire had been started in a nearby campground. The campers lost control and brush along the river started to burn. The fire roared up the canyon and burned the bridge. We were shocked and saddened. A bit of history had been lost.

We met EK and Marianne in Moab and were introduced to their friends. We had a meal and spent the night in a motel. The next morning, we boarded an old school bus that was driven by a guy who had grown up in Hawaii. We bumped along on some pretty poor desert roads and came to a stop on the rim of the river canyon.

Our driver informed us that because of the danger we would be required to walk down this steep and rutted road. We were in high spirits and enjoyed the exercise. We arrived at the river and found six rubber rafts lashed together. There was a beehive of activity as rafters were briefed, supplies were loaded, and boats were assigned. Our boatmen pushed out onto the river. Another adventure had begun.

The weather was perfect and the scenery spectacular. Our only duty was to try to take it all in. We had not been briefed as to the overall conduct of the trip. At around noon the flotilla was guided into a sand bar and we were told to disembark. We were about to have lunch but had not been told. Again, we had no duties as coolers were off-loaded and a table was assembled. In only a few minutes we were presented with a very nice lunch which included several kinds of delicious melons. During the entire trip the crew amazed us again and again as they created gourmet meals out of seemingly nowhere.

Privacy? The Expedition Company joined our group with a group of women. The merged group consisted of about equal numbers of men and women who were strangers before we were introduced that morning. On the first lunch break Glenda and another lady wandered away from the group in search of a little privacy. They walked along a line of small trees to the end of our little sandbar. They disappeared from sight. Suddenly the other lady shot into full view feet first with her clothing around her ankles. The slight incline had been quite slippery.

A porta-potty was set up each evening but during the day people took care of their light work behind any obstacle that was available. Gradually, modesty slipped away. Near the end of the trip nearly all the women lined up only about ten yards from the men and proceeded to get the job done.

During the first few days we remained lashed together. The water was mostly flat, and we gently drifted along. One day our leader announced that we were getting a "divorce." The water had become a bit more vigorous. Rather than being one big unit we were now six separate boats. The water seemed to be getting restless.

There were enough tents on board to allow everyone to sleep inside if they so chose. The weather was nice and on several nights, we just rolled out our sleeping bags and slept under the stars. Deep into this wilderness there were no city lights, therefore the stars were a sight to behold. A thunderstorm popped up late one afternoon. Tents were set up, just in case. Just after dark the thunder and lightning began in earnest. The sound of thunder echoing down the canyon and the lightning display were slightly frightening but special. There was wind but no rain.

This trip was marketed as being a floating/hiking adventure. We stopped the boats and walked to an old cabin. It was on the top of a small hill that was surrounded by some relatively level ground. It was believed that a pioneer had made an effort to farm on that spot.

Another short walk enabled us to see a seven-foot by seven-foot rock face that was covered with petroglyphs. We wondered what sort of life the people had led that made these drawings. Indian drawings and a few cliff dwellings were visible on several occasions from the river.

On two occasions we climbed out of the canyon. The trails were quite steep, and Glenda chose not to take part in the second climb. One of our stronger men lost his footing and almost tumbled down the cliff. He could have been seriously hurt if he had fallen.

Not long after our "divorce" we approached the white-water portion of Cataract Canyon. On several occasions the boats were halted just above white-water areas. All the boatmen walked along the water until they had a view of the upcoming rapids. They would stand, talk, and point. Finally, with the nodding of heads they returned to their boat and went into the attack mode.

The boat would move into the white water slowly at first and then all hell would break loose. We often rushed directly toward waves that appeared to be impossible to survive. With us hanging on for dear life the rubber boat would either float above or dive beneath the big waves. Suddenly, the boat with its full load of crew and passengers would pop out below the rapids. I would immediately use our assigned five-gallon bucket to bail as much water from our boat as possible before we reached the next rapids.

We repeated the above many times. Suddenly the water went flat, it was almost like waking from a dream. The excitement slowly receded. As we were served our last shore lunch, I noticed a high bridge over some nearby trees across the river. Civilization was just around the next bend.

What a trip. Another major entry into our list of wonderful adventures. Thank you so much, EK and Marianne. If it were not for you, we probably would not have enjoyed such a trip.

HAVASUPAI CANYON

Supai Village

Glenda was waiting on the south rim as Roger and I struggled to the top of the Bright Angel Trail. After a nearly five-thousand-foot climb and a ten-mile trek, we were completing our hike from the Phantom Ranch at the bottom of the Grand Canyon. A pint of cold beer at the nearby pub was a welcome treat. My old body was weary but a good meal and a night between clean crisp sheets within reach of a warm soft body put me firmly on the road to recovery.

Years ago, Glenda and I had departed New York City aboard the MS *Prinsendam*, a Holland American cruise ship. This fifty-six-day cruise along the east coast of the United States, through the Panama Canal, and down the west coast of South America ranks as one of our favorite adventures.

We met many new friends including Bob and Carol Jarboe. Bob and I had served in Vietnam as Marine attack pilots and therefore had something in common. Since that cruise we had maintained a casual relationship. They were a friendly, adventuresome couple and we had enjoyed their company.

The Jarboes invited Glenda and me to join them for a hike to Supai, a Havasupai Indian Village. This village is located at the bottom of the Grand Canyon about seventy or so miles west of the South Rim tourist venue. Even though the trailhead and the village were off the beaten trail, they were still located within the Grand Canyon National Park. Bob and Carol had completed this trek some years earlier and had enjoyed it to the extent of wanting to do it again. The feeling was that this adventure offered a pretty much tourist-free chance to view the canyon and interact with the Native American residents.

Due to previously planned obligations we reluctantly turned down their first invitation but expressed the desire to make the hike at some later date. A year later everyone was available, and we made plans to attempt this adventure. Everything seemed to fall into place. I had already planned a hike to Phantom Ranch from the south rim and we were already in the area.

After trekking to the Phantom Ranch and back, I looked forward to another trip into this magnificent canyon. I had several days for my body to recover. We decided to spend those days exploring the Indian culture and villages to the east of the Grand Canyon.

This mostly desert area is the homeland of the Navaho and Hopi Indians. During the next few days we explored this harsh land and observed how the natives lived. Unfortunately, we came to realize that too many members of these Indian tribes were living in what seemed to be rather severe poverty. In general, the housing was poor, and in one case the homes of a small village were almost covered by drifting sand. The natives were friendly and did not seem to resent our presence. We were amazed that the people could live in such dry conditions. We were left with a slight feeling of depression. There seemed to be no way out.

As our appointment with our friends neared, we turned our trusty old Lexus westward. We stayed overnight in historic Williams, Arizona. A steam-powered train makes a daily roundtrip to the south rim of the Grand Canyon from this town.

Once established in our motel we made our way to a recommended restaurant a few blocks away. The weather was quite brisk; therefore, we maintained a good pace. The restaurant lived up to the hype and we had a great meal.

The next day dawned clear, calm, and still cold. We do not remember seeing even one other car as we made our way through the desert to the trailhead. The Jarboes had arrived slightly earlier from Laughlin, NV to the west and were busy arranging their backpacks. It was very cold. Pack animals were being loaded for their daily trek down into the canyon. Most of the supplies for the village are carried by these animals.

Anxious to leave the biting north wind behind, we hurriedly donned our light packs and started down the trail. A helicopter lifted off and it seemed very strange since it almost immediately was flying below us as it descended from the parking lot into the canyon.

Shortly after starting down the switchback trail we met a mule train on its way to the rim. The guy in charge nodded slightly from his horseback perch and raised one finger in greeting as we passed. We got the impression that the locals tolerated visitors but did not go out of their way to be welcoming. Very soon after leaving the trailhead we encountered warm and pleasant weather. It was a lovely day for a hike.

At first the canyon was quite wide, but the walls gradually closed in leaving only a narrow passageway. As we wandered into the village, we saw no people but there were several horses. As we reached the center of town, we saw more human activity. There were kids playing in the street and two older men sitting on a bench in front of the small store. As we proceeded to the motel, we observed a church, school, and the restaurant building.

The noise of a helicopter caught our attention and we stopped to watch. It approached and landed in an open field right in town. The engine continued to run as people and supplies were deplaned. This was the helicopter that had departed the parking lot as we began our hike. After only a few minutes, with a new load of people and baggage it kicked up a cloud of dust as it headed back to the rim.

Bob had made the reservations and therefore did the talking as we checked into our "Motel 6"-like accommodations. There was a slight misunderstanding as to how much deposit had been paid. Bob asked the check-in lady a question and she snapped, "I have been doing this job for a long time and I know what I am doing." As we walked around town, we learned that the two guys on the bench did not want their picture taken. When they were not looking, I snapped one anyway.

We soon learned that the only restaurant in town was closed. The small grocery store was open, and we were able to buy bread, cold cuts, and soft drinks. I remember that we ate our evening meal at a picnic table near the motel.

We enjoyed a comfortable night's sleep and during breakfast we made a plan for the day. We followed a dusty trail farther down the canyon. Shockingly, the stream that flowed vigorously through the valley was a beautiful shade of blue. We found and enjoyed two spectacular waterfalls, the first of which is often seen in TV ads. The trail descended along the left side of this first falls, giving us many interesting views. Below the falls, Bob and Carol slipped out of their boots and waded in the blue water.

The second falls was probably higher than the first but not as beautiful. Snooping around, we found a rickety old ladder with rope and chain handrails that led through a tunnel to the stream below. Bob used this damp and moss-covered contraption to make his way to the bottom. I watched from the top since I could not muster the courage to go along.

As we made our way back up the trail, we passed through what appeared to be an old campground. The camp did not appear to be in use but sitting in the open on a small platform were two toilets. We assumed that they were not functional but the girls, fully clothed, demonstrated their use. We made our way back to the village, ate at the restaurant and turned in, tired but happy.

There was no wind, the sky was blue, and the temperature was perfect on our trek back to the rim. The trip out was a bit more strenuous, but the group had no problems. We arrived at the parking lot in good spirits and in good shape physically. We stowed our packs and after saying our goodbyes, we were ready to leave. Bob instructed us to follow them for a mile or so. We parked the cars and he produced a bottle of champagne. We touched glasses and sipped the sparkling beverage. A fitting end to another of life's little adventures.

Bob and Carol, thank you so much for allowing us to tag along. You are good people and we enjoy your company.

Kilt Lifter

Bruges, Belgium
2007

Reference books had been referenced, a cruise had been chosen, reservations had been made, airline tickets had been bought, and a long overnight flight had been endured. We were now in Copenhagen, Denmark, a clean, safe, and beautiful city from which the good ship Star Princess would be boarded for a thirty-day European cruise.

Glenda and I and our traveling partners, Anne and Ed Dougherty, had arrived in this great city two days before the ship was to sale. We had booked into different hotels and did not join up until just before boarding. It was good to see them in person since there always seems to be a bit of uncertainty associated with international travel. We had been friends for many years, but this was our first joint cruise. Spirits were high and we were ready for a fun trip.

We were among the earlier boarding passengers and therefore had some free time during which we explored the ship and chatted over a leisurely lunch. So far, so good. After finishing our meal, we wandered toward our assigned cabins. We noticed that musicians were gathering on the dock. We were told that for the entire summer Copenhagen had served as this ship's home port. This was the ships last departure.

There was a small celebration and the band played. There was also a fireworks display and everyone sang and waved. We felt loved.

Everything had gone as planned, but we had still felt some stress. We slowly began to relax. Over cocktails, we discovered that both couples had read books by Rick Steves, the renowned European travel authority and author. His expert advice is always presented in a straightforward and easy-to-read manner. He seemed to suggest that the traveler should have fun and see the sights without breaking the bank.

Our first port of call was Rotterdam. We were surprised to learn as we walked about that this city loved elephants. There were many statues of these animals around town, each with its own special paint job. We later learned that local people had founded a movement called "Elephant Parade". The primary goal of this project was the attempt to protect the endangered Asian Elephant.

Tired and happy, we trudged back to the ship for a great evening meal at sunset as the ship slipped out of port. As we slept, the ship's crew steered a course toward Zeebrugge, Belgium. None of our little group had ever visited this city. In fact, we were not even sure as how to pronounce the name. Rick Steves' book enabled us to make a plan.

We decided to travel to Bruges, a small but picturesque town about 20 to 30 miles to the south. A taxi driver in his Mercedes insisted that he would deliver us to the center of town and return at an agreed upon time for the return trip. He made good on his word.

The weather was almost perfect—sunny and warm. We strolled around this historic and scenic town enjoying the old buildings, statues, and the lovely homes. The many tourists were being entertained by tour boats plying the many canals that meandered through the city. Thinking this would be a pleasant adventure, we were informed that there were no more seats available.

Our feet were tired, and the thought of food caused us to look for an interesting place for lunch. Anne had read the night before of a restaurant that was recommended by Rick Steves. The streets were not well-marked. We wandered about but eventually found the pub-like establishment. Evidently this recommendation had been taken seriously by a lot of the town's visitors as it was a bit crowded.

To our surprise we were immediately escorted to an upstairs dining room. As we made our way to our table Glenda stumbled on a slight step-down and immediately received an enthusiastic round of applause from the already-seated guests. It became apparent that most of the tables were filled with young men who had already downed a few pints. They were in a festive mood.

Anne, being the outgoing type, engaged some of these guys in conversation and learned that they were from Scotland and were in town to celebrate an upcoming wedding. This was a bachelor party. It was observed that the groom-to-be was dressed in full Scottish costume, including the traditional highlander kilt.

With a smile I asked the groom if it was true that the Scots wore "nothing" under their kilts. He was a large man. Hesitating for only a moment, he stood and faced the wall. Bending over slightly, with both hands he flipped up his kilt. There in this crowded restaurant he exposed his larger than life hairy butt. We had been mooned. Too much information.

We have fond memories of that cruise but the "Kilt Lifter" is the story that is most often told. Due to Rick Steve's book we had several interesting adventures. We consider him to be the master and will continue to look his way for suggestions.

Trailers for Sale or Rent

At the age of 68 I was introduced to a simple little book called *Deals on Wheels*. It was written by Lonnie Scruggs in which he explained how he was able to make a very good return on investment by working with old mobile homes. I bought his book and read it, cover to cover, in one evening. His business plan was to buy older mobile homes at a low cost, make minimal repairs, and sell them at a profit using a rent-to-own contract. He indicated that this could be a good deal for everyone involved.

The average family that lives in a mobile home normally does not have and cannot borrow the money required to buy a home of their own. Most, however, have jobs and can make reasonable monthly payments. *Deals on Wheels* explained how Scruggs used these two truths to make a good profit and become a hero to his customers. The customer, with very little money down, could make payments for four or five years and end up with title to their homes rather than a stack of rent receipts. The buyer could own a functional home with monthly payments that would be similar to a rent payment.

Our son Darrel Jr. had worked in the home-building industry for many years. He had started as a roofer and framer but gradually worked himself into the position of site manager. His last job was to oversee the completion of a 175-unit project. As this job was coming to an end he fully expected to move to another development and continue as he had done for the last several years. His employer, a nationwide company, deeply cut back on its activity and therefore laid off most of their employees in the Minneapolis area. He was without a job.

I had worked in real estate for most of my adult life; therefore, it was normal for us to team up. He and I began buying distressed houses, fixing them up, and reselling. The banks liked our product and happily furnished the required capital. The housing market crashed, and the ensuing financial crisis caught us, and our bankers, totally by surprise. Our business came to a screeching halt—making it impossible for us to sell or lease the houses that we owned.

Trying to deal with this inventory of houses that had lost 40% or more of their value put a tremendous strain on our financial situation. In most cases the houses sat empty. We found renters for two houses, but they soon stopped making payments and refused to leave. When they finally did move, we discovered thousands of dollars in damage. It was a disaster.

The money was going out much faster than coming in. We were losing our limited net worth at an alarming rate. I had worked all my life trying to do the right thing, but suddenly my back was against the wall. It was a desperate time. I don't remember the sequence of events that led me to Lonnie's book, but I will forever be grateful.

At first I was skeptical--how could this simple little business plan work? How could a mobile home be bought for the low prices suggested in the *Deals on Wheels* book and then resold at about twice that price? I agonized over whether or not this crazy idea should be attempted.

I didn't have much money to get started but not much was required. I drove through a number of trailer parks, some were in poor condition and at times it felt that my safety might be in jeopardy. One fifty-lot park had at least ten trailers sitting empty and overall it looked pretty shabby.

I was tormented. The desire was there but I was afraid to take the plunge. Many people seem to think that folks who live in trailer parks should be considered "trailer park trash." There is a definite stigma. Finally, I mustered the courage to call a park owner to inquire about an empty trailer.

The trailer was abandoned and had an orange plastic net stretched across the driveway. Pete, the park owner, met me at the trailer on a very windy day. As we approached the front door my cap blew off and flew over the trailer into an open field. The trailer had been vacant for many months because of a suspicious bathroom fire. The tub, vanity, toilet, and all electrical wiring had been destroyed and the entire house was coated with a heavy layer of soot. The floors were covered with all sort of trash. It was a wreck.

Pete informed me he would reluctantly sell me this burned-out trailer for $1,000. I did not know if that was a good deal or not. We had another meeting a few days later and I convinced him to make me a gift of the trailer and allow me several months of free lot rent. The work began. In the long run Pete's decision to give me the trailer was a good deal for him. He has now received nine years of monthly lot rent payments.

Glenda and I soon decided that we would never again buy a fire damaged trailer. We worked on this wreck for several months and it slowly began to look more livable. Late one afternoon a small "For Sale" sign was stuck in a window. Tired and hungry, I headed for home. I had driven only a few miles when Tom called to say that he and his wife had seen the sign and would like to view the trailer. Reluctantly, I returned to show them this old rebuilt trailer.

To my great surprise they seemed excited and wanted to move in as soon as possible. We drew up a simple contract and they agreed to buy the trailer for about twice the money that I had invested. The many, many hours that Glenda and I had worked were not taken into consideration. If they made the reasonable monthly payments the trailer would be theirs in five years. They would own their own home for less than buying a used automobile.

To make a long story short, they made every payment. After the last one Glenda and I drove to the house and delivered the title with a bottle of champagne. We had a small celebration since they now owned the trailer free and clear. Tears rolled down their cheeks.

Only a few months later they decided to move to a much larger manufactured home. They tried to sell the trailer but an agreed upon deal fell apart. They were suddenly very motivated sellers, just wanting to be done with this house. They asked me how much I would give them in cash. I informed them that I did not want to get involved.

Glenda and I told them that we had only $2,700 available in cash and they both eagerly shouted, "Sold." We sold that trailer for $9,000 the same day on a rent-to-own agreement. The new buyers made every payment and we again transferred the title. Everyone was happy.

This trailer has been bought and paid for twice. We initially put about $6,500 and a lot of labor into it and sold it for $11,000. The second time I invested $2,700, no work involved, and sold it for $9,000. There is profit to be made in mobile homes but you must realize that you are working with the folks on the bottom rung of the economic ladder. There is no way these folks could borrow the money to buy a home. We financed them, without cheating them, so that they could become homeowners. They seemed to love us.

Over the years we have bought, sold, or rented many mobile homes. We have met some great people and also some real losers. All in all, it has been a positive experience. The folks we deal with come from many walks of life. We have done business with Army and Marine Corps snipers, strippers, airline owners, retired Air Force personnel, ice cream truck owners, welfare recipients, drug dealers, world champion professional wrestlers, and many more. There is never a dull moment.

We have struggled to recover from the collapse of the housing market. Progress has been made. Dealing with these old mobile homes has given us an insight into a phase of life that we would have never known. These folks are real people with real dreams, fears, and feelings-- they should not be referred to as "trailer park trash".

Example deals:

I once looked at a trailer and rejected it because it was in horrible shape. My son walked through it and said, "I can fix it." The total out-of-pocket cost was about $3,500. That unit has now been rented for five years with a monthly net income of $300, about $18,000 total. Annual income has been $3,600 which is a 100% return on investment.

An old mobile home was being sold at auction by the county in an effort to recover unpaid taxes. After walking through the place, the doors were open, and curtains were blowing through window openings, I decided not to bid, wanting only to observe an auction. Only two people showed up, the park owner and myself. We were informed that $126 was owed in back taxes. The park owner asked the deputy what it would take to buy this old wreck. One dollar above the taxes due would be the minimum bid. The park owner bid $127.

I was asked if I wanted to bid. I said, "Of course not. I don't want to bid against the park owner." The park owner stated emphatically that he did not want that trailer. I bid $128 and became the proud owner. After the sale was complete, I asked the park owner to walk with me through the mobile home. It was so bad he refused by saying, "I am not going in there." That trailer was fixed up for about $4,500 and has been rented, with a few short periods of vacancy, producing a very nice return on investment.

That one purchase has led to my buying seven trailers in that one park. I sold one for cash but still own the remaining six. With very little work I receive an income of about $2000 each month.

On the downside, we have made deals with seemingly nice people who soon stopped paying, trashed the house, left infestations of bugs, and disappeared in the night. The laws generally protect these people.

BLACK-BACKED

He Gave Me the Bird
Thanks, Kevin.
Summer of 2013

The wind was blowing and the trees, mostly dead from a recent fire, were being bullied. The noise of this typical South Dakota breeze made it almost impossible to hear the tell-tale tapping of my prey.

An article in the Rapid City Journal by Kevin Woster was enough to make me drop my tools (I fix-up old mobile homes) and head out Sheridan Lake Road to the recent forest fire area at Dakota Point. He had written of his recent trip to this burn, looking for a fairly rare bird, the Black-Backed Woodpecker.

I had been a casual bird watcher for many years and was eager to add one more sighting to my life list. This seemed to be a good reason to take a walk in the woods. Arriving at the trailhead, I had hopes of getting a glimpse of this bird but knew that failure was a real possibility.

According to my reference books, the normal range of the Black-Backed is mostly north of the Dakotas, stretching from the east coast all the way to Alaska. We are fortunate that there is a small population here in the Black Hills of South Dakota. Kevin explained in his newspaper article that the Wood Borer beetle normally moves quickly into any forest where trees have been killed by fire. The Black-Backed Woodpecker soon follows to feed on the larvae of this beetle.

I parked my old pickup near the only other car at the trailhead. After passing through an iron gate, I turned to the right and proceeded up the hill through a stand of blackened trees. I was encouraged since there was an abundance of holes in the burned trees. Woodpeckers were definitely in the area.

The fire, which had destroyed about 250 acres of pine forest, had been started by lightning the previous summer. As Mother Nature dictates, Wood Borer beetles had arrived, closely followed by the Black-Backed Woodpeckers, to begin the natural regeneration of the forest. Now, only one year later, the trees were already beginning to decay.

Walking slowly, I wandered through this devastated landscape hoping to get a glimpse of the Black-Backed. A nuthatch and a chickadee were the only living things observed during the hour or so spent in the woods. Failure.

Several days later, I discussed the desire to find the Black-Backed with Glenda and she agreed to accompany me for a second look. Frankly, we arrived at the parking area with very low expectations.

We quietly walked up the same hillside that I had previously explored but on this day there was very little wind. The near silence gave us a chance of hearing the Black-Backed at work. After reaching the top we decided to turn to our left with the intent of descending to a trail that ran around the hill.

Our slow descent took us through a grove of dense pine trees, most of which had been killed by the fire. We were standing in this grove when Glenda, who could hear much better than I, announced that she could hear pecking sounds.

I cupped my hands behind my ears and listened intently. These faint sounds were very encouraging, but they seemed to come from far away. We tried to determine the location of the bird that was pecking away.

Suddenly, a slight movement only about twelve feet away made us aware that the woodpecker was much closer than expected. We were shocked and excited—this semi-rare bird paid us no mind. It leisurely went about its normal daily routine giving no indication that we were even there.

We pointed without speaking, afraid that we would scare our new friend. After a while we started to whisper and then began talking normally, the Black-Backed seemed to take no offense. We watched for a while and then simply walked away, leaving this little bird undisturbed.

GERBER

A Handy Tool

I am 78 years old and although I love them, have had very little to do with babies. One Gerber Company produces products directed toward the care and nourishment of young human beings. Their products have nothing to do with the subject of this story.

The Gerber Company that I am so familiar with produces and sells some of the most useful and practical multi-tools available. During my professional flying career, I flew Marine attack aircraft and large passenger planes for a major airline. During the year that I spent in Southeast Asia, as a Marine pilot, I always carried a .38 Special revolver in a shoulder holster. I felt naked if the weight of that piece of hardware could not be felt against my body.

After retiring from flying, I gradually became involved in buying, rehabbing, and selling or renting older mobile homes. This is a hands-on type business that involves many varied tasks involving all the systems required to produce a safe, functional, and inexpensive home.

Many years ago, I happened to buy a Gerber multi-tool. I soon became dependent on it in my everyday duties. I now feel naked, as with my .38 Special, when it is not on my belt. Even at social events when certain circumstances arise, my hand automatically reaches for my Gerber. This tool has become a part of me.

The model name is not evident as I examine my trusty multi-tool, but it has my admiration. It has never failed me. It still looks new although it has been mistreated on numerous occasions. It is normal for me to sharpen the blade as I watch football on television.

My son, and my handyman, ended up with multi-tools manufactured by another well-known company. These devices are useful, but they do not measure up to my Gerber. On two occasions the well-known tool that my handyman uses failed. In both cases it was repaired or replaced but he was without its use for weeks.

My Gerber has been flawless. I have used it many years and experienced no malfunctions. The original carry case had to be replaced and could possibly need to be replaced again. I love my Gerber. I take pride in using a dependable product that is made in the USA.

We spend three months each winter in Arizona to avoid the cold weather in South Dakota. My wife and I take regular hikes into the desert. I feel it is necessary to have my Gerber on my belt. Recently, the pliers were used to pull cactus thorns from a hiker's boot.

PS: I lost my original Gerber. I ordered and received a replacement. The new Diesel is now on my belt. Oh, darn. I found my old Gerber. Now I have two completely functional utility tools.

LUNCH IN EAST ST. LOUIS

2014

On the 18th of June 2014 Glenda and I began yet another little adventure. I don't remember how we came up with the idea, but we decided to drive the GRR, the Great River Road.

The United States Government has designated a series of roads along or near the Mississippi River as national treasures. This network of roads follows the river from its source in northern Minnesota to a place near New Orleans, Louisiana, more than two thousand miles away.

We consider this trip worthwhile in that we learned and saw so much. The simple act of having lunch in the "hood" of East St. Louis stands out as the one highlight that we think of when we reflect upon this drive.

Near noon in East St. Louis, we had lost our way; our intended route had been closed due to construction. As we slowly cruised a very questionable neighborhood, houses with boarded-up windows and lawns gone wild, looking for a street name that we would possibly recognize, we saw smoke. It was coming from a building that had once been a restaurant but now had plywood over the front windows and door. I noticed that the back door was open. There were several people standing in what appeared to be a line, and smoke was coming from the concrete block chimney.

I attempted to approach this building by turning down a one-way street but a black man in an old car blew his horn loudly and waved me away. He gave me a friendly wave and a big smile as I realized my error.

Making my way back to this derelict building, I eased the car into the unpaved parking lot out back. On the door, where the people stood in line, the word "OPEN" was painted in block red letters.

As I approached, a very large black man asked in a rough, seemingly unfriendly voice, "Can we help you?" I replied in my best imitation of a firm voice, "I just want to know what is going on here. I see people waiting in line, I see smoke, and the aroma is wonderful. There must be something good to eat around here somewhere." The big man mellowed, gave me a big smile and said, "Just step inside--that woman probably has exactly what you are looking for." He was the driver of an eighteen-wheeler that was patiently waiting out in the street with its engine running.

Through an open window, I ordered a half-slab of ribs and two 7 UP soft drinks. While waiting for our food, a woman in an orange shirt came out of the kitchen and asked if everything was okay? I thought she was part of the restaurant staff. We exchanged pleasantries and I confessed that the only reason we had found this eatery was because we were lost.

She asked where we were trying to go. I told her to ask Glenda. I watched them study a map and point in every direction. As I approached with our lunch, they seemed to have come to an understanding. "Orange Shirt" started to walk away but I asked if she would allow me to take her photograph. She agreed, and I now have a photo of Glenda and her smiling with their arms around the other's waist.

"Orange Shirt" soon returned, telling Glenda that there was a more direct route that we should consider. This new route was much easier and we chose to use it. She then put water, food, some sort of headset and recorder into her car, and waved as she drove away.

While we were eating from the trunk of our car, the restaurant owner approached us twice with extra napkins. Our lunch was great and with sticky fingers we continued our drive along the mighty Mississippi. After only a mile or so, as we passed a road construction site, we observed "Orange Shirt," headset in place, working near the business end of a large digging machine.

Later, upon reading the guidebooks, we learned that East St. Louis should be avoided if possible. It seems that gangs control the area and any outsider could immediately be in trouble. We found no hostilities but lots of friendliness-- maybe we were just lucky. This little encounter was a very pleasant and memorable part of our Great River Road tour.

Our trip was a great adventure with little happenings like this making it even better. We loved "Orange Shirt" and the food.

Glenda with "Orange Shirt"

Baja Whale-Watching

Stand by Your Van

On November 19th, 1999, the old but sturdy Aegean One departed Athens, Greece with about 400 excited passengers for a four-month around-the-world cruise. For most of us this trip was a once-in-a-lifetime event. I will never forget Glenda leaning against me as we stood on the aft deck watching the lights of the port of Piraeus slowly disappear into the night. The ever so slight vibration of the deck caused by the engines was evidence that the adventure had begun.

The extended time on board, the rather small number of people, and the mode of travel caused many of the passengers to form special bonds. Many will remain friends for life. Flossie Ferlic from the Minneapolis, Minnesota area often publishes newsletters with news of that group and on many occasions has organized reunions.

One of these reunions was held in San Diego, California in February of 2015 and was attended by about 50 travelers from the Little Ship that Could. Glenda and I had decided not to attend this gathering but after hearing of a planned adventure we changed our minds since we tend to enjoy doing things that may seem a bit strange to some. Chris Foster had planned and organized an unusual whale-watching trip. He came up with the idea of renting three vans, each with over 100,000 miles on the odometer, and inviting 33 people for a 600-mile drive into Mexico. The goal was to get up close and personal with gray whales.

Arriving at our California hotel in the late afternoon, we soon found ourselves laughing and talking with friends that we had not seen for years. The conversations usually drifted to that world cruise of so many years ago. It was a fun night.

The next day everyone boarded a sightseeing boat with hopes of seeing whales in and around the San Diego harbor. We were in luck. No whales were seen at first but suddenly a humpback breached near our boat. The captain followed and for the next hour or so this lone whale put on a wonderful show. Over and over again, it heaved its huge body into the air and crashed back into the water.

We had seen whales very often while living in Hawaii, but they were generally at a distance. Considering that experience and having observed this whale at very close range, we questioned our decision to take a long drive into Mexico in an attempt to see more. Even with having a seed of doubt, we chose to follow through with the plan to travel along the Baja Peninsula. We are very glad that we decided to go and this trip has become one of our favorite adventures.

Flossie and Chris assigned each person to a specific van. However, there always seemed to be some confusion. Sometimes it seemed complicated and we old people found it difficult to get it right. As the van boardings continued to be a bit of a problem, we were often directed to "Stand by Your Van." Someone connected this phrase with the county western song "Stand by Your Man", hence the sub-title.

Daylight arrived just as we arrived at the Mexican border. Several times during the trip there seemed to be disagreements between our group and management people or officials. This border crossing was the first of this type of disagreement. I felt that we were about to be denied entry into Mexico because of some technicality. The officials kept shaking their heads and saying, "No" or "Impossible." Chris did not seem to be worried. He had spent a lot of time in Mexico and knew how to conduct himself. The conversation gradually turned in our favor. Not only were we allowed to cross the border, but we were not required to pay the normal tourist tax. Chris was able to negotiate our way out of situations that seemed to have no easy solution. He knew what to say and do. He spoke the language and would not accept "no" as an answer.

Initially, the roads were like freeways, four lanes with limited access but that would soon change. After a few miles all roads had only two lanes, and at times there was no shoulder. If one of our drivers had allowed a wheel to slip off the pavement the van could have possibly flipped and in places, tumbled down steep embankments.

What a great group of travelers. The vans were crowded and for hour after hour we rapidly passed through the desert-like countryside. The large cities turned into smaller towns which turned into small villages. There were endless mountains and many different types of cactus. This ride was not for the faint of heart. Everyone maintained a positive attitude and I don't remember hearing even one complaint or cross word. Good troopers, all.

Enduring the grueling first day, we finally arrived at a hotel in a small town with the entire group in good health and high spirits. It was cold. Glenda and I felt that going south of California would bring warmer weather. Therefore, we had not packed coats or sweaters. This was a big mistake.

Chris set up a makeshift bar near the hotel swimming pool from which he served some really great margaritas. The day of misery on the road was soon forgotten. We had been told that this first day would be the longest and toughest. It was a hard day but some of the next few days proved to be just as trying.

We were now 300 miles down the Baja Peninsula and there was no chance of quitting now. Like it or not, everyone was now committed to the entire trip. As usual, we were a bit apprehensive but happy to be a part of this adventure. We noticed that Osprey nests were common on any available pole along the road. The Osprey is a large fish-eating hawk whose wingspan can be almost six feet. The condition of the roads and the quality of the hotels would decrease but the sense of adventure would only grow.

The cramped traveling conditions, beautiful scenery, good food, decent hotels, and lots of margaritas became a pattern. On several occasions we took short breaks to stretch our legs, usually in small towns. The street vendors were plentiful and served some of the best food that we had tasted. Maybe the location and situation were factors in our assessment of their offerings.

The day and time arrived. We boarded 10 or 12 passenger, outboard-powered boats. After a twenty-minute ride, during which we observed sea lions resting on buoys, we saw our first gray whales in the distance. Everyone pointed and chattered excitedly but I noticed that our boat driver seemed very uninterested. We would come to understand his attitude.

The next several hours provided a very unique adventure. Whales could be seen in every direction. The boat drivers would slowly motor about, watching for whales near the surface. As we approached, these huge animals would slowly submerge or swim away. Many of the females had babies that they kept near their sides.

At near noon our boat captain shut down the engine allowing us to dive into our bag lunch. We felt we were very privileged to be able to munch on a sandwich and chips while sipping from a can of Coke as we watched huge whales surfacing all about.

It seemed to me that the whales had a slight change of attitude after our lunch break. As we slowly motored up to them, they were slower to move away. They seemed to have some curiosity about us and our boats. Some would just relax on the surface and allow us to pull alongside. They did not react when several people would pat their rubbery sides.

On several occasions, the mother whales maneuvered their babies to right beside our boats. It was almost as if they were proud and wanted to show off their young. We were allowed to touch these youngsters. At times a whale would put its head out of the water just beside the boat and look us in the eye. I had my cap blown off when one of these friendly giants hit me with a vigorous expulsion of air. I was able to pat another one on the cheek as it looked me over.

They showed no fear and, as mentioned, seemed to be curious. Their way of seeing what was happening in the area was quite interesting. Standing vertically in the water, they would slowly push their pointed noses into the air. The eyes were out of the water and this position was held while they took a look around. As much as eight or ten feet of their nose would be out of the water.

As could be imagined, this was a very exciting day. We had a similar experience the next day, but because the tide was out, we had to wade about one hundred yards to our boats. Our close encounter with these huge creatures will always be remembered. The discomfort that we had experienced in the vans was well worth it.

In reflecting upon attempting to get this little story into print, I feel that I would be remiss should our three van drivers not be given proper credit. Bob Nielson, retired Naval Officer, Chris Foster, educator and world adventurer, and Gene Byron, medical doctor and surgeon, stepped forward and shouldered the responsibility of driving these used vans, loaded with old people, deep into a foreign country. They had to deal with bad roads, overloaded vehicles, and hectic traffic in the process of delivering us to our destination and back home safely. There was not even one questionable incident. Nice job, guys.

Experiencing hours and days of crowded conditions, marginal roads, exceptionally beautiful countryside, and an abundance of margaritas enabled us to safely arrive back at the border crossing. As usual there was a substantial delay, causing many of our group to need a potty break. There were no devastating accidents, but it was close. The pressure reached a peak as we approached the hotel causing a mad dash toward the appropriate facilities.

Glenda and I have traveled the world, climbed high mountains, and experienced many unusual circumstances; but this adventure will always be ranked as one of our greatest endeavors.

Thank you, Chris and Flossie.

These Old Hands

If ten people, including myself, laid their hands palms down on a table, mine would look very similar to the others. All the hands would have ten fingers and various scars and imperfections that were collected through years of living.

Should these hands be presented with the palms upward they would still look very similar. No one would be able to tell that my normal looking hands had flown aircraft across vast oceans, carried collegiate footballs across goal lines, milked cows, cleaned sewage lines, or created functional housing for the disadvantaged.

There would be no way to know that the thumb on my right hand, by touching a small button on an aircraft control stick, had released more than 300,000 pounds of high explosives on an enemy that was never seen. War is what it is. I am sure that thumb caused tremendous damage to the enemy, but very likely also caused people to die who did not deserve to die.

My right forefinger could tell a very similar story. That finger, with a movement similar to pulling the trigger on a gun, unleashed untold violence. Day after day, this finger sent rockets and automatic weapons fire into the forests and rice paddies below. I will never know the damage that these old hands have caused.

I have always considered my hands to be kind. They have held babies, aided in the birth of many farm animals, escorted my granddaughter down the aisle at her wedding, and helped many people who were in need.

The fingers are now bent, and the age spots are plentiful. The sight of these old weathered hands makes me appreciate the time that I have been granted on this earth and regret the destruction that they have caused.

I never had any intention of hurting anyone. My country called, and I answered. The Marine Corps signed me on, and I swore to do as they directed. They sent me to war, and I did my job to the best of my ability.

These old hands will soon lie still. The world will go on and I suspect that there will continue to be wars and rumors of wars. Other hands will assume the duties that my hands performed. It would be wonderful if the people on this earth could join hands for the good of all. I fear that this will never happen.

I did my part to the best of my ability. I was at times afraid for my life, but I pressed on. I am not unique. There were many strong young men who flew and marched into the face of danger.

They Come in the Night

In the dark of night, while most people are sleeping, without making a sound or being seen, they come. Only hours before, innocent and unsuspecting children played only a few feet from where the next horrific deed would take place. They come when least expected and show no mercy or guilt.

This latest intrusion was not a surprise. Everyone knew, without a doubt, that they would return. It was just a matter of time. The folks who lived in the area had complained many times but the authorities either had not cared or were powerless to provide protection.

Many individuals had attempted to take defensive measures into their own hands. In most cases their efforts had failed miserably. It seemed that there was no hope. Most folks finally just gave up, realizing that this menace would forever be a part of their lives.

Glenda and I were leaving a Walmart Store when we noticed some, not so appealing, rose bush plantings that were on sale. They looked dead, but the price was right. We had recently purchased a home that had a small rock garden in which the planted tree was obviously totally dead. We wondered if one of these rose bushes would survive in that little plot of ground. This was the beginning of our latest close encounter with the Monsters of the Black Hills. I shudder as I write this story.

We bought one of the dead-looking bundles and hauled it home. The rose bush sat in our garage until Glenda insisted that something had to be done. The two of us took a spade, pulled back the rocks, and planted it with no great hopes of success. It was soon forgotten.

We watched with interest as it sent out a number of branches, each producing several buds and eventually many very beautiful red blossoms. Not belonging to the Green Thumb Club, we were proud of our minor success.

"The little rose bush that could" gave us a lot of pleasure but then it just quit producing. There were no buds, therefore, no blossoms. After a few weeks it began its second productive cycle. Some of the many new buds quickly developed into beautiful flowers. We were excited that our little plant was again providing us with more floral pleasure.

Then it happened. Glenda had stepped out onto the front porch to get the newspaper when I heard her gasp. I thought she had seen a large spider or a snake. But no, she was not in danger, only in shock.

During the night, members of our local deer population had wandered into our yard and reduced our little rose bush to nothing more than bare branches with thorns. All the buds, leaves and blossoms were gone.

Deer are plentiful here in western South Dakota. We enjoy sitting on the back deck in the late afternoon, watching them feed on the distant hills. They normally stay out on the prairie or up in the high country during the summer, but in winter they come to town, making themselves right at home. Custer, South Dakota residents joke that the deer are so accustomed to city life that they even wait for a green light before crossing the street.

I called them monsters and they can be quite annoying. Collisions between deer and automobiles happen frequently. It is common to see several dead deer along the roadways each morning.

In general, we like having them around. We have learned to accept them for what they are, realizing that they bring more to our lives than they take away.

Radiation Vacation

Loma Linda, California

Lisa was not satisfied. She was the thin, shy, and persistent Physician's Assistant who oversaw my initial foray into the world of prostate cancer.

I was in shock when told that Lisa would soon walk into my life as my advisor. Within only a few minutes of our first meeting she instructed me to drop my trousers and bend over the examination table. This was a rather awkward event but seemingly necessary. She proceeded to explore my nether regions with a gloved finger. Cancer had not been detected in my two previous biopsies therefore I felt that a bullet had been dodged. Lisa insisted that one more test be conducted. I hate her and love her for her persistence.

A biopsy for this disease is a rather painful procedure which includes rectal penetration with an instrument which is capable of penetrating the large intestine wall and retrieving minute samples of the prostate gland. It was very uncomfortable, but this doctor said, "If cancer is there, we will find it." That terrible snapping sound went on for way too long. I felt violated.

Long story short, a few cancerous cells were found. Lisa, wherever you may be today, I thank you from the bottom of my heart. Your persistence may have extended my life.

Cancer had been found. Now what? As with most men who have had a positive diagnosis of prostate cancer, the research began. There are several ways that this condition can be treated. I sat down and discussed my condition with several experts. I found that the specialists who performed a certain treatment wholeheartedly felt that their approach was the best.

Most of these doctors were very open and honest in the description as to how the treatment would be carried out. The surgeon talked of a lot of blood, a rather long recovery period, and a probable loss of all sexual activity. The implant doctor felt that his treatment would be effective, but the possibility of further sexual activity was very unlikely.

Someone told me about the Loma Linda program of neutron radiation. I tried to educate myself. The general feeling was that this procedure would stop or slow the cancer while having very few side effects. I spoke with several men who had completed the program--they reported a painless treatment and very low incidents of problems thereafter. No blood, no pain, and a chance of future sexual activity enticed me to lean toward this type of treatment.

Loma Linda, "Pretty Hill" in Spanish, is a lovely little town in the eastern reaches of the city of Los Angeles. The Seventh Day Adventists supported the beautiful and progressive hospital. I had decided to utilize their proton radiation as treatment for my prostate cancer. For nine weeks I was to be zapped with radiation that was designed to rid me of my prostate gland and the cancer--forty-five treatments in all.

The hospital staff treated us as if we were special. We were encouraged to eat properly and exercise regularly. The patient and spouse were welcomed into a beautiful workout facility which featured modern equipment and organized exercise classes. Glenda got rather involved in various dance and stretching classes. She sometimes spoke almost angrily about some of the instructors who drove the class, showing no mercy.

One of the first procedures for the patient was to create a personal pod. I showed up at the lab, more like a warehouse, and was instructed to strip naked and climb into a large plastic half tube. It appeared to be a large PVC pipe. After being carefully positioned, liquid Styrofoam was poured into my piece of culvert. I was instructed to remain still, the liquid quickly turned to a solid. This pod was now my personal tool which would enable me to assume the same position for each treatment.

Glenda and I found and rented a very basic upstairs apartment. It was simple but met our needs. Most of the folks who lived nearby were working their way through the same radiation program. We bonded with these strangers.

This treatment program had no severe side effects. The most noticeable was that after a few weeks I found that there would be periods of a sudden desperate need to urinate. I played golf with my fellow patients and we found that the privacy of the large trees on the course was greatly appreciated.

After some delay I showed up for my first treatment. I was directed to a very small room where freshly laundered hospital gowns were stacked. We were to strip nude, put on one of these garments and wait, while tucking as much as possible. These first appointments made us feel self-conscious, but we would soon get over it.

I am sure it was planned. My name was called. Holding my gown in place, I responded and was situated into my pod. A most attractive, dark-haired young woman approached and said, "Mister Smith, turn over." She held in her hand a probe with an inflatable balloon attached. She proceeded to insert the probe into my rectum and then inflate the balloon with a small amount of warm water. The research had determined that an inflated balloon would move something out of the line of fire of the proton radiation.

We soon forgot any feeling of modesty as we paraded from the dressing room to the treatment room with our hospital gowns flapping in the breeze. This attractive young woman had seen the butts of too many old men.

Another patient wrote about this experience and called it a "radiation vacation." We tried to make this time in Loma Linda as just that. I soon requested that my treatments be early in the morning. I would slip out of bed well before daylight and take the short walk to the treatment facility. The treatments were scheduled for 15 minutes after which I dressed and had no further duties for the day. I usually returned to the side of my sleeping wife and we napped until a normal breakfast hour. The whole day lay ahead.

We walked in the nearby hills many times, climbed rather demanding mountains, visited museums, went to the beach, played golf, and explored national parks. We, in fact, made the time during my treatment a radiation vacation.

The big selling point for this type of treatment was that there would be very minimal side effects and the fact that any cancer would be set back by maybe ten years. Prostate cancer in some cases progresses very slowly. The feeling was that after delaying the cancer by those years, something else would probably cause my demise.

This treatment happened about ten years ago and there has been no further indication that the cancer has returned. So far, I have been happy with my choice of treatment measures.

I checked a chart concerning life span in the United States. Men were projected, on average, to live to 76 years of age. Very soon I will turn 78. I am now, for once in my life, above average. I can only try to keep my weight under control, get a bit of exercise and enjoy each day. Glenda and I have had an eventful life. We hope to have a few more adventures. When our time on this earth comes to an end, we hope to still be wearing our adventure boots.

Random Thoughts

As a young person I did not enjoy the drudgery of life on a small farm and dreamed of living a different life. I had no idea what I wanted but knew there had to be something better.

As children, my brother and I spent the summers shirtless and shoeless. Our feet became tough enough to run barefoot down a graveled road with no pain.

Mules and other draft animals lived a life of hard labor. They seemed to simply endure. They were gentle animals and spent their lives working and never rebelled. During certain times of the year these animals worked in the fields six days a week. On Sundays after church we rode them for fun. Once we were carefully leading the old gray mare across an old bridge over a creek. Suddenly, her back legs broke through the rotten bridge planks. She fell about ten feet into the creek below. She remained calm and simply looked up at us holding her reins on what was left of the bridge. After leading her out of her spot of bother we mounted up and rode her home.

My early life was very basic. Water was drawn from an open well and much of our food was produced on the farm. Every farm in those days had a calf and hogs that were destined for slaughter. Pork hams and shoulders were salted down in a four-foot by four-foot square wooden box. From raw to cured, the process made the meat edible many months later. Folks looked forward to salt-cured pork and redeye gravy.

In the farm country of West Tennessee, it was common to address folks with titles such as Miss, Uncle, Auntie, and Cousin. Cousin Poppy was an old lady cared for by her daughter, Cousin Willie. In those days old people were cared for by family. As a teenager I was helping Cousin Thurmond stack hay into the loft of his barn. I noticed that his head was near a large active wasp nest. I warned, "Watch out for that wasp nest."

He turned, saw the nest, and with his hard, calloused, weathered, and bare hand, simply reached up and crushed the nest and its many angry occupants into oblivion. His hands were so tough that the wasp stings had no effect. He continued to stack hay with no comment.

During my youth our farm community consisted of a mixture of white landowners and a few scattered black families. These black folks survived by doing physical labor on the nearby farms for a meager wage. I can remember in the middle of the night my mother, who had only an eighth-grade education, was called upon to aid in the birth of a black child. She did not hesitate. It did not matter the skin color of this new baby. She was needed, and she stepped forward. She was known as Miss Mable.

My dad, a good man, knew nothing of teaching. When a job on the farm needed doing, he would simply tell me to go do that job. I felt inadequate when the job gave me difficulty. Years later I was amazed, when at every step the flight school instructors gave me detailed instruction as to what was expected of me. It seemed that this was somehow cheating.

During my days of playing on independent baseball teams, I was usually the youngest player on adult men's teams. I just kept quiet but learned of activities and thoughts that my teammates frequently discussed. I was so young, but they talked to each other without taking this kid into consideration. Wow, I never would have guessed.

I found it difficult to believe that a female would join with this poor farm boy for a life together. Glenda, who is now sitting on the couch with me, took on that challenge. The two of us have been lucky to have experienced so many of the wonders of this world. She is a dear and enduring woman.

During my athletic career I never had exceptional strength, speed, or size, but I always hung in there. The quarterback gave me the ball and I ran with it. Even though I was selected as a small college All American, I never felt that I was special. My teammates always kept me in check by ribbing me without mercy anytime an award came my way. Some called me "Turkey tail" because of the way I ran…it cannot be explained. The Montreal Alouettes, a professional Canadian football team, sent me a letter of inquiry but I never replied. I knew that I was not good enough to be a professional.

I showed up in Pensacola, Florida for flight training with a little hope and the intention to never give up. During the training program the pressure was constant, and I was always in fear of failing. Looking back, I completed the program with no unsatisfactory flights and not even one below average grade on any specific maneuver. I felt as if I were failing but in fact I was doing as well or better than most.

On a training flight in the advanced phase of my jet training, I had completed my high-altitude work and was ready to return to the airfield for practice landings. To keep the instructor informed, I announced, "I am fixin' to start down." He asked, "What did you say?" I repeated that I was indeed "fixin'" to begin a descent. This was a normal southern saying and I could not understand why he was questioning me. In Tennessee, fixin' meant that you were preparing to begin an activity. We both had a laugh and I explained that my hillbilly upbringing was a part of me.

The Marine Corps made every effort to accommodate the major events of a pilot's life. I was granted extra leave to be present for the birth of our daughter, but I missed it. Later, I was halfway around the world in a combat zone when our son was born. I bought cigars and passed them around. I tried to smoke one but collapsed into a chair.

Once on a dark night in Vietnam, I was flying a TPQ-10 radar bombing mission. Leveling at 15 thousand feet, in the clouds and distracted with other duties, I allowed the aircraft to slow to the point of activating the stick shaker, or stall warning. I added full power and recovered easily. This reminded me that I still had so much to learn. This event happened more than 50 years ago, and this is the first time the story has been told. I was not proud.

The outdoor toilets in Vietnam looked much like the outhouses on any farm of my youth. Beneath the seats of a two-holer were 55-gallon barrels that had been cut down to about two feet. At regular intervals, enlisted Marines would use homemade hooks to drag these containers out into the open. The residue was soaked with jet fuel and set afire. The black smoke and unpleasant odor became familiar. Do these same Marines now wear caps that proclaim, "Vietnam Veteran"? The urinals were simply three-inch PVC pipes buried at an angle into the sand. These pipes stood about two and a half feet above the surface. We stood in the open and got the job done.

Very near my childhood home was a fenced area that had once been the hog lot. The swine were long gone, and the weeds had taken over. My dad was over 90 years of age and his mind was stronger than his body when he asked me to use his old John Deere tractor to cut these weeds. I made several passes, but he was not satisfied. He waved me down and yelled, "If you can't do it right, then just get off and I will take over." He was growing old and could not have even climbed onto the tractor. I smiled and told him that I would finish the job. He thought for a moment and then simply walked away.

The writing of this book has been an important part of my life. Glenda and I have enjoyed eventful lives. The process of putting these stories into print has brought to mind so many memories that had been long forgotten. I truly hope that a few of you have enjoyed or identified with some of these stories.

OBITUARY

Old Darrel

I am still alive and kicking but have written this to be used at the proper time:

Do any of you remember Darrel F. Smith who was born and raised on a small farm in Tennessee, enjoyed active sports, graduated from college, married Glenda M. Cousar, served as a Marine Corps officer and pilot, participated in an active war, flew large aircraft as a profession, served as a Chief Pilot, enjoyed travel, experienced numerous adventures including climbing several tall mountains, wrote stories of his life, worked hard, and loved Glenda, the kids and their families? Well, if you haven't already heard, Darrel died.

Should you happen to recall this guy, he hereby requests that you raise a glass of your favorite beverage skyward and say, without fear of telling a lie, "Of all the people I have known during my lifetime, Old Darrel was one of them."

I, Darrel, wrote this while alive and of sound mind. I lived my life to the best of my ability but fell short in so many ways. Under the stress of living, I never allowed myself to laugh enough. Please don't make the same mistake. I believe that we live on this earth only once, so make the best of this gift.

Life is short, sometimes hard but generally good. Live strong. Disregard what others might think. Be yourself.

I was born 01Jan1940 and died ————TBD

My life has been rich and blessed. Do not grieve. Celebrate.

ABOUT THE AUTHOR

Darrel came into this world on a cold night in an old farmhouse on a hard-scrabble farm in West Tennessee. To an outside observer, it would have seemed evident that this lowly child was destined to a life of near poverty and hard work. As he grew older, however, a feeling of wanting something more slowly crept into his mind. A life of hard work did happen, but with effort, good luck, and the help of others, he was able to rise above this basic existence.

Possessing some natural athletic abilities, he attended the University of Tennessee at Martin, UT Martin Branch at the time, on a football scholarship. During his sophomore year the Marine Corps presented him with the possibility of becoming a Marine Corps officer and even a pilot. Upon graduation, he reported to the Naval Aviation Flight Training School at Pensacola, Florida.

Upon completing flight school, he was assigned to a Marine Corps attack squadron in North Carolina. He was soon designated as a combat-ready attack pilot. A one-year tour of duty in Vietnam and a year as an instructor in the advanced jet training command completed his obligation and he opted to leave the Marine Corps.

He secured a job with Northwest Airlines and spent thirty years as a commercial pilot and instructor while flying various types of company aircraft.

After retirement, he spent several years in Reno, Nevada before he and his wife Glenda chose to live and travel in a motorhome. Several winters were spent in Gold Canyon, Arizona. The motorhome was sold but they still made the "valley of the sun" their winter destination.

During the winter of 2012, Larry R. Gibson, an old Marine buddy, encouraged him to write and possibly publish stories of his life, as Larry had done in his book, "Recollections of a Marine Attack Pilot." Over the next five or six years he worked at putting into print his memory of events in his life. The effort to write these stories brought many forgotten memories to mind. His life became much richer due to the influence of his old friend Larry.

Glenda Marie Cousar Smith, Darrel's wife, faithfully stood shoulder to shoulder with him facing every adversity and enjoying the good times. She lived many of the stories included in this book. He was very fortunate to have her as his partner in life.

This book is a compilation of the memories that came to mind as he reflected upon his life. It is his hope that this book will be of interest to his family, friends, and even others.

Made in the USA
Lexington, KY
08 November 2019